How

FREE WILL
WORKS

THE BLUEPRINTS TO TAKE CHARGE OF
YOUR LIFE, HEALTH, AND HAPPINESS

DOVID LIEBERMAN

Published by:
Viter Press
1072 Madison Ave.
Lakewood, NJ 08701
ViterPress@live.com

Distributed by:
Feldheim Publishers
208 Airport Executive Park
Nanuet, NY 10954
POB 43163 / Jerusalem, Israel
www.feldheim.com

10 9 8 7 6 5 4 3 2 1

ISBN: 978-1-4675-6353-6

Printed in the United States of America

Written by: Dr. Dovid Lieberman
Cover and layout design: Sonnshine Publishing | Shaya Sonnenschein | 732-961-2169

This edition is lovingly dedicated by

Asher David Milstein

In memory of

His grandparents

Rabbi Elazar Kahanow ז"ל ∿ Henrietta Milstein ע"ה

His brother

Betzalel Binyamin Milstein ז"ל

His great uncles

Aaron Kahan ז"ל ∿ Yankel Basch ז"ל

And his great aunt

Hanka Kozlovsky ע"ה

∾∾∾

And in honor of his parents

Lazer and Ziporah Milstein

His grandparents

Monroe and Judy Milstein ∿ Rebbetzin Rochel Kahanow

His brother

Elisha Shlomo Milstein

∾∾∾

And in tribute to

Rabbi Jeff Seidel, Rabbi Efraim Weingot
and Rabbi Ezriel Munk

בס"ד

שמואל קמנצקי
Rabbi S. Kamenetsky

2018 Upland Way
Philadelphia, PA 19131

Home: 215-473-2798
Study: 215-473-1212

ר"ח כסלו, תשע"ג

Dr. David Lieberman is a wonderful individual who dedicates his life on behalf of the Klal. He is a very gifted writer with a track record of writing very important books that help to educate the Tzibur and brings them closer to HaKadosh Baruch Hu. His Avodas HaKodesh is continuing with the publication of his new book, <u>How Free Will Works</u>.

The book addresses the topic of free will in a very clear manner and demonstrates how we can better control our Yetzer Hora by understanding this concept properly. Based on Chazal, Dr. Lieberman offers practical skills and strategies to help us grow and realize our full potential. When we appreciate the gift of free will and recognize the power that it yields over our emotional, spiritual and physical lives, we will come to make healthy choices in our Avodas Hashem.

We live in trying times, and a book such as this helps us appreciate the tools that HaKadosh Baruch Hu gave us with which we meet these challenges.

I wish him great hatzlacha in all his endeavors.

S. Kamenetsky

TABLE OF CONTENTS

SECTION TWO: DREAMS INTO ACTION

ACKNOWLEDGMENTS

This work was made possible due to the input and expertise of many, many people. It is with great gratitude that I acknowledge HaRav Shmuel Kamenetsky sh'lita, whose interest and support have been immeasurable.

It is with appreciation, warmth, and respect that I acknowledge Mr. Asher David Milstein. He is a person of a rare breed—one whose desire to make a difference corresponds with his actions, which actually make a difference.

I am most thankful to the prolific and talented Rabbi Moshe Goldberger sh'lita for his ongoing and always-sage advice and observations. This book has been improved because of his many contributions. Special recognition goes to Rabbi Yechezkel Auerbach sh'lita for his sharp analysis and insight. Much appreciation goes to my wonderful editors, Rabbi Moshe Armel, Mrs. Sorelle Weinstein, Ms. Patricia Waldygo and Mrs. Sara Miriam Gross, who helped transform this book into a clear and cogent work.

I am indebted to my extraordinary parents and most grateful for my incredible wife and generally well-behaved children, who make it all possible and worthwhile. A big thank you, as well, to my amazing in-laws for their never-ceasing thoughtfulness.

I am eternally grateful to *HaKadosh Baruch Hu*, for His many blessings and Whose infinite kindness and benevolence have allowed this book to be written.

PLEASE NOTE

While this work has been vetted to offer information that is sound in *hashkafah*, if you find anything objectionable, please bear in mind that this in no way reflects on the integrity of those individuals who offered their kind words to this book and who lent their names in support. Editorial changes may have affected content such that it no longer supports their position or opinion. *Sole responsibility for any errors, omissions, or inconsistencies lies with the author.*

Throughout the editorial process, the material has undergone many revisions, and it is possible that a misquote or an omission of credit—be it citation, source, or Torah insight—may have occurred. To this end, any comments and corrections are welcome so that this book can be revised for future editions.

A spectrum of non-Torah sources from poets to physicists to psychologists is included in this work. This was not done to lend credence to the sagacity of Torah or to validate insights from rabbinic commentators. No stamp of approval is necessary. Rather, these sources are offered to help the uninitiated reader to more intensely appreciate the depth and beauty of Torah wisdom. Certainly, these inclusions should not be construed as a wholesale endorsement of the respective author's ideology. As we will learn, intelligence and talent do not make one wise or immune to a corrupted worldview.

INTRODUCTION

Personal transformation is not only the cornerstone of our faith but lies at the core of our purpose. Beginning with our forefather Abraham, who at seventy-five set out to remake himself and the world, the Torah is filled with accounts of those who rose above their nature to succeed in transforming their character and fulfilling their Divine service.

Whether slicing through obstacles or trudging through discomfort and difficulties, great people throughout history have possessed the ability to minimize temptations and galvanize their resolve. They move through life with clarity and confidence—a knowing invincibility.

Most of us, though, become stuck along the way, barely scratching the surface of our lives. Encased in a cocoon of negative habits and fears, we are alive, but there's no freshness or vitality. Our personalities have become stifled and suffocate under the weight of our insecurities.

We wade through life, but we are not living it; and thanks to twenty-first-century advances, instant shrink-wrapped entertainment offers escape into other worlds, a vast labyrinth of toys, tools, and distractions from which to concoct elaborate avoidances.

But there is no escape. Our fruitless attempts to hide from life only bring us greater pain and despair. Depression is aptly described in Torah sources as a taste of death. When we die, our soul—the real us—separates from the body. A person who is not growing and moving forward in life will force a rift between the body and soul—the very experience of death itself.

Our soul is rigged to revolt against negligence and indifference, and the system will faithfully keep dishing out new symptoms—both emotional and physical—to remind us that we are in this world for a reason. Every soul has a distinct mission, infused with its own spiritual DNA. It longs to rise above the masses and to light up creation by unleashing its unique spark of the Infinite. The purpose of this book is to help rekindle our passion for life by tapping into this deep, fervent yearning for self-expression.

Once we recognize the power and process of free will, we will understand unquestionably what is to be gained and what is to be lost; and then we would not—could not—behave irresponsibly, much less contradictory to our long-term interests and objectives.

This enhanced mindset brings us to the point where we are no longer eager to deny the truth—the pain of forfeiting our destiny is too great, and the genuine pleasure missed, too palpable. We are then propelled forward with a renewed desire to actualize our free will and to extract the greatest potential from our God-given talents and opportunities.

THE STRUCTURE OF FREE WILL

Free will operates within a framework of clearly defined rules and parameters: laws. As with all laws, there are cause and effect. In this section we discover that our decisions do not always carry immediate and clear consequences and affect us in ways we might never have imagined—ranging from the imperceptible to the unmistakable, and extending from this world into the next.

As our knowledge of free will crystallizes, we move in a world that offers us a different experience, and it will become increasingly difficult—if not inconceivable—for us to ignore the one truth that will become so patently obvious: we control the quality of our lives—and our afterlife.

PART 1

THE MECHANICS
OF CHOICE

We begin by exploring the drives that come together in the decision-making process and then connect the dots to discover how and why our choices—even small and seemingly inconsequential ones—ripple predictably into the entirety of our emotional, spiritual, and physical lives.

THE CLASH AND THE CONSEQUENCES

1

An endless stream of decisions flows through our lives from the beginning until the end, but not all choices are created equal. Whether we wiggle our right finger or left finger or pick a red blanket over a blue one is a matter of preference. It is a choice, yes, but without moral significance. Regardless of the outcome, we will neither beam with pride nor experience pangs of shame.

Of course, life is filled with hard choices that have real consequences, and as we know, making the right choice is not always easy or comfortable. Self-esteem helps.[1] It stimulates the desire to invest in ourselves and provides the energy for self-discipline, pushing us toward responsible behavior. Moreover, each and every time we rise above our nature, we bolster this key ingredient to psychological and spiritual health.

To the extent that we do not love ourselves, though, our willingness to endure short-term pain for a long-term gain wanes. Who wants to put in effort—enduring heartache and hardship—for someone whom they do not even like?

The mindset is understandable but quite problematic. If we frequently shirk our obligations and shun new opportunities, we lose more than we might expect.

NOTES

1. Confidence is often mistaken for self-esteem, but the two are quite different. Confidence is how effective we feel within a specific area or situation, while self-esteem is defined as how much we recognize our inherent worth, feel deserving of happiness and good fortune, and know that we are precious in the eyes of God. As we will discuss at great length, our feelings of self-esteem are shaped by our free will behavior, rather than by the assets at our disposal. One who attempts to fortify his self-image by taking pride in a specific trait may exhibit signs of high self-esteem to the untrained eye, but in fact, such a person often suffers from low self-esteem because all he has is an inflated ego.

Findings show that the tendency to avoid the pain inherent in taking responsibility for our lives is the primary basis of all mental illness and is central to nearly every emotional issue, including anxiety, depression, and addiction.[2] This is how it happens:

LIVE OR LET DIE

Within all of us exist three inner forces that are often at odds with one another: the soul, the ego, and the body.[3] In short, the soul seeks to do what is right; the ego wants to be right and see itself in the optimal light; and the body just wants to escape from it all.

Doing what is comfortable or enjoyable is a body drive. Examples of indulgences of this force are overeating or oversleeping—in effect, doing something merely because of how it feels. An ego drive can run the gamut from making a joke at someone else's expense to making a lavish purchase that's beyond one's means. When the ego reigns, we are not drawn to what *is* good, but to what makes us *look* good—in our own eyes and in the eyes of others.[4]

Over time, these choices erode our self-esteem because when we routinely succumb to immediate gratification or live to protect and project an image, we become angry with ourselves and ultimately feel empty inside.[5]

When we do not like who we are, we punish ourselves with activities that are disguised as pleasurable: excessive eating, alcohol or drug abuse as well as meaningless diversions and excursions. We long to love ourselves, but instead we lose ourselves. Unable to invest in our own well-being, we substitute illusions for love. These ethereal delights mask our self-contempt, and since the comfort sought is rewarded instead by greater pain, we descend further into despair.

As our behavior becomes increasingly reckless and irresponsible, the ego

---

NOTES

2. See M. Scott Peck, *The Road Less Traveled: A New Psychology of Love, Traditional Values and Spiritual Growth* (New York: Simon & Schuster, 1978), 17-19. See Roy F. Baumeister, Todd F. Heatherton, and Dianne M. Tice, *Losing Control: How and Why People Fail at Self-Regulation* (California: Academic Press, 1994). Also see Christopher Peterson and Martin E. P. Seligman, *Character Strengths and Virtues* (Oxford, UK: Oxford University Press, 2004).

3. The soul's influence is called the *yetzer tov*, "good inclination," or "conscience." The ego is the false self and is referred to as the *yetzer hara*, "evil inclination."

4. See Dovid Lieberman, *Real Power* (New Jersey: Viter Press, 2008), 76.

5. Both the quality and quantity of our choices factor into the equation. This means that a single egregious act can infect our belief system and the unwillingness to face the resultant guilt or shame may stain our entire worldview.

swells to compensate for feelings of guilt and shame. Our perspective narrows, and we see more of the self and less of the world; this makes us even more sensitive and unstable.

PERSPECTIVE = MENTAL HEALTH

The clearer our perspective, the more reality we allow in, and the more objective and rational are our attitudes, thoughts, and behaviors. As the ego grows, the seedlings of emotional instability take root because any distortion of our true self produces a misrepresentation of the world;[6] and if our grasp of reality is flawed, then our adjustment to life will suffer.[7]

When a person loses his sanity—the ability to see, accept, and respond to his world—it means that he has lost all perspective.

The Talmud states that Adam HaRishon ("Adam, the first man") could see from one end of the world to the other.[8] Before eating of the *Eitz HaDaas* ("Tree of Knowledge"), Adam had no *yetzer hara* ("ego"). This entity was represented by the serpent and was external to Adam. So his perception was unfettered.[9]

The *yetzer hara* entered only when Adam ate of the tree and became alert to the difference between good and evil, which shifted his perspective.[10] Man's awareness was reduced from the objective world of "truth and falsehood" to the subjective world of "good and bad."[11] After the sin, human beings would forever see their world through the cloudy lens of "I."

NOTES

6. To the degree that we cannot accept our imperfections and limitations, we are forced to shift fault elsewhere. In other words: *If there is nothing wrong with me then there must be something wrong with you.* In order for us to remain unblemished, we distort the world around us. The ego has a variety of these defense mechanisms which are detailed in the following chapter.

7. Ralph Waldo Emerson wrote, "People do not seem to realize that their opinion of the world is also a confession of character." "...we were like grasshoppers in our eyes, and so we were like in their eyes!" (Numbers 13:33). The spies believed that the current inhabitants in the Land of Israel viewed them as people who could easily be conquered. Because the spies felt like grasshoppers in their own eyes, they were convinced that others also perceived them in this way (*Sfas Emes*, ibid.).

8. *Chagigah* 12a.

9. A fetus is also able to see from one end of the world to the other (*Niddah* 30b). This is because the *yetzer hara* does not enter a person until the moment of birth, as it is written, "Sin crouches at the door" (Genesis 4:7, cf. *Sanhedrin* 91b).

10. See Rashi on Genesis 2:25.

11. See Rambam, *Guide for the Perplexed* 1:2.

Emotional instability is, fundamentally, a lack of clarity—the degree to which the ego infects us. To this extent, we are all somewhat sick.[12] At whatever point we have clarity that a given behavior is wrong, *bechirah* ("free will") emerges, and it becomes a genuine choice. That is, to choose good over evil. To the degree that we fall short, we are all somewhat evil.[13]

12. The Rambam writes that in any instance, the only reason we come to sin is that we do not know fully what we are doing *(Hilchos Geirushin* 2:20).

13. This is an oversimplification of the decision-making process because a lack of clarity is not always self-induced and intellectual awareness—distinguishing right from wrong—is not enough to put a behavior within the scope of free will. A person must have the equal capacity to act. This will be explained in the upcoming chapters.

2 | ROOTS OF UNHAPPINESS

On a conscious level we cannot easily admit to ourselves that we are selfish or lazy, much less a failure or flawed.[14] The ego is thus equipped with an elaborate array of defense mechanisms to thwart the harshness of reality. As these defenses emerge, instability, which can be seen as the chasm between the truth and our ability to accept it, develops. Defense mechanisms are categorized based on how they affect an individual's functioning:[15]

Level III—Neurotic defenses (i.e., intellectualization, reaction formation, dissociation, displacement, repression, rationalizing). These neurotic mechanisms are fairly common and cause greater challenges for those who default to them regularly.

Level II—Immature defenses (i.e., fantasy, projection, passive aggression, acting out). These mechanisms temporarily lessen distress and anxiety provoked by an uncomfortable situation and, with constant engagement, lead to serious problems in a person's ability to develop genuine coping strategies with minimal distortion of the facts.

Level I—Pathological defenses (i.e., psychotic denial, delusional

---

NOTES

14. It is not uncommon for a person to declare himself worthless—so damaged, bad, and broken that he is beyond repair or reproach. This unconsciously motivated, ego-driven tactic cleverly absolves him of responsibility because he doesn't "deserve" to be happy. He thereby avoids the pain of accountability and the burden of obligation. He may also choose to lay blame outside of his control: a victim of inexorable desire or of a callous society. See Chapter 35, "The Force of Habit" for further discussion.

15. Based on George E. Vaillant, *Ego Mechanisms of Defense: A Guide for Clinicians and Researchers* (Washington, DC: American Psychiatric Publishing, 1992), 327–238.

projection). The mechanisms on this level are severely pathological and effectively recreate external experiences to do away with the need to cope with reality.

Our ego colors the world, so that we are not tarnished. Before we airbrush reality, however, a collision occurs in the unaccessed caverns of the unconscious, between truth and falsehood—producing the psychological phenomenon *cognitive dissonance*: the feeling of uncomfortable tension and stress that comes from holding two contradictory ideas simultaneously. From a Torah standpoint, cognitive dissonance is the by-product of tension between the *yetzer tov* ("soul") and *yetzer hara* ("ego")—a choice to either accept reality or reduce dissonance by any of the above-mentioned mechanisms. The most common of these are (a) avoidance, (b) denial, or (c) justification.[16]

Smoking offers a classic illustration of cognitive dissonance. The smoker may acknowledge that cigarettes cause a wide range of negative health effects, but he probably also desires to be healthy. The tension produced by these inconsistent ideas can be reduced by (a) not thinking about it; (b) disputing or denying the evidence; (c) justifying one's smoking ("A bus could come and hit me tomorrow," "I need to smoke, or I'd gain too much weight"); or (d) accepting the truth, and taking steps to quit.[17]

Physiologically speaking, research shows that "reasoning areas of the brain virtually shut down when we are confronted with dissonant information; and the emotion circuits of the brain light up unreservedly when consonance is restored."[18] Similarly, our Sages say, "There is no happiness like the resolution of doubt," which is why the ego seizes any opportunity to reconcile the internal conflict.[19] The following anecdote typifies this process, particularly when our self-image is on the line.

NOTES

16. Denial is a defense mechanism where one is faced with a truth that is too uncomfortable or threatening to accept and therefore rejects it. The person may refuse to accept the reality of the unpleasant fact completely (plain denial), admit the fact but deny its seriousness (minimizing), or admit both the reality and the gravity but totally deny responsibility (transference). (Definition based on Wikipedia.)

17. In 1969, celebrated psychologist Eliot Aronson refined the theory to reveal a deeper, universal (and Torah-aligned) conflict. He posits that all people want to see themselves as good individuals and in control of their behavior. Hence, all attempts to reduce dissonance are really a desire to preserve this self-concept.

18. Drew Westen, et al., "The Neural Basis of Motivated Reasoning: An fMRI Study of Emotional Constraints on Partisan Political Judgment in the 2004 U.S. Presidential Election," *Journal of Cognitive Neuroscience* 18, no. 11 (2006): 1947–1958.

19. See *Metzudas David* on Proverbs 15:30.

There was a man who woke one day convinced that he was a zombie. When he told his wife he was a zombie, she tried to talk him out of this outrageous opinion.

"You are not a zombie!" she said.

"I am a zombie," he answered.

"What makes you think you are a zombie?" she asked rhetorically.

"Don't you think zombies know they are zombies?" he answered with great sincerity.

His wife realized she was not getting anywhere, so she called his mother and told her what was going on. His mother tried to help.

"I'm your mother. Wouldn't I know if I gave birth to a zombie?"

"You didn't," he explained. "I became a zombie later."

"I didn't raise my son to be a zombie, or even to think he is a zombie," his mother pleaded.

"Nonetheless, I am a zombie," he said, unmoved by his mother's appeal to his identity and sense of guilt.

Later that day his wife called [a psychiatrist].

The wife was given an emergency appointment, and within the hour the husband was in the psychiatrist's office.

"So, you think you are a zombie?" the psychiatrist asked.

"I know I am a zombie," the man said.

"Tell me, do zombies bleed?" the psychiatrist asked.

"Of course not," said the man. "Zombies are the living dead. They don't bleed." The man was a little annoyed at the psychiatrist's patronizing question.

"Well, watch this," said the psychiatrist as he picked up a pin. He took the man's finger and made a tiny pinprick. The man looked at his finger with great amazement and said nothing for three or four minutes.

"What do you know," the man finally said, "zombies do bleed!"[20]

FROM SHIELD TO SHELL

Denying reality does not come without a price. Exhausted and on edge, our ego edits our world to ensure that we leave in nothing that will hurt us or reveal us, either to ourselves or to others. Preoccupied with potential threats to our self-image, we are on guard 24/7.

NOTES

20. Robert Fritz, *The Path of Least Resistance: Learning to Become the Creative Force in Your Own Life* (New York: Fawcett Columbine, 1989). (Passage edited.)

We hide behind a carefully crafted façade, and the identity that we build to shield ourselves soon becomes a shell that encases us. Over time, we fall into a hellish gap of unrealized potential, our true self weakens, and our inside grows hollow. We no longer live for ourselves. We exist only to protect our image. This includes all of the games we play and the masks we wear to provide the rest of the world with what we believe is the right persona.

We may not even realize how much of our attitude and behavior—indeed, our very identity—is self-styled to avoid self-reflection, to compensate for self-hatred, and to project an image that betrays neither.

In the exchange, we lose ourselves, contorting to the images demanded by others to win their praise.[21] The great *mussar* leader Rabbi Simcha Zissel Ziv writes, "If you observe people carefully you will see that someone who loves the approval of others will, as it were, sell himself as a slave to those who flatter him. He will not even realize what is happening to him, however obvious it may be to an outside observer."[22]

Unsurprisingly, we are never truly satiated. When we do not love ourselves, we cannot give love and we cannot feel loved. Even when the supply is plentiful, with adulation beyond measure, we experience a different reality. Ultimately, we remain empty inside.

Imagine pouring water into a cup that has no bottom. As someone pours in the water, the cup feels and looks full. As long as the cup is constantly being filled, we are content. But the minute someone stops filling it (with undivided attention, respect, or adoration), the cup quickly becomes empty, and we are left as thirsty as ever.[23] A shattered cup will never be full, and our thirst can never be quenched, no matter how much we receive.[24]

NOTES

21. Certainly, there is a positive side. Ethics of the Fathers 1:12 states, "Be among the disciples of Aaron ... loving people and bringing them close to Torah." The Rambam, in his commentary on this *Mishnah*, quotes from *Avos d'Rabbi Nassan* (12:3), which describes how Aaron would make an effort to befriend a person who behaved wrongly, knowing that the offender's shame would encourage him to mend his ways, so as not to disappoint his honorable new friend.

22. Rabbi Simcha Zissel Ziv Broida, *Chochmah u'Mussar*, Vol. 1, 219. *Mussar* is the practice of personality development (through exercising moral discipline), moving toward perfection of character, cultivation of morality, and emulation of Divine qualities.

23. This hunger compels us to become braggarts so that others will hear of our greatness. "A sign of complete ignorance is self-praise" (*Zohar* 193b). "One coin in a pitcher makes a great deal of noise" (*Bava Metzia* 85b).

24. Much unhappiness in life stems from failing or failed relationships, with our emotional health feasting on, and fueling, the quality of our relationships. Dr. William Glaser writes, "From the perspective of forty years of psychiatric practice, it has become apparent to me that all unhappy people have the same problem: they are unable to get along with the people they want to get along well with." *Reality Therapy*, 5.

Herein lies the basis for many failed relationships. When we lack self-esteem, we push away the very people we so desperately want in our lives because we cannot fathom why anyone would love someone who is so unlovable. And whatever affection or kindness forces its way through to us is hardly embraced. Such overtures do not serve to comfort, but to confuse. To compound matters, the less self-control we have the more desperate we are to manipulate the events and people around us, especially those closest to us—either overtly or passive-aggressively.[25] Since self-control leads to self-respect, we need to feel as if we are in control of someone, something, anything, to gain a sense of traction. Low self-esteem can thus trigger a powerful unconscious desire to usurp authority, to overstep bounds, and to mistreat those who care about us. When we do not like ourselves, we suffer. Our relationships suffer. Everyone suffers.

25. A passive-aggressive person is generally described as one who retreats to avoid a confrontation. He is unable to face the situation head-on, so he chooses to back down, only to get back at the person in another way, at another time—whether it is by being late, "forgetting" to do something important for the person, or just generally inconveniencing him. This behavior is rarely consciously examined.

PART 2

THE SHAPE OF REALITY

As self-esteem fades and the ego's noose tightens, our entire decision-making system becomes corrupt, and our lives are reduced to a network of conditioned responses. The following chapters explain how seemingly smart people fall victim to irrationality and become vulnerable to the whims and the will of the world around them.

3 | TRUTH OR CONSEQUENCES

Irrationality lies at the root of the classic proclamation "If God showed Himself to me just once or performed a miracle right in front of my eyes, then I would be a believer and do everything that He says." First, such unearned clarity removes the possibility of free will. Man would then believe in God because he had no choice. We would, in effect, be no different from angels—for who could act against God when in His undeniable presence?[1]

Yet our quest for absolute proof is utterly illogical. It is an emotional argument offered up to grant ourselves permission to do whatever we want.[2] We require little proof to do what we feel like doing; and we often go against flawless logic when it is convenient or comfortable.[3] It's not about reason and rationale. It's about emotion and desire.

With cigarette warnings of severe consequences in plain view, tens of millions of people still smoke. An avalanche of literature on the hazards of obesity and

---

NOTES

1. A direct, known, and immediate consequence also removes the opportunity for free will. If the impact of our choices—positive or negative—were always observable and obvious, then our ability to choose would be compromised.

2. Lot made a decision to leave his uncle, Abraham, to settle in the spiritually depraved city of Sodom (Genesis 13:10–11), because he saw that land to be the most fertile. Rashi, citing *Chazal* ("our Sages") (*Nazir* 23a), explains that the underlying reason Lot went to Sodom was because he was drawn to the immorality of that place but was unaware of his own motivations.

3. The clear and evident problems with evolutionary theory are a prime example. People cling tightly to this inane theory because it absolves them of accountability. Indeed, atheists have no fewer questions than do people who believe in God and follow His commandments, yet they contend that they are not convinced enough to believe. In truth, however, it really is a lack of will to change their behavior and a desire to avoid the pain of dissonance that drives their thinking—or lack thereof.

the importance of exercise is ignored by 67 percent of the population who remain overweight or obese. With hundreds of studies bringing us to near-universal agreement that money doesn't buy happiness, 55 percent of the adult population are in debt. What does proof have to do with it?

Open miracle after open miracle were performed on behalf of the Jewish people in Egypt. And then they all stood as a Nation and heard the voice of God at *Har Sinai* ("Mount Sinai"), where each and every Jew experienced mass prophecy in the form of a direct revelation from God. They even received the first two of the Ten Commandments directly from Him, but a mere forty days later they permitted the worshiping of an idol, the Golden Calf.[4]

Nature is designed to reveal God's Presence to those who learn to see it. At the same time, nature is designed to mask God's Presence from those who cannot see beyond themselves. This is precisely why He only shows us reality but does not give us unearned clarity—it simply does not stick.[5] We do not need a new landscape. We need to open our eyes.

The Torah states that everyone was aware that a Hebrew slave had risen to great prominence in Egypt, and, in spite of an uncanny sequence of events and hints, "they did not recognize him."[6] A stunning series of clues as to the viceroy's true identity was overlooked by the brothers, even though they had it in mind to look for Joseph when they entered Egypt. Against what must have seemed like astronomical odds, Joseph seated his eleven brothers in age-order, calling them each by name. Undoubtedly, the occasion itself should have been suspect, in that the leader of Egypt invited these "spies" to a lavish meal and even showed that the meat had been slaughtered in strict accordance with *halachah* ("Jewish law").[7] Furthermore, the *Midrash* relates that when the viceroy was about to reveal his true identity, he said, "Your brother whom you sold is in the house," and the brothers began looking around the room but never thought to look in front of them.[8] We read in the *Midrash*:

---

4. The Torah (Exodus 32:38) states that three thousand out of three million people (a mere .1 percent) were actively involved. Yet the entire Jewish nation was held responsible because of their failure to intervene in its construction and its worship. (To be clear, the Golden Calf was not created as a deity to replace God, but as an intermediary to replace Moses whom they thought to have died.)

5. The Ramban, Rabbi Moshe ben Nachman (*Toras Hashem Temimah*) writes, "The great public miracles which can confound the weak in faith are not performed for every generation, for the generations are not worthy ... or because there is no need for them to be performed."

6. Cf. Genesis 43:32; ibid., 42:8.

7. Genesis 43:33.

8. *Bereishis Rabbah* 93:8.

Their eyes darted to every corner of the house.

Said Joseph, "Why are you looking from side-to-side—you are looking at him! I am Joseph."

His brothers were stunned and speechless.[9]

Joseph's brothers were just feet away from him, but they simply could not fathom that they had been wrong for all of those years. They stared at reality, and reality stared back, yet they could not see.[10]

A STUBBORN STREAK

When our ego rules, we become stuck in a perpetual cycle of bad decisions, such that we feel further compelled to justify our previous actions, regardless of the consequences. We will eat food that we don't want because we ordered it. We will read a book that we really don't want to read because we went all the way to the library in the rain to get it. Our primary concern is with being right, even if it means compromising our present judgment in order to justify past behaviors. The folly of this mindset is poetically condensed by Ralph Waldo Emerson: "A foolish consistency is the hobgoblin of little minds."[11]

A revealing application of this mentality is the process of cult recruiting. We may wonder how an intelligent and aware person could ever become involved in a cult—where the member gives up his family, friends, possessions, and, in some very tragic instances, his life. The method employed in cult recruitment is to involve the person slowly over a period of time, so that each new step of involvement lulls the person into justifying his previous behavior. Then, once the person is past the point of indoctrination, a period of harsh rebuke and magnification of personal flaws and failings is instituted to chip away at the follower's self-esteem.

The higher a person's self-esteem, the less likely he will be to subject himself to the prey of a cult (once he becomes aware of its true agenda)—primarily because a person with a positive self-concept can admit to himself, and to others, that he

---

9. *Tanchumah, Vayigash* 5.

10. "A wise man was asked: 'What is the easiest thing for a man to do?' He replied, 'The easiest thing a man can do is to fool himself.' It takes a lot of forethought and planning to fool others, but he can fool himself in a moment and at any moment." *Ya'aros Dvash* (Vol. I, No. 3), Rabbi Jonathan Eybeschutz (1690–1764).

11. "Self-Reliance," *Essays: First Series,* 1841. Ralph Waldo Emerson (1803–1882) was an American essayist, lecturer, and poet.

has done something foolishly dangerous. Those whose egos reign cannot afford to question their judgment, worth, or intelligence.

Our commitment to staying the course tends to become stronger once we have invested time, money, or energy into something—whether it's a tumbling stock, a doomed relationship, or a dead-end job. If we make a bleak investment, it's easy to succumb to the sunk-cost fallacy: *I can't stop now because everything I've invested so far will be lost*. This is true, of course, but it's irrelevant to whether we should continue down a wasteful path.

The Torah speaks of God changing His mind in the days of Noah. "God saw the great evil of Man on the earth and that all the designs of the thoughts of his heart were only evil the entire day. God regretted that He had made Man on the earth and it caused mourning in His heart."[12] This cannot be taken literally. After all, we know that "God is no man that He should reconsider."[13] Instead, "The Torah speaks in the language of men."[14] It is meant to teach us the lesson of responsible decisions. God saw mankind's corruption for what it was and then acted accordingly. God did not refrain from wiping away every living creature simply because He had "invested so much time and energy." Even the suggestion of it is ludicrous. The same logic, though, applies to us. Justification binds us to the past and drags mistakes into the future.[15]

Irrational commitment was the opening salvo of the *yetzer hara*. Eve said to the serpent, "Of the fruit of the tree which is in the center of the garden God has said: 'You shall neither eat of it nor touch it, lest you die.'"[16] (God had commanded that she not eat from the tree, but she herself added the prohibition against touching it.) The serpent pushed her against the tree and said, "Just as you did not die from touching it, so you will not die from eating it."[17] The serpent ("ego incarnate") injected itself into her thinking, and because she did not want to retreat from her previous statement, she relented, accepting the logic put forth, even though she knew it was tainted by her own lie.

NOTES

12. Genesis 6:5–6.

13. I Samuel 15:29.

14. *Ibn Ezra*, ad loc.

15. The impact of our choice carries forward. Once we commit to something, we use *adaptive self-serving biases* to support our decision. For example, after we buy a certain product, we are more likely to notice evidence that confirms that we made the right choice.

16. Genesis 2:17.

17. *Midrash*, Rashi on Genesis 3:3. According to another tradition, it was Adam who expanded God's prohibition to include touching the tree, but he neglected to clarify this point with Eve. We see from this interpretation that falsehood is the opening to the *yetzer hara*.

RIGHT TO THE END

Even after the facts become obvious, an intelligent but egocentric person may not only stay the course of a bad decision, but persist in engaging in outright self-destructive behavior. The ego wants us to see ourselves as victims of fate, circumstance, or others' cruel behavior in order to avoid taking responsibility for our actions and our lives. We become locked into these patterns in order to manipulate reality and to cause it to unfold in accordance with our expectations. It's how we need the world to be.

Being right becomes more of an emotional priority than doing what is right. We act against our own best interest because, unconsciously, we need to prove to ourselves and to others that we have been damaged, and so we perpetuate our own misery. Renowned psychologist Dr. Nathaniel Branden writes,

> I am thinking of a woman I once treated who grew up thinking she was "bad" and undeserving of kindness, respect, or happiness. Predictably, she married a man who "knew" he was unlovable and felt consumed by self-hatred. He protected himself by being cruel to others before they could be cruel to him. She did not complain about his abuse since she knew that abuse was her destiny. He was not surprised by her increasing withdrawal and remoteness from him since he "knew" no one could ever love him. They spent 20 years of torture together proving how right they were about themselves and about life.[18]

When we suffer from low self-esteem, we often feel that something bad will happen to us after something good happens. When unexpected fortune comes our way, there is an anxiety brought on by this feeling of unworthiness. In order to reduce the emotional tension, we may even sabotage our success to fulfill our personal prophecy, which gives us a contrived sense of security. The world is as we predicted. Our beliefs—no matter how damaging and distorted—have been reaffirmed. We will be right, even if it kills us.

18. Nathaniel Branden, *The Power of Self Esteem* (Florida: HCI, 1992), 14–15.

THE LURE OF CONFORMITY

4

In nonphysical space, closeness is measured in terms of similarities. Conceptually, the space between low self-esteem (an egocentric mentality) and the *yetzer hara* is shorter—because it's more similar—than between high self-esteem (elevated presence of the soul) and the *yetzer hara*.

For what really is the difference between a self-centered person and his *yetzer hara*? This is why such a person can abruptly shift from being reasonable one moment to grossly reckless the next. He lives on the cusp of these intermingled forces.[19]

To illustrate with a real-world metaphor, all objects are attracted to each other by the force of gravity. The strength of the attraction depends on the size of the objects (mass) and the distance between them. The more we identify with the *yetzer hara*, the greater our attraction or susceptibility to unhealthy influences, because it is "heavier" and closer in proximity to the world of falsehood.[20]

Simply, the less control we exert over ourselves, the more sway our surroundings

---

NOTES

19. Mood is the shadow of self-esteem. The higher our self-esteem, the more consistently positive and stable is our mood. We all have our bad days and good days, but true emotional stability remains fairly consistent, regardless of our daily ups and downs.

20. The Sages say, "The greater the person, the greater [the lure of] the *yetzer hara*" (*Kiddushin* 52b). Regardless of our spiritual standing, none of us are exempt from trials tailored to our own specific level (*Succah* 52a). The difference lies not in the metaphorical size of the competing negative force, but in our ability to fight off its influences. An egocentric person has a lower resistance to the outside world because his spiritual immune system is compromised. Minimal exposure to any germ—in other words, negative stimuli—can contaminate his entire belief system.

hold over us. We must all, however, be vigilant. Because we are a mélange of body, ego, and soul, no one is impervious to the hidden force of social influence that imperceptibly recalibrates one's moral compass to accommodate the need for acceptance and recognition (and to sanction self-indulgence).

REALITY BY CONSENSUS

In this classic experiment, subjects were asked to find the best match for the line in the box on the left from the lines in the box on the right. When asked privately, almost every person judged line C as the correct match. When the subject, however, first listened to several other people who were in on the experiment and

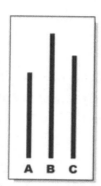

who unanimously gave a wrong answer, 76 percent of the subjects responded, at least once, in accord with the group, rather than trust their own eyes and judgment. There was no pressure to conform, only the subtle influence of the others.[21]

A philosopher once mused, "Insanity in individuals is something rare, but in groups, parties, nations, and epochs, it is the rule." An illustration of this idea is the mob mentality, the phenomenon in which people in groups tend to support more extreme ideas than they would individually. The events surrounding the actions of Pinchas serve as a poignant example. Many Jews, particularly from the Tribe of Shimon defied God's will in support of the sinful and adulterous behavior of their prince, Zimri ben Salu.[22] Embers of shame were all but extinguished, and much of the Jewish nation was caught in the wave of madness.[23]

A weakened core-self collapses altogether under the weight of social influence, but we can withstand only so much external pressure before it begins to wear us down.[24] King Solomon warns, "Withdraw yourself from a fool," because to some

NOTES

21. "If the conduct of a man is in constant change, he is a stranger to the right way: but one of inner purity, his doings are straightforward" (Proverbs 21:8).

22. Some of the *Shevet* ("Tribe") actually sinned first, and they then pleaded with their head who joined them. See Rashi on Numbers 25:6.

23. Numbers 25:1–9.

24. Alice M. Tybout and Richard F. Yalch, "The Effect of Experience: A Matter of Salience?" *Journal of Consumer Research* 6, no. 4 (1980), 406–413.6. "In general, a person who is being particular about his

degree, we all become a product of our environment.[25] According to Rabbi Bachya ibn Pakudah,

> Many people think that the environment exerts a significant influence only on children and the weak-minded. This is not true. The environment has important effects even on the greatest... . It is irrationality and poverty of spirit [to] patiently endure injuries which might be averted. This sort of humility is found among foolish and ignorant people [and is not really humility], but rather spiritual poverty and blindness.[26]

The Ramchal is forthright: "If someone says to you, 'A man's mind should always be associated with his fellow men,' tell him, 'This refers to people who conduct themselves as human beings and not to people who conduct themselves as animals.'"[27] Our identity is very much tied in with where we live, and the Torah alerts us to the hazards of being around those who will negatively impact our spiritual well-being.[28] This is the lesson of the well-known excerpt from Ethics of the Fathers:

> Rabbi Yossi ben Kisma said: One time I was walking along the way and a certain man met me. He greeted me and I returned the greeting. He said to me, "Rabbi, where are you from?" I responded, "I am from a great city of scholars and scribes." He said, "Rabbi, would you be willing to dwell among us in our place, and I will give you thousands of thousands of gold coins, precious stones, and pearls?" I replied: "Even if you would give me all the silver, gold, precious stones, and pearls in the world, I would not dwell anywhere other than in a place of Torah."[29]

NOTES

mitzvah observance, the main challenge is in standing alone, and he needs courage not to be swayed by his environment" (Chazon Ish, *Emunah U'Bitachon*, Ch. 4).

25. Proverbs 14:7. A person who kills another accidentally is exiled to an *Ir Miklat* ("a city of refuge"). Here, such a person did not dwell among crooks and thieves. On the contrary, the city was inhabited by the spiritually refined Levites, who played an integral role in the rehabilitation of its inhabitants.

26. Bachya ibn Pakudah, *Chovos HaLevavos*, Vol. 2, 75.

27. Ramchal, *Mesillas Yesharim*, Ch. 5, 71.

28. "A person is drawn after the society he lives in" (Rambam, *Hilchos De'os* 6:1). "Fortunate is he who does not walk in the council of the wicked or sit in a place of scoffers" (Psalms 1:1). "Do not associate with the man of temper and do not come near a man of wrath, lest you learn from his ways and endanger your soul" (Proverbs 22:24–25).

29. Ethics of the Fathers 6:9.

This explains why a person may act totally out of character while on vacation or visiting another city. We are, in part, a product of our surroundings, and the pull from our environment—both positive and negative—is strong. Naturally, it's not always a bad thing.[30]

Referring to the *mitzvah* ("commandment") of *hakhel* for all of the Jewish people to gather together every seven years on the festival of Succos, the Rambam writes, "Such a gathering results in a renewal of the Torah, this being a result of the people being affected by it and the fraternity that comes about because of it."[31] The environment is indeed a double-edged sword. The word *hakhel* is also used in reference to the sin of the Golden Calf. It came about because the people gathered—*va-yikahel*.[32]

WRONG BECOMES RELATIVE

Even something that we know to be wrong becomes more alluring when we discover that others are engaged in this very behavior. For this reason, municipalities are aware, for instance, that graffiti must be removed as quickly as possible, because as soon as it appears, it creates a breeding ground for vandalism perpetrated by others who previously thought it unacceptable. A sign at Arizona's Petrified Forest National Park reads:

> *Your heritage is being vandalized every day by theft losses of petrified*
> *wood of 14 tons a year, mostly a small piece at a time.*

Researchers marked pieces of petrified wood along the trails to see how many of them the visitors would steal. When the above-worded sign was taken down, 2.92 percent of the pieces were stolen. When the sign was up and in plain sight, 7.92 percent of the pieces were stolen.[33] The National Park management did not realize

30. The Sages warn us that we should not separate ourselves from the community (Ethics of the Fathers 2:5); those weaker, in particular, need the framework of society to ensure that they act appropriately, even if it is out of fear. "Pray for the welfare of the government, for without fear of governmental authorities people would swallow each other alive" (ibid., 3:2).

31. Rambam, *Guide for the Perplexed*.

32. In parallel, the *parashah* (Leviticus 25:9) reveals that on Yom Kippur of the *Yovel* year, a *shofar* is to be blown throughout the land, even on Shabbos (Rashi 25:9). The *Sefer HaChinuch* states that this is to publicize the edict that all Jewish slaves must be released. He explains that it is not easy for most people to free their slaves and that the *shofar* blast reminds the people that others, too, are faced with the same difficulty; it offers solace and makes it easier to part with one's slave when one recognizes that everyone is in the same proverbial boat. He writes, "There is nothing that provides comfort and strength to the hearts of man like the fact that many people are in the same situation as him" (*Sefer HaChinuch, Mitzvah* 331).

33. Noah J. Goldstein, Steve J. Martin, and Robert B. Cialdini, *Yes! 50 Scientifically Proven Ways to Be Convincing* (New York: Free Press, 2008).

that the sign would promote stealing (in fact, doubling it), because it revealed that theft was socially acceptable—even though it is obviously wrong.

The impact of social influence is even more concerning and disturbing in an age when technology streams the world to our fingertips. The media calls it the "copycat effect," but to psychologists it's the "Werther effect." It is based on the principle that human beings use others' actions to decide on what is proper behavior for themselves (again, the lower our self-esteem, the greater our dependency).[34]

For example, when people learn of another's suicide, a number of them decide that suicide may make sense for themselves—even some who were not actively planning to end their lives! (Some will commit suicide without caring that people know they killed themselves, but others do not want their deaths to appear to be suicides.) Thus, research shows that three days following a report in the media about a suicide, the rate of automobile fatalities increased by 31 percent.[35]

The chilling effect extends beyond numbers, in that fatalities are most frequent in the region where the suicide story is publicized, and the more similar we are to the victim, the more likely we are to be influenced (due to ego-identification). Hence, when the media reports that a young person committed suicide, the number of crashes by young people increases. When news about an older person committing suicide is reported, the number of crashes by older individuals increases.

This insidious phenomenon invades all areas of our lives, with research at Harvard University revealing that obesity, smoking, and drinking—among a range of unhealthy behaviors—can spread, as they put it, "from person-to-person, through social networks, much like a virus during an epidemic," and compare these behaviors to "emotional stampedes" or "a social chain reaction."[36]

NOTES

34. Biologically speaking, our vulnerability is partly due to specialized brain cells called mirror neurons, which seek out signals that serve as cues for what is considered proper behavior given the situation. Mirror neurons are responsible for *mass psychogenic illness* (also called *conversation disorder* and previously named *mass hysteria*). A person with this disorder has neurological symptoms—ranging from uncontrolled outbursts to paralysis—that are not related to any known neurological condition and that spread throughout a cohesive group (such as a class in a school or an office) with no root cause, other than the subconscious influence of those around them.

35. The "Werther Effect" was coined by Dr. David P. Phillips. He writes, "The increase in the suicide rate was not due to the effect of weekday or monthly fluctuations in motor vehicle fatalities, to holiday weekends, or to yearly linear trends, because the effects were corrected for in the selection and treatment of the control periods, with which the experimental periods are compared." D. P. Phillips, "Suicide, Motor Vehicle Fatalities, and the Mass Media: Evidence toward a Theory of Suggestion," *American Journal of Sociology* 84, no. 5 (1979).

36. Nicholas A. Christakis and James H. Fowler, "The Spread of Obesity in a Large Social Network Over 32 Years," *New England Journal of Medicine* 357, no. 4 (2007): 370–379. See also Nicholas A. Christakis and James H. Fowler, "The Collective Dynamics of Smoking in a Large Social Network," *New England Journal of Medicine*

We must keep in mind that even the greatest among us are vulnerable to these hidden pitfalls. The only weapon we have—in addition to increasing self-esteem to reduce the ego—is to sensitize ourselves by constantly, consciously reminding ourselves of the truth.[37] In this way we are alert, rather than oblivious, to contradictory stimuli, which helps insulate us from blindly absorbing the attitudes and values of others.[38] The Ramchal writes,

> We must constantly—at all times, and particularly during a regularly appointed time of solitude—reflect upon the true path [according to the ordinance of the Torah] that we must walk upon. After engaging in such reflection we will come to consider whether or not our deeds travel along this path.[39]

Naturally, the ego, does not want us to consider such matters, and the deeper it pulls us into the darkness, the more vested we become in closing our eyes to the remaining light.

When we become desperate for an anchor to orient our lives—because we no longer believe in ourselves—we attach ourselves to inane ideals and beliefs. Our ego seeks to identify with something secure and permanent because the soul's connection to the Infinite—true security—is frayed. We are then forced to rely on the ever-shifting sands of ethics, rather than on the bedrock of morality.

NOTES

358, no. 21 (2008): 2249–2258; and James N. Rosenquist, Joanne Murabito, James H. Fowler, and Nicholas A. Christakis, "The Spread of Alcohol Consumption Behavior in a Large Social Network," *Annals of Internal Medicine* 152, no. 7 (2010): 426–433. See Chapter 33, "Mental Reserves" for details on these studies.

37. We also become more attuned to whatever will help us foster our objectives; "... a tailor who sees a person will look in particular at his clothes. A cobbler—at so-and-so's shoes. A hat maker—at so-and-so's hat. Similarly, a shopkeeper in the market will be very alert to speech or action that will bring him some gain in his sales. Unlike another person, who wouldn't hear or see these things, for his heart isn't given over to ask and look into these things, for he has no desire for them." Rabbi Simcha Zissel Ziv, *Chochmah U'Mussar* (Vol. 2, 113). The Reticular Activating System (RAS) is the brain's filtering mechanism and keeps us from becoming overwhelmed by unnecessary stimuli. Our objectives (and in some instances, our fears) dictate what we deem as necessary and whether or not something is unconsciously dismissed or consciously accepted.

38. Cf. Maimonides, *Eight Chapters* (Introduction to *Pirkei Avot*); cf. Rabbi Simcha Zissel Ziv, *Chochmah U'Mussar*, Vol. 1, 452. See also Chapter 28, "Freedom from Fear," and our discussion on *terror management theory* and the necessity of having a definitive purpose.

39. *Mesillas Yesharim*, (*The Path of the Just*), Ch. 3.

CULT
OF
PERSONALITY

5

As we noted, right and wrong are value concepts that are not always aligned with the world of absolute truths.[40] This is the difference between morality and ethics. Morality is unchanging—it is from God. Ethics exists within the context of a social or professional framework: soft clay, kneaded and molded to suit our sensibilities.[41]

In Roman times, infanticide was a common and acceptable practice, as, indeed, it remains today in certain parts of the world. Any person of conscience would consider this practice abhorrent, but when it becomes the norm—and is endorsed by those in authority—our indignation and guilt are assuaged.

As trust in ourselves slips away, we look to the world because we dare not look to ourselves. The involvement of an expert or an authority figure further ratchets up the social pressure, and it requires great vigilance for us to hold our intellectual ground and to think for ourselves.

We are all to some degree susceptible to our conditioning regarding authority because, as children, we are taught—and rightly so—that obedience to authority is good and necessary. Yet the abuses of our vulnerability are flagrant and rampant because we will tend to obey authority figures even when it flies in the face of reason, much less common sense. Leading social psychologist Dr. Robert Cialdini explains that symbols of authority—titles, clothes, and trappings—influence our

---

NOTES

40. See Rambam, *Guide for the Perplexed* 1:2. He explains, "Right and wrong are value concepts that are applicable to the mundane world, not to the world of absolute truths. For example, you cannot say that the statement 'the heavens are spherical' or the contention that 'the earth is flat' is bad. But you can say that one is true and the other is false" (ibid., 2:2).

41. "A system of morality which is based on relative emotional values is a mere illusion, a thoroughly vulgar conception which has nothing sound in it and nothing true" (Socrates).

behavior and lead to mechanical obedience. He cites one such experiment involving a "doctor" prescribing an unusually high and dangerous dose of medication over the phone that resulted in a 95 percent compliance rate. The nurses disregarded hospital policy (which forbade orders from doctors by phone) and their own judgment (that the dose was clearly unsafe). The researchers concluded that the intelligence of the nurses following the orders was "nonfunctioning."[42]

DO AS YOU ARE TOLD

Probably no study pulls back the curtain on the darker side of social influence more than the mesmerizing experiment called the Milgram Obedience Study. Dr. Stanley Milgram writes,

> After watching the learner being strapped into place, he is seated before an impressive shock generator. The instrument panel consists of thirty lever switches set in a horizontal line. Each switch is clearly labeled with a voltage designation ranging from 15 to 450 volts. The following designations are clearly indicated for groups of four switches, going from left to right: Slight Shock, Moderate Shock, Strong Shock, Very Strong Shock, Intense Shock, Extreme Intensity Shock, Danger: Severe Shock... .When a switch is depressed, a pilot light corresponding to each switch is illuminated in bright red; an electric buzzing is heard; a blue light, labeled "voltage energizer," flashes; the dial on the voltage meter swings to the right; and various relay clicks sound off.[43]

Each willing but unwitting participant took the role of a teacher who would deliver a sequence of shocks to another so-called participant (termed the "learner")

42. Robert Cialdini, *Influence: The Psychology of Persuasion* (New York: HarperBusiness, 2006), 225. A person who questions authority does not necessarily have high self-esteem. There are those who challenge it at every turn because they have no respect for authority, let alone social norms. They are not honestly bothered by any self-proclaimed injustice, nor do they seek the truth. They are only interested in advancing their own agendas. Rashi (*Parshas Korach*) notes that Korach was extremely intelligent, astute, and even worthy of prophecy. But envy took hold, and he led a rebellion against Moses and Aaron's leadership under the guise of truth seeking. As the commentators point out, Korach was motivated only by self-interest. He was willing to send all of his supporters to certain death because he believed (as it turns out, wrongly) that he alone would survive. When our perspective is a reflection of our own desires, we cannot see the truth, much less consider another person's point of view.

43. Stanley Milgram, "The Perils of Obedience," *Harper's,* 1974. Abridged and adapted from *Obedience to Authority.*

every time an incorrect answer was given (from a simple word-pairing game). In actuality, the learner was really an actor who was only pretending to be shocked, but the participant fully believed that he was delivering real shocks, because they were in separate rooms and a tape recorder was integrated with the "electro-shock generator," which played prerecorded, increasingly escalating cries of pain at each shock level. Dr. Milgram continues,

> Conflict arises when the man receiving the shock begins to show that he is experiencing discomfort. At 75 volts, he grunts; at 120 volts, he complains loudly; at 150, he demands to be released from the experiment. As the voltage increases, his protests become more vehement and emotional. At 285 volts, his response can be described only as an agonized scream. Soon thereafter, he makes no sound at all.

Past this point, the learner would refuse to answer any further questions, and the participant was directed to treat this silence as an incorrect response and to continue to issue shocks accordingly.

Whenever a participant questioned whether or not he/she should continue, the experimenter issued a series of commands to prod the participant along:[44]

"Please continue."

"The experiment requires that you continue."

"It is absolutely essential that you continue."

"You have no other choice, you must go on."

The results were disturbing. Of the 40 participants in the study, 26 (two-thirds) delivered the maximum shock level of 450 volts. While the other 14 participants stopped before reaching the highest level, all of them—without a single exception—continued to 300 volts.

Many of the subjects became agitated and even angry with the experimenter. A few participants began to laugh nervously or exhibit other signs of stress once they heard the learner crying out in pain—yet they all continued to follow instructions.

Interestingly, two factors changed compliance rates. First, if the subjects saw other subjects refusing, they would start to resist as well. They were not strong enough to say "No" on their own, but with an ally felt more confident in voicing

NOTES

44. Stanley Milgram, "Behavioral Study of Obedience," *Journal of Abnormal and Social Psychology* 67, no. 4 (1963): 371–378. Text adapted from http://psychology.about.com/od/historyofpsychology/a/milgram.htm

their objection—once again revealing the sheer power of social influence. Second, if the subjects did not directly administer the shock but supervised those who did, they were far more inclined to continue.

Dr. Milgram elaborated on two theories in explaining the results. Note that the first is a function of a lack of faith in one's judgment, and the second, an abdication of personal responsibility.

- A subject who has neither ability nor expertise to make decisions, particularly in a crisis, will leave decision making to the group and its leaders. The group then becomes a model for this person's own behavior.

- The fuel of obedience is ignited when a person comes to view himself as the instrument for carrying out another person's wishes, and he therefore no longer sees himself as responsible for his actions. Once this critical shift in mindset occurs, all the essential features of obedience will follow.[45]

Milgram summarized the experiment in his 1974 article "The Perils of Obedience":

Stark authority was pitted against the subjects' [participants'] strongest moral imperatives against hurting others, and, with the subjects' [participants'] ears ringing with the screams of the victims, authority won more often than not. The extreme willingness of adults to go to almost any lengths on the command of an authority constitutes the chief finding of the study and the fact most urgently demanding explanation.... Ordinary people, simply doing their jobs, and without any particular hostility on their part, can become agents in a terrible destructive process. Moreover, even when the destructive effects of their work become patently clear, and they are asked to carry out actions incompatible with fundamental standards of morality, relatively few people have the resources needed to resist authority.[46]

The resource he speaks of is the emotional strength that comes with moral clarity—producing the capacity to choose responsibly and to hold tight to our convictions, regardless of the perceived cost or consequence.

45. Ibid.
46. Stanley Milgram, "The Perils of Obedience," *Harper's*, 1974. Abridged and adapted from *Obedience to Authority*.

Attempts to put our virtue into practice are made evermore difficult as the truth becomes a moving target. A distinguished psychiatrist observes how so-called experts are increasingly quick to relieve our overburdened conscience by blurring the line between truth and falsehood. She writes about the murky waters of moral relativity that exist today and that use "deceptive rhetoric, combined with a simply amazing and mind-boggling talent of being able to ignore objective reality under any circumstance." She continues,

> If you can convince children that objective reality is an illusion; that A does not equal A; that black is white; and that good is bad; if you can make them accept that everything is subjective and relative; then you own them. They will believe any drivel.[47]

As a person moves away from doing what is right, he moves away from God and toward moral relativism. When we come to believe that there are no absolute truths, then we will believe almost anything. For who is to say what is good and what is evil, when there is no God to say this is truth and this is falsehood?

THE OTHER HALF

While a weaker *yetzer tov* increases a person's subconscious susceptibility to outside influences, the egocentric person is certainly not without his own beliefs—they are just shackled around the need for acceptance (and self-indulgence). Some people become quintessential people-pleasers, perpetual doormats, trying to please the world in a fruitless attempt to gain love and approval.[48]

The other main personality type presents an attitude of defiance and self-righteousness, but this surface behavior does not reveal the ego's true fragility: namely, the need for recognition and respect. If this person wishes to amass a great fortune, for example, he may certainly run roughshod over others, with obvious disregard for making a favorable impression. Nonetheless, his ego-based drive is ultimately a societal-based pursuit—one that will leave him perpetually lacking—because he is dependent on others to tell him when he has achieved success. He thinks that he

---

NOTES

47. Dr. Pat Sanity. Retrieved: http://drsanity.blogspot.com/2007/05/children-of-postmodern-nihilism.html.

48. Much goes into the psychological mix, because even as the ego is compelled to satisfy its needs, the body seeks comfort and ease. Therefore, one who does not pursue ego-oriented goals cannot be assumed to be spiritually elevated, for, in actuality, he may be losing the battle to his body, rather than to his ego.

lives life on his own terms, yet this iconoclastic free-thinker becomes a strange mix of confidence and dependency: so brazen on the outside, and so brittle on the inside.

Since our perspective generates our reality, the more egotistical a person is, the more his worldview becomes the right view. His opinions become facts, and his preferences, truths, but unlike his people-pleasing counterpart, this person thirsts for power and control. And, when extreme arrogance meets talent and drive, more alarming than blindly following authority is that we become that authority.

Human beings are intrinsically driven to change the world, and those who are capable of great devastation and destruction are endowed with an equal ability to put forth goodness and to effect positive change.[49] As we quoted, "The greater the person, the greater his *yetzer hara*."[50] In the next chapter we will see that without wisdom it is impossible to operate with moral clarity—the ability to see clearly and respond appropriately. Without the faculty for both, we cannot stand up for the truth when it is uncomfortable or unpopular, and we will either speak out in ignorance or remain silent in shame.

49. "Great ambition is central to great potential. Those endowed with it may perform very good or very bad acts. All depends on the principles which direct them" (Napoleon Bonaparte).
50. *Kiddushin* 52b.

6 | WISDOM SPRINGS ETERNAL

The Hebrew word for *melech* ("king") is understood as an acronym for *mo'ach* ("brain"), *lev* ("heart"), and *kaveid* ("liver"). A king must exercise great wisdom and self-discipline and should be in complete control of these three organs. The order of the words in the acronym also alludes to a hierarchy of priorities. The brain or intellect must rule the heart, which represents emotions, and the liver, which represents a person's base desires, must be subservient to his thoughts and feelings.[51]

The Torah elucidates what life experience confirms: The decision-making process should be intellectual, with our emotions reinforcing our choices and infusing them with passion, inspiring us to take action and to follow through.[52]

INTELLECT WITHOUT EMOTION

He was known in medical literature as Elliot and became a famous figure in brain research on suffering damage to the frontal lobes of his brain as the result of a tumor. Although he enjoyed a superior IQ, he would become lost in triviality and foolish pursuits. After a battery of tests, his physician, leading scientist Dr. Antonio Damasio, realized that Elliot was incapable of emotional expression. While intellectually he could weigh the pros and cons of any decision, when it came time to actually make a decision he found himself completely lost. Dr. Damasio states,

---

NOTES

51. "Don't be misled by your heart and your eyes" (Numbers 15:39).

52. We are not stating that a visibly passionate person is less morally sound than one who prides himself on his cool and detached demeanor. Whether or not a person presents himself as emotional is more a function of personality, not perspective, and is thus immaterial.

"His decision-making landscape was hopelessly flat."[53] In his book *Descartes' Error*, Damasio describes trying to set up an appointment with Elliot:

> I suggested two alternative dates, both in the coming month and just a few days apart from each other. The patient pulled out his appointment book and began consulting the calendar. The behavior that ensued, which was witnessed by several investigators, was remarkable. For the better part of a half hour, the patient enumerated reasons for and against each of the two dates: previous engagements, proximity to other engagements, possible meteorological conditions, virtually anything that one could think about concerning a simple date. [He was] walking us through a tiresome cost-benefit analysis, an endless outlining and fruitless comparison of options and possible consequences. It took enormous discipline to listen to all of this without pounding on the table and telling him to stop.[54]

Indeed, it did stop. All it took was for Damasio to interrupt the man's deliberations and assign him a date and time to return. Without hesitating, the patient said, "That's fine," and went on his way.

When there is no drive that mobilizes our passion, we have nothing to reinforce the intellectual process that moves us in one direction or the other—this is one of the primary functions that emotions serve. We need emotions, but when we lead with our feelings, our intellect then fortifies a distorted conclusion.[55] This truism is expressed in the *Aleinu* prayer: "You are to *know* this day, and *take to your heart* that *Hashem* [God] is the only God."[56] First, we are to understand intellectually and, afterward, align our emotions to our intellect.[57]

NOTES

53. Antonio Damasio, *Descartes' Error: Emotion, Reason and the Human Brain* (New York: Avon, 1994), 193.

54. Ibid.

55. The Torah does not view the act of making a *neder* ("vow") lightly. However, it is possible to annul a vow through reconsideration and unforeseen circumstances (cf. *Nedarim* 27a). If it can be determined that a person made the vow without thinking through the consequences, this may offer the Sage an opening through which to annul it. After all, the vow was fueled by an emotional reaction to a set of circumstances and does not reflect the person's true will. Conversely, if a person makes a vow when in full control of his intellect and is not under stress or duress, then the vow is seen as a conscious free will declaration of intent.

56. *Aleinu* is a prayer that concludes all three daily prayer services.

57. This concept is also expressed in the arrangement of the holy emanations known as the *Sefiros*. According to Kabbalah, *Keser* (or *Da'as*), *Chochmah*, and *Binah* form the first triad of mind or intellect. Then *Chesed*, *Gevurah*, and *Tifferes* form the second triad of heart or emotion, and *Netzach*, *Hod*, and *Yesod* form the third triad of behavior or physicality.

INTELLIGENCE VERSUS WISDOM

Many of us have had the experience of trying to explain an objectively obvious point to someone who firmly disagrees with us. We persist in the belief that if we just present a rational argument and explain the facts clearly and logically, he will arrive at the only natural conclusion and see things as we do.[58]

We must cease believing that we are only one perfectly crafted sentence away from helping this person realize the error of his ways. Attempting to reason with such a person is often futile, if he cannot see past his own emotionally charged point of view. We are looking for reason in an infrastructure devoid of wisdom. What causes a person to deviate from sound evaluation and judgment? Again, to the degree that the ego is engaged, we unconsciously distort (or consciously ignore) reality and are pulled toward the less responsible choice. Therefore, in any given situation, it's quite possible for a smart person to make an astonishingly poor decision, while his less-intelligent counterpart will make the wiser, more prudent choice.

Intelligence does not make a person rational. Findings show that a person with a high IQ is no more inclined to be open-minded or able to weigh both sides of an issue than is someone of average intelligence. Intelligence can only put us in the driver's seat with a map in hand.[59] Wisdom—the ability to see clearly and respond appropriately—is one of the most powerful by-products of emotional health and gives us the capacity and fortitude to steer our lives in the right direction.

In fact, not only is wisdom distinct from intelligence, but, ironically, intelligent people are particularly prone to four fallacies that actually inhibit wise action.[60] These four fallacies are all ego-driven.[61]

NOTES

58. This thinking is reminiscent of the person who, when in conversation with someone who does not know his language, speaks slower and louder, enunciating each word with animated facial expressions. On one level, he recognizes that the other person does not understand a single word that he utters, but his emotional self cannot fathom how this can be when the words seem so clear to him.

59. It is significant to note that self-control is a better predictor of academic success than an IQ test is. B. J. Casey, L. H. Somerville, I. H. Gotlib, et al., "Behavioral and Neural Correlates of Delay of Gratification 40 Years Later," *Proc Natl Acad Sci* USA 108, no. 36 (September 6, 2011): 14998–15003. Epub August 29, 2011.

60. The *Mishnah* provides an evaluation: "Who is wise? One who learns from all people" (Ethics of the Fathers 4:1). We further learn that there are seven characteristics of an uncultured person and seven of a wise man. Not surprisingly, all of these qualities are related to the ego and its effacement. A wise man (a) does not speak before one who is superior to him in wisdom; (b) does not interrupt the words of his fellow; (c) is not hasty to answer; (d) asks pertinent questions and answers to the point; (e) speaks about the first thing first and the last thing last; (f) regarding what he has not heard, he says, "I have not heard it"; and (g) admits the truth. The opposite of these is characteristic of an uncultured man (Ethics of the Fathers 5:7).

61. Robert J. Sternberg, ed., "Intelligence and Wisdom," in *Handbook of Intelligence* (Cambridge: Cambridge

- The Egocentrism Fallacy: Thinking that the world revolves, or at least should revolve, around us. Acting in ways that benefit only us, regardless of how that behavior affects others.
- The Omniscience Fallacy: Believing that we know all there is to know, and therefore we do not have to listen to the advice and counsel of others.
- The Omnipotence Fallacy: Believing that our intelligence and education somehow make us all-powerful.
- The Invulnerability Fallacy: Believing that we can do whatever we want and that others will never be able to hurt or expose us.

Case in point: When awarded the Nobel Prize for discovering DNA, Dr. James Watson declared, "Let us redefine birth. Birth shall no longer be regarded as taking place at the moment of parturition but as occurring seventy-two hours after the emergence of the infant from the birth canal. Since the baby is not yet born, in the event that it is found to be physically or mentally defective it could be destroyed with impunity up to the moment of 'birth.' "

His genius-level IQ, stripped of wisdom, teeters on insanity and presumes that if he changed the meaning of life, then reality would simply fall in line with his definition. Not to be outdone, his partner, England's celebrated biologist and Nobel Prize laureate Dr. Francis Crick, advocated compulsory death for all who reach the age of eighty as part of a "new ethical system based on modern science."[62] Such is the blindfold of arrogance.[63]

THE BIBLICAL PROTOTYPE

Of course, the more objective and obvious a truth is, the larger the ego needs to be, and the sicker the person must be, in order to be unaware of what is in plain sight. But clarity itself, we recall, does not guarantee the *direction* of choice, only

---

University Press, 2000), 631–649. We all have the capacity for such erroneous thoughts, but the intellectual—though emotionally stifled—person is more adept at rationalizations that solidify this way of thinking. Hence, some of the smartest people can do the most foolish things.

62. Quoted in Fred Rosner and Rabbi Dr. J. David Bleich, eds., *Jewish Bioethics* (New York: Hebrew Publishing Co., 1979), 268–269.

63. "Man is wise only while in search of wisdom; when he imagines he has attained it, he is a fool" (Ibn Gavirol, *Mivchar HaPeninim*, c. 1050, no. 21). Emotional illness is borne out of a limited perspective, which stems from arrogance. "He whose *da'as* [knowledge] is full of pride and takes honors unto himself and thereby feels respected, sins, and is a *shoteh* [foolish or crazy]" (Rambam, *Mishneh Torah, Hilchos Lulav*, 8:15).

Let us organize what we have discussed as additional intricacies to the free will schematic are introduced. All of the following will be explained further in the upcoming chapters, particularly in the companion chapter, Chapter 24, "The Battlefield."

A. The aggregate of our free will choices orients our perspective:

- Responsible choice→self-esteem increases→ego shrinks→perspective widens→we become healthier and wiser
- Irresponsible choice→self-esteem decreases→ego expands→perspective narrows→we become more sick and foolish

    Although the ego encrusts our clarity, our perspective can become compromised by three main factors outside of our control (which will be explained).

B. A free will choice exists only where there is an objective truth—a moral component in the decision-making process.

C. In order for a particular decision to meet the free will threshold, we must have (a) objective clarity—a recognition of right from wrong, meaning an awareness of the truth, and (b) moral clarity—an attraction to and appreciation for the truth.

D. When a decision falls short of the free will threshold, we are not necessarily exempt from accountability because we are responsible for previous free will conduct that pushes a current behavior outside of the free will arena.

E. If we are completely drawn to what is right and we are not tempted to deviate from the truth, then free will is not actuated. This is, in essence, wisdom. The rare contrast—pure evil—may have total clarity, but it is attracted not to truth, but to falsehood.

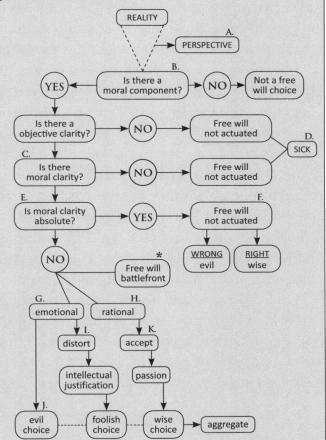

F. Once again, the absence of free will does not automatically exempt us from accountability—for better or worse.

G. If we felt 100 percent confident that we could face anything and everything with complete success and total ease, we would meet life head-on—boldly seeking out the truth no matter where it takes us. But our unwillingness to accept our faults and failings engages one of two primary emotions: fear. Fear and the ego go hand in hand, with each fortifying the other. The greater one's ego is, the greater his fear of exposure to himself, to others, and to the truth; and the greater this fear, the more the ego expands. As a result, investment in our real selves is minimized while the pull of the ego and body intensifies.

H. The other primary emotion is love, which is soul-based. This is not a selfish love in that "we want something because it makes us happy." This type of "love" distorts our thinking because it is "I" based and more accurately called *lust*. A soul-based love is pure and undistorted.

I. An emotionally warped thought process—through the lens of fear—is intellectually justified and often leads to a foolish choice. As we observed, intelligence and talent legitimize our worldview, and for the egocentric person, this means greater confidence in his ideas and thinking no matter how bizarre.

J. When we choose foolishly, we rationalize our behavior because we know that it is wrong. But when we act without regard for anything other than our own desires—but could nonetheless justify ourselves or, more so, choose differently—the act (certainly not the person) is appropriately labeled as *evil*.

K. An objective evaluation with a passion to connect to the truth—to do what is right—often leads to the wise choice.

L. The choice itself—wise, foolish, or evil—then feeds back into the aggregate, widening or narrowing our perspective.

*See Chapter 24 for a magnified view of this battlefront.

the possibility *for* choice. It also means that a person may fight to the bitter end to defend his decision, whether for good or evil.[64]

Our Sages are swift to warn, however, "Do not judge your fellow until you are in his place."[65] Since each person is at his own level, it is impossible to ever judge another person, as we can never really stand in his place. Thus, we do not know at what point a person has free will in a given situation.

Intriguingly, the Torah provides an example of one person, who despite perfect clarity—via prophecy—sought to contravene the will of God. The wicked Bilaam's obsession with cursing the Jewish people is the classic example of how the ego can cause one to blithely rebuff reality.[66] Balak, king of Moab, sent for Bilaam to come and curse the Israelites and thwart their plans to conquer the Land of Israel. That night, God came to Bilaam in a dream and told him, "Do not go with them; do not curse the people, for they are blessed." In the morning, Bilaam told the messengers, "Go back to your country, for God does not permit me to go with you." Balak sent Bilaam a new set of messengers, "more numerous and prestigious" than the first, and although God had already refused his request, Bilaam once more pushed for Divine permission to curse the Jewish people.[67]

God did not want him to curse the people and would not allow him to do so—and yet Bilaam did everything he could to bring a curse upon them.[68] It was not his intellect or even his emotions that caused him to sin.[69] Bilaam was perfectly aware. In spite of his egocentricity, his prophetic abilities allowed him a near-unprecedented degree of clarity.[70] In speaking of the Jewish people, he says, "Let

64. "Moses and Aaron came to Pharaoh and they said to him, this is what God, the Lord of the Hebrews said: How long will you refuse to humble yourself before Me?" (Exodus 10:3). Because of Pharaoh's arrogance, he could not see the truth, let alone accede to God's will (Rabbi Bachya, ad loc.). "When pride comes, disgrace comes; but with humility comes wisdom" (Proverbs 11:2).

65. Ethics of the Fathers 2:4.

66. Cf. Numbers 22:1–24:13.

67. God then allowed Bilaam to go to Balak but issued a stern warning: "Only that which I tell you may you say!" This was followed by Bilaam's miraculous speaking donkey that saw the angel blocking their way to Balak, but Bilaam did not heed. Only once he admitted that he had unjustly hit his donkey did God uncover Bilaam's eyes, and he saw the angel holding a drawn sword. "I oppose you because you have taken the path against me," said the angel. Still, Bilaam could not grasp what was happening. He said, "I have sinned, for I did not know that you stood in my way."

68. The Gemara (*Sanhedrin* 105a) relates that Bilaam was blind in one eye, and without both eyes a person is unable to see his physical world in perspective, because two eyes are needed to provide depth perception.

69. "God said to Bilaam, 'Do not go with them …'" (Numbers 22:12). "Bilaam thought, because I am so righteous He does not wish to inconvenience me …" (*Midrash Shochar Tov* 1:22).

70. Bilaam's level of prophecy was equal to that of Moses (*Bamidbar Rabbah* 20).

my soul die the death of the righteous and let my end be like theirs."[71] Yet unearned clarity does nothing to change a person's basic nature. The *Midrash* explains that he was so ensconced in decadence and depravity that spiritually, he was stunted, misshapen. He saw the truth and cursed it.[72] He was not sick. He was not foolish. He was evil.

A fool averts his eyes from truth to avoid the sting of conscience, but evil stares lovingly, longingly at falsehood and lunges toward it with eyes wide open.[73] In comparison, a wise person seeks out truth and acts in accordance with what he finds because *chochmah* ("wisdom") penetrates the outer layer of reality to reveal the hidden beauty of truth—awakening the desire to attach to what is good and true. The Chazon Ish writes that "seemingly the difference in character traits should have no connection with the degree of wisdom of each individual, and being morally corrupt should not interfere with wisdom." But, he explains, "this is not so."

> A flaw on the nobility of the soul and a lack of good character traits interfere with the acquisition of wisdom.... Even if he is granted the talent for wisdom as part of his soul, and even if a double portion of understanding has been delegated to him, he cannot prosper in his studies, because bad habits, a closed heart, and a closed mind shut the doors of wisdom from him and lock the gates of understanding. The secret of wisdom lies in the fine points, in delicate sensibilities that cannot be sensed by an ordinary eye—only a refined eye, behind which there is a refined heart.[74]

Arrogance, the hallmark of a swollen ego, destroys our relationship with God.[75] Even a Biblical paradox—a prophetic egotist—who heard the voice of God, could

71. Numbers 23:10.

72. "These words [of Torah] are not empty. If they appear empty, the emptiness is in you" (*Yerushalmi Peah* 1:1).

73. The Malbim explains that, "a fool knows *chochmah* [wisdom]; he is not deficient in his ability to understand it, but he rejects it because it demands that he not indulge his every desire." Quoted in *Mishlei*, Vol. 1, (New York: Artscroll, 1998), 27.

74. *Emunah U'Bitachon*, Ch. 1.

75. The Torah demonstrates that the equation of *humility* = *wisdom* is not self-contained. Humility is the path to maximize our potential for wisdom, within the confines of our allotted capacity. Shlomo Hamelech ("King Solomon") was the wisest of men, while Moses was the greatest prophet and the most humble of men. King Solomon understood the whole Torah, except the *chok* ("Biblical law for which there is no apparent logic") of the Red Heifer, while Moses understood this as well (*Vayikra Rabbah, Chukas* 19:3).

not bring himself to actually listen.[76] In stark contrast, King Solomon asked of God, "Grant Your servant a listening heart to govern Your people and to distinguish between right and wrong."[77] The essence of his request was for the ability to see a situation with such clarity that no other path, other than the right one, would be appealing. This is wisdom.

76. If Divine inspiration extends from humility, why does the Torah have examples of non-righteous, even evil men who prophesize? "And God came to Abimelech in a dream by night and said to him, 'Behold you are to die because of the woman you have taken; moreover she is a married woman'" (Genesis 20:3). Even though prophecy is usually reserved for those on a refined spiritual level, God appeared to Abimelech to warn him not to touch Sarah, in order to protect the honor of His righteous ones. For this reason, God will sometimes appear even to heathens, provided that they are people of some stature (Radak, ad loc.). In the days of Joseph, Pharaoh received prophetic dreams. This, too, was not due to his merit but only as the catalyst for Joseph's release and ascent. This also explains God's revelations to Bilaam. To protect His nation and to elevate them in the eyes of the nations, God gave prophecy to Bilaam. The Torah therefore uses a word insinuating God's reluctance, as it were, to speak with Bilaam: "God happened [*vayikar*] upon him" (Numbers 23:4). Whenever God spoke to Moses, however, the Torah uses a term of endearment, *vayikra*, "and He called to him."

77. II Kings 3:9. The greater a person's wisdom, the closer the perceptional gap between "right and wrong" and "truth and falsehood." King Solomon speaks of this clarity; and when we use the term "right and wrong" throughout this work, we mean to imply a similarly truth-based clarity.

PART 3

EMOTIONAL LAWS OF FREE WILL

All roads out of reality lead to the Land of Escapism. Yet mask it, conceal it, dilute it—the pain doesn't go away. Avoidance is not coping. It's crashing in slow motion. In this part, we will see how moving away from truth and morality not only injures our self-esteem, but leads to anxiety and depression. We will then shift to explore the inverse: how our emotional equilibrium is automatically reestablished through positive, productive choice.

7 | THE GREAT ESCAPE

The Torah describes the Jewish labor in Egypt as *avodas parech*—work that has no purpose and is meant just to keep the slave busy.[1] Pharaoh understood how painful futility is, and thus, cites the *Midrash*, he had the Jewish slaves build entire structures on a foundation of sand—structures that promptly collapsed.[2]

The more meaning something has, the greater the inherent pleasure.[3] No matter how much effort we expend, the satisfaction dissipates if the end objective is not meaningful. Being comfortable and having fun are not enough. Our soul gnaws at us not just to do more, but to *become* something more.

Lying on the couch and leafing through a stack of magazines is undoubtedly comfortable, but it is not meaningful, and so, by definition, it offers no lasting pleasure. The pursuit of comfort is basically the avoidance of life and not only denies us of pleasure, it moves us into the waiting arms of emotional disease.

CHASING COMFORT = PAIN

Pursuing comfort at all costs becomes expensive, because making good choices—which is the gateway to self-esteem—often requires effort. In an attempt to bypass

---

NOTES

1. See Rambam, *Hilchos Avadim* 116.

2. See *Even Shleimah* 1:2.

3. The axis of psychology has long consisted of the following theories regarding our motivation: Freud (human beings are motivated by pleasure), Adler (we are motivated by power), and Meaning Theory (we strive primarily to find meaning). From a Torah perspective, we can see how these three paradigms synthesize into a single model. The pursuit of meaning gives us maximum pleasure, the prerequisite of which is self-regulation, which is the highest form of power: the ability to maintain control over oneself.

pain, we short-circuit our emotional health.[4] Let us examine the deeper connection.

Our Sages say that idleness leads to mental illness, and accordingly, research shows that the more modern a society, the higher its rate of depression.[5] Technology leaves idle hands and the prospect of either time well spent or of time misused and abused.[6] From the time that Adam sinned, if a person planted wheat, thorns and thistles also sprouted.[7] This kept Adam and his descendants perpetually occupied. "Through the sweat of your brow shall you eat bread…."[8] The curse became necessary because once the *yetzer hara* became internal, man needed to engage in the world in order to maintain his emotional solvency.[9]

In Noah's generation, this curse was mitigated with the invention of farm tools, offering more time to pursue other activities because less time was needed for farming. The people, however, chose ease and indulgence over Torah, and so began the decay of morality and then of civilization itself. "The earth became corrupt before God and was filled with robbery."[10]

A PREMATURE DEATH

Hamlet: Act 3, Scene 1

To be or not to be, that is the question.
Whether 'tis nobler in the mind to suffer
The slings and arrows of outrageous fortune,
Or to take arms against a sea of troubles,

NOTES

4. The celebrated anthem that life should be comfortable leads to despair and dysfunction, and sprouts the king of all negative traits after arrogance: laziness.

5. *Kesubos* 59b. Cited by Stephen S. Ilardi, *The Depression Cure: The 6-Step Program to Beat Depression without Drugs* (Cambridge, MA: Da Capo Lifelong, 2009).

6. People without work are more likely to suffer psychological trouble and stress-related illnesses, such as diabetes, heart disease, and stroke. They also have diminished life expectancy. Michael Argyle, "Causes and Correlates of Happiness," *Well-Being: The Foundations of Hedonic Psychology*, ed. Daniel Kahneman, Ed Diener, and Norbert Schwartz (New York: Russell Sage Foundation, 2000), 353–373.

7. Rashi, Genesis 3:18.

8. Genesis 3:19.

9. Torah scholars may not need to toil physically, for their learning provides sustenance for their emotional fitness. The Talmud (*Yoma* 75a) teaches that the more righteous a person was, the closer to his home the *manna* fell. For the true *tzaddikim*, the *manna* fell on their doorsteps. In light of our discussion, we see that physical exertion is necessary to maintain our emotional health to the degree that one does not occupy his mind with Torah thoughts and concepts.

10. Genesis 6:11.

And by opposing, end them? To die: to sleep;
No more; and by a sleep to say we end
The heart-ache and the thousand natural shocks… .

Hamlet speaks of the pain and distress that fill human existence. He contemplated his choices: either I endure the trials of life or I end it with suicide. And by suicide, we do not mean one tormented action to end it all, but rather the discreet death of escapism.[11] That is the challenge we are confronted with each day. Will we rise to meet life head-on or turn away and sink into the deceptive comfort of a counterfeit existence?

We observed earlier that free will is the moral essence of a choice. Peeling back another layer, we find that morality is more than just choosing between "right and wrong." In a larger sense, it is a choice between life and death. God says, "I have put before you life and death … choose life so that you may live."[12] Choosing responsibly means engaging life, rather than choosing evil, which is leaving life and dying, ever so slowly.[13]

As noted in the Introduction, a person who is not truly living in this world forces a chasm between the body and the soul—the very experience of death itself.[14] This lack of harmony is felt as depression. Our soul aches to grow, and stagnation feels like death—because it is, a spiritual death.[15]

For this reason, we are more distraught to learn of the injury, or death, God forbid, of a young person than we are of an elderly person. Loss of life is unequivocally

---

NOTES

11. The pursuit of ego-oriented objectives—those that bring money, power, or fame as a means unto themselves—takes us out of reality as completely and as quickly as the pursuit of amusement and recreation as goals unto themselves.

12. Deuteronomy 30:19. God continues to lay out the unambiguous consequences: "But if your heart will stray and you will not listen … I tell you today that you will surely be lost" (ibid.).

13. Who more than Esau rejoiced over ephemeral delights? "Pour me some of that red stuff, because I'm tired of it all" (*Midrash*, Genesis 25:31).

14. "The task of the soul is the refinement of the body. When the soul is able to fulfill this duty [the soul] becomes perfected … [and] fulfills the purpose for which it was created" (Ramchal, *Way of God, Derech Hashem* 1:3:12).

15. A person can literally be bored to death. As evidence of this, 7,500 London civil servants ages thirty-five to fifty-five were asked to fill out a simple questionnaire. They were asked if they had felt bored at work during the previous month. The researchers followed up to determine how many of the participants had died after approximately ten years. Workers who reported they had been "very bored" were two and a half times more likely to die of a heart-related ailment than were those who had reported "not bored." Annie Britton and Martin J. Shipley, "Bored To Death," *International Journal of Epidemiology* 39, no. 2 (2010): 323–326.

sad, but it is the loss of assumed potential that we find particularly heartbreaking.[16] The wider the gap between potential and (opportunity for) actualization, the sadder it seems. Likewise, the extent to which we fall short of our own potential, the greater the waste and the more distress we experience.[17]

NO ESCAPE FROM TRUTH

God looked into the Torah and created the world.[18] We find that there is no word for entertainment in *Lashon HaKodesh* (ancient Hebrew—lit., "the Holy Tongue").[19] The concept itself does not exist. Entertainment is a diversion from reality, and extracting genuine pleasure from something that is not real is not possible. Authentic, sustainable happiness—let alone emotional health—is found in our connection to reality, not in our escape from it.[20]

Mental health requires an allegiance to reality regardless of the pain or effort involved.[21] Any time we move from the swift current of life, we become less stable because we are disconnecting from truth. Should we move too far into our "own world" even an insignificant event puts our fertile imagination into overdrive, consuming us with mushrooming fear and anxiety.[22] Our lives become filled with "never-ending tragedies" that never actually happen.

NOTES

16. We say "assume" because we cannot presume to know whose mission in life was fulfilled and whose was not.

17. We are speaking of potential, not productivity. To identify worthiness based on productivity is to devalue one as he grows older or becomes incapacitated—an idea antithetical to Torah ideals and values. Moreover, the *Shulchan Aruch* ("Code of Jewish Law") explains the *halachah* that "One person's life does not take precedence over another's." This comes to teach us that even potential is not a benchmark of worth, and that a person lying in a vegetative state has the same "value" and rights as does a person who is endowed with extraordinary potential.

18. *Zohar* 2:161b.

19. Modern Hebrew concocted the word *bilui*, "recreation," but it is not rooted in Biblical Hebrew. The word is derived from the verb *bidur* ("to scatter" or "to disperse") and carries the connotation "to waste."

20. Likewise, some people engage in high-risk behavior in order to shaking themselves from their lifelessness. They risk death for the jolt—the adrenaline rush—so that they can, at least in the moment, feel alive. There is no word in Biblical Hebrew for "adventure," either, since it is an artificial experience meant to simulate a zest for life itself.

21. Living in the world of truth brings genuine pleasure with a side effect of temporary pain or discomfort. Escapism brings permanent, persistent pain punctuated by brief periods of comfort.

22. Emotionally unstable people often have an ongoing internal dialogue, always analyzing how they are feeling and their feelings about those feelings. The rumination is endless, and this very policing of their emotions stimulates neuroses. They are continually labeling their feelings in response to questions such as *Am I happy? Is this okay? Why do I feel this way?* and *What does this mean?* Unable to move through the day

Paradoxically, the more neurotic a person is, the more he believes in his ability to see, know, and predict the world around him. In actuality, he is less able to recognize cause-and-effect relationships. To compensate for his impairment, to feel some sense of control, he creates his own associations between action and consequence. Naturally, this compounds his neurosis because when the inevitable breach occurs, he retreats deeper into his assumptions.[23]

Superstition is nothing but a diluted form of paranoia—the desire to make connections where none exist. All of reality is an undifferentiated facet of the whole, so patterns and connections are everywhere, but when a person cannot see beyond himself, the soul's desire to make connections is supplanted by the ego's own self-oriented correlations. Since he cannot find meaning, he invents it. (In fact, psychosis—and, to a lesser degree, neurosis—and prophecy lie at opposite ends of the spectrum. The latter is an all-encompassing perspective, while the former is exceedingly myopic.)[24]

Often compounding the emotional strain is the confusion between affliction and accomplishment—when we make distress the objective, rather than success, and where pain equals progress.[25] While it is true that "According to the effort is the reward," a person cannot heap challenges on himself.[26] We are rewarded for the effort put forth and the pain endured, but we are not compensated for self-inflicted wounds.

Yet all too often, we unconsciously create obstacles to give ourselves the feeling of growth without movement. An example of a common tactic: the file that we absolutely cannot afford to lose, our cellular phone, vehicle registration—just about everything and anything that we can misplace, we will misplace. Essentially, we

---

NOTES

without a complete emotional inventory, they have no energy left with which to lift themselves up from the couch.

23. Stress and anxiety increase neurosis and false beliefs. "If your brain is distracted or under pressure, you will tend to believe statements that you would normally find rather dubious ... even if you were told they were untrue." John A. Bargh, Mark Chen, and Lara Burrows, "Automaticity of Social Behavior: Direct Effects of Trait Construct and Stereotype Activation on Action," *Journal of Personality & Social Psychology* 71 (1996): 230–244.

24. Multiple Personality Disorder is a serious emotional illness. A patient with MPD develops additional personalities as a way of coping with a traumatic event. Later chapters expand on this theme: how wholeness corresponds to reality and multiplicity with falsehood.

25. It is too easy to become lost in our thoughts and somehow feel that if we spent the day feeling guilty or worried, then we have put in a full day's work. Actual contemplation is good, but ruminations of the ego—fear, guilt, worry, and the like—are neither thought nor progress. They are self-flagellation disguised as thinking.

26. Ethics of the Fathers 5:22.

manufacture a challenge in a controlled environment that, once overcome, gives us a sense of excitement and accomplishment.[27] It is a sorry attempt to feel the rush of life, without the effort of living.

Some people are miserable even though by all accounts they are making good choices. This is because we each stand on a never-ending ladder whose starting point is irrelevant. We might be capable of climbing easily but choose to be complacent and climb only a few rungs at our leisure. Genuine progress—and therefore self-esteem and emotional health—is assessed only through looking at our effort in relation to our ability. Pioneering psychologist Abraham Maslow succinctly summarizes this point: "If you plan on being anything less than you are capable of being, you will probably be unhappy all of the days of your life."[28]

27. In some instances, we create these little challenges because, unconsciously, we want to inconvenience ourselves. Feelings of guilt and self-recrimination cause us to inflict harm upon ourselves. Note that this is the very epitome of self-destruction.

28. Abraham Maslow, *Motivation and Personality* (New York: Harper, 1954), 46.

8 | LIFE
IN
CONTEXT

Living a life with meaning not only brings pleasure and bolsters our emotional, spiritual, and physical health, but it also means that we experience less suffering. That is not to say that difficulties do not come to a person who always seeks to do what is right. Rather, life's painful challenges are not felt as intensely.

We certainly are not saying that people who endure great misfortune in any way bring it upon themselves. On the contrary, the Sages tell us that God gives challenges to those whom He loves.[29] These painful circumstances are often beyond our finite understanding and are not necessarily the result of our actions, but, as our Sages explain, "Suffering is caused only by some transgression."[30] We all experience pain, but suffering is the emotional consequence of our choices.

How we feel about ourselves determines how long pain lingers and whether it will morph into suffering. The equation is simple: self-centered = suffering. This explains why an overly immature person, one with low self-esteem (or a child, perhaps), becomes agitated over every little thing that goes wrong.[31]

Lacking the emotional shock absorber of perspective, we feel only pain—that persists. This is because it is perspective that gives context, and context allows

29. Proverbs 3:12.

30. *Shabbos 55*a. In the words of the Prophet Yirmeyahu, "Your evil will cause you suffering" (*Yirmeyahu* 2:19).

31. The attributes of a narrowed perspective can be characterized as childlike. Small children, by virtue of the fact that they lack a *yetzer tov*, are egocentric beings. They react to their environment with sudden tantrums, mindless exuberance, wild mood swings, and an absolute black-white view of events. They are quick to misread or misinterpret the behavior of others and overreact to perceived insults, slights, and criticism.

for us to more easily extract and attach significance. We can see how seemingly disparate facets are integrated in a larger whole, and each new piece of the puzzle that is identified helps clarify and define what is already known. Without context there is no recognition, much less appreciation for our experiences. Everything God does is for the good.[32] How much of that good we are able to recognize is partly up to us.

Imagine the wings of a butterfly magnified a thousand times. Being so close, we can't tell what it is, what it does, or why it exists. We must take a step back to see what it really is. Then its design, details, and meaning become clear. The wings are part of a larger organism. Everything begins to make sense when we have perspective. The Gemara recounts the following:

> While traveling, the great Rabbi Akiva came to a town to look for lodging, but to no avail. He said: "Everything that God does, He does for the best." He went and slept in a field, and he had with him a rooster, a donkey, and a candle. A gust of wind came and extinguished the candle; a cat came and ate the rooster; and a lion came and ate the donkey. He said: "Everything that God does, He does for the best." The same night an army came and took the city into captivity. Had the rooster crowed or the donkey neighed or the candle been lit, he would have been discovered and been captured along with them. He said to them: Didn't I tell you? Everything that God does, He does for the best.[33]

CONTEXT IS KING

The pinnacle of perspective even insulates one from physical pain. A person can crawl across broken glass to escape from a burning room, experiencing little or no pain. His focus is on the larger, more important picture.[34] The Romans arrested Rabbi Akiva and executed him by brutally tearing the skin from his body with hot iron forks. As he was being tortured, Rabbi Akiva joyously recited the *Shema* blessing: "Hear O Israel, the Lord our God, the Lord is One." He smiled to his students in the moment just prior to his death and said that he was overjoyed to have finally

32. A person should accustom himself to saying, "Everything that God does is for the good" (*Berachos* 60b).

33. *Berachos* 60b.

34. Perspective—which is locked into time and space—exists only in the physical world. Rabbi Akiva's nullified ego brought him perfect perspective, which freed him from the grip of physicality.

achieved serving God with all of his being. The Gemara relates that Rabbi Akiva stretched out the word *echad* ("one") until his soul departed with complete recognition of God's total unity.

In a word, he had *context*. When a person recognizes that his pain has meaning—and perhaps discerns the message God is showing him—the pain does not metastasize into suffering, the experience becomes more bearable and, for those on the highest of levels, even joyous. (This is the true meaning of *mesirus nefesh*, discussed in Chapter 23, "Anatomy of a Choice.")

Research in physical pain management also shows us that pain severity depends on the context in which the pain occurs. The pain threshold increases as the patient better understands the body's healing process and the role of pain in the healing. This explains why major depression is associated with a decreased pain threshold.[35] As a person becomes increasingly focused on himself, he loses perspective, then context, and then meaning. We are left with only pain, and much of life—even living itself—becomes hard.

WHAT DOESN'T BREAK US

We are all aware of people who have led charmed upbringings, but a succession of stunningly irresponsible choices dragged them down a path of misery. We are equally mindful of those who have been dealt one challenge after another, yet soared above even the most daunting heartaches, embracing their futures with steadfast courage and trust in God. This very lesson is woven throughout the text of the Torah, beginning with our forefathers.

Abraham faced ten trials, including the enigmatic command to offer up his son, Isaac, who himself was ready to be slaughtered by his father, and later contended with the jealousy of the Philistines and was deceived on his deathbed by his wife and his son. Who can count the troubles faced by Jacob? He had a wicked brother who sought to kill him, a dreadful father-in-law, and mourned his beloved son Joseph for twenty-two years.

A range of rotating heartaches and anguish—imprisonment, betrayal, treachery, and murder—awaited every great figure in the Torah without exception: Adam, Noah, Sarah, Rachel, Leah, Joseph, Moses, Aaron, King David, King Solomon, and the list goes on. Who could argue that the lives of these Torah giants were not

35. Bruno Silvestrini, "Trazodone: From the Mental Pain to the 'Dys-stress' Hypothesis of Depression," *Clinical Neuropharmacology* 12 (Suppl. 1) (1989): S4–10. PMID 2568177.

difficult? Yet who would say that their lives were not the paradigm of meaning and fulfillment?

King David writes, "Had I not been preoccupied with Your Torah, I would have perished in my suffering."[36] Despite a life full of trials and tribulations, his Psalms exude joy and gratitude because when one lives a meaningful life, pain and pleasure coexist.[37] It is essential to understand that pain does not make a person unhappy—suffering does, and suffering is, as we said, a consequence of an egocentric lifestyle. Meaning fills our lives with pleasure and douses the flames of suffering. Struggles and setbacks are a part of life, but without perspective, they become our lives.

Psychologist Boris Cyrulnik, who is a Holocaust survivor and world-recognized expert in the study of emotional resilience, explains that we have to give meaning to tragedy as soon as possible in order not to remain stuck. Otherwise, he writes, "we bring ourselves back to life by inflicting pain on ourselves ... repeating the same story."[38] Perspective gives us the natural ability to frame a trauma in a meaningful context before it becomes fused with our identity and becomes part of a self-sustaining story that defines us.

HAPPINESS IS IN OUR HANDS

Findings confirm that those who place a high priority on money and fame are significantly less happy and emotionally solvent than are those who strive to bring meaning into their lives by pursuing healthy relationships, developing their potential, and becoming involved in social causes.[39] God sets forth the choice:

> See, I present before you today a blessing and a curse. The blessing: that you hearken to the commandments of *Hashem*, your God, that I command you today. And the curse: If you do not hearken to the commandments of *Hashem* your God.[40]

NOTES

36. Psalms 119:92. "You have turned my grief into dance. You have loosened my sackcloth and girded me with joy. So that my soul might make music to You and not be stilled, *Hashem* my God, forever will I thank you" (ibid., 30:11–12).

37. "Happy is the man whom You afflict and teach him Your Torah" (Psalms 94:12).

38. Boris Cyrulnik, *The Whispering of Ghosts: Trauma and Resilience* (New York: Other Press, 2005), 38.

39. Peter Schmuck, Tim Kasser, and Richard M. Ryan, "Intrinsic and Extrinsic Goals: Their Structure and Relationship to Wellbeing in German and US College Students," *Social Indicators Research* 50, no. 2 (2000): 225–241.

40. Deuteronomy 11:26–28.

Rabbi Moshe Feinstein explains that for those who keep the Torah, life is a blessing, because they enjoy all of the blessings God gives them. But those who ignore their purpose in this world can never fully appreciate the good in their lives.[41] Life becomes a curse because as much good fortune as they receive, they are never fulfilled; they cannot enjoy what they have, and they always want more.[42]

Our Sages define happiness as the ability to find pleasure in what we have and not pain in what we don't. "Who is wealthy? He who is happy with what he has."[43] The Talmud affirms, "Who sets his eyes on what is not his, loses also what is his."[44]

Without perspective, all of the good in our lives remains out of focus. We are left in a state of restless desire, goaded on by a sense of entitlement, with an inescapable finale: disappointment and despair.[45] By comparison, a healthy perspective advances an attitude of gratitude, which itself changes the quality of our lives.[46] A summary of research:

> In an experimental comparison, those who kept gratitude journals on a weekly basis exercised more regularly, reported fewer physical symptoms, felt better about their lives as a whole, and were more optimistic about the upcoming week compared to those who recorded hassles or neutral life events. A related benefit was observed in the realm of personal goal attainment: Participants

---

NOTES

41. "No one leaves this world with even half his desires fulfilled" (*Koheles Rabbah* 1:13). "One who has one, wants two" (ibid., 1:34).

42. See *Drash Moshe* (Artscroll, 1994), 296–297. The brain is not even deterred by an irrational or useless gain. So insidious is our desire for more, that even when it comes to the score of a video game, where the goal is the mere accrual of points, the expectation mechanism is just as active. The ego doesn't care how useful something is—where there is something to be had, it wants it. M. J. Koepp, et al., "Evidence for Striatal Dopamine Release during a Video Game," *Nature* 393 (1998): 266–268.

43. Ethics of the Fathers 4:1.

44. *Sotah* 9a.

45. The Hebrew word for *humble—anav—*means "undistorted," which denotes an objective perspective void of personal bias. Humility does not spring from inferiority but bubbles forth from the fountain of reality. Proper perspective yields the ability to see our greatness and potential but, at the same time, to appreciate that all that we have, all that we are, exists as a gift of kindness from our Creator (perspective→humility →gratitude→joy).

46. The power that positive thinking wields over our emotional and physical health is well established in scientific literature. As such, we should always try to be positive. However, a person whose perspective does not allow for him to see, much less appreciate, all of the good in his life, will have a hard time maintaining this way of thinking.

who kept gratitude lists were more likely to have made progress toward important personal goals (academic, interpersonal and health-based) over a two-month period compared to subjects in the other experimental conditions. In a sample of adults with neuromuscular disease, a 21-day gratitude intervention resulted in greater amounts of high energy positive moods, a greater sense of feeling connected to others, more optimistic ratings of one's life, and better sleep duration and sleep quality, relative to a control group.[47]

The Rabbis say that before a person is born, God decrees whether that person will be clever or foolish, strong or weak, healthy or diseased, rich or poor.[48] The only thing that is not preordained is whether the person will be a *tzaddik* ("righteous person") or a *rasha* ("wicked person").[49] That depends on free will—how we choose to live our lives.

Findings show what our Sages taught long ago: circumstances do not relate to life satisfaction, but subjective feelings do—and subjective feelings are a direct reflection of our choices, not conditions.[50] The following is research out of Harvard University:

> Only 10 percent of our long-term happiness is predicted by the external world; 90 percent of our long-term happiness is dependent on how our brain processes the external world... . The external world does not predict your happiness, which is a freeing scientific realization about how much control you actually have over your happiness.[51]

NOTES

47. See Emmons, R. A., McCullough, M. E., & Tsang, J. (2003). "The Measurement of Gratitude," S. Lopez and C.R. Snyder (Eds.), *Handbook of positive psychology assessment* (pp. 327-341). Washington, DC: American Psychological Association. Retrieved: http://psychology.ucdavis.edu/Labs/emmons/PWT/index.cfm?Secon=4.

48. Chapter 17, "Reconfiguring *Mazal*" discusses how even these decrees may be alterable.

49. *Niddah* 16b.

50. While psychological or emotional problems may be classified under the broad umbrella of mental health disorders, they can take a tremendous toll on our physical health. Yet the converse is not necessarily true: physical ailments need not affect our emotional status. A person who is physically ill can (though not always) still lead a successful life and move toward actualizing his potential. A person who is emotionally unwell, however, cannot easily enjoy any of the good in his life, even though he may be in peak physical condition. For this reason, praying for our emotional health takes precedence over our physical health.

51. Shawn Achor, *The Happiness Advantage: The Seven Principles of Positive Psychology That Fuel Success and Performance at Work* (New York: Crown Business, 2010).

In the upcoming chapters, we will discuss God's providence and the means to rise above a heavenly decree. Should we fail, however, in our sincerest efforts to alter life's difficult terrain, we must know that more important than the road we travel is who we become along the way. The *yetzer hara* too easily tricks us into accepting that what happens to us is the yardstick of significance. Yet it is not the circumstances we face, but how we face our circumstances that determines the true nature of the experience, and this is something we always have complete providence over.

9 | EMPATHY
MATTERS

When a person experiences physical pain, it is difficult for the mind to drift; one cannot help but become absorbed in the moment. Emotional pain has the same capacity to bring us into the present.[52] Pain, however, is only a fulcrum. It does not move us but gives us the opportunity to respond in one of three ways: (1) we can choose to avoid or dull the pain with endless distractions and excessive indulgence; (2) we can fortify our false self and become indignant to compensate for feelings of weakness and vulnerability; or (3) we can act responsibly, accept the outcome and seek meaning in the experience.

If we see God during difficult times—and get the message—then the pain pierces our shell, the ego. Instead of merely denting our image, the hurt penetrates straight through to our soul. The experience is productive because through it we are inclined to ask questions, instead of demanding answers, thereby fostering humility and a relationship with our Creator.

If we ignore what we know we must do, then God reminds us. First, God whispers to get our attention. If we do not listen, then He shouts. As a last resort, He knocks down the door. Then we ask why.

The *Midrash* teaches us that the three manifestations of *tzora'as* (typically translated as "leprosy" but more akin to a spiritual form of vitiligo) are to be perceived as stages of warnings. First, God places *tzora'as* on our home, and if we don't mend our ways, we get *tzora'as* on our clothing, and if we still fail to heed the message, then finally our bodies are directly afflicted.[53]

NOTES

52. "I can feel guilty about the past, apprehensive about the future, but only in the present can I act. The ability to be in the present moment is a major component of mental wellness" (Abraham Maslow).

53. *Vayikra Rabbah* 17:4. The Gemara speaks of a similar pattern of repercussions if one does business with

God does not punish for wrongdoing as much as He creates natural consequences out of love, for our ultimate good. A parent would prefer his child to do the right thing without being asked. Short of that, the parent would hope that the child listens after being told. At some point, a scolding or discipline may become the only recourse. Again, this is not punitive. On the contrary, it is an act of love, to educate the child or to protect him from harm, and it is always for the child's own benefit.

Analogously, a person who has gangrene in his finger may have the finger amputated or risk having the infection spread throughout his body, killing him. The finger is a part of a larger organism, and while it serves an important function, there is more that needs to be considered. This is the message that God tries to communicate to us: we cannot ignore the pain. If we fail to heed this warning, our real selves, our souls, will pay the greater, more devastating price.[54]

PAIN = DISTANCE FROM GOD

Is a person lying in a vegetative state, oblivious to pain, better off than one who endures life's daily struggles? We feel pain and label it as bad, but something that causes us emotional hurt is not necessarily a bad thing. Pain equals distance from God. If our greatest pleasure is to cleave to God by being like God (see Chapter 11, "The Purpose of Free Will"), then anything that moves us away from God is truly bad, and anything that moves us closer to God—to ultimate meaning—is good.[55]

Pain is absolutely necessary, because it is the catalyst for growth. And growth is non-negotiable—it is why we are in the world. The question is on whose terms. Life's lessons need not always be earned or learned through personal hardships. Growth—the acquisition of necessary traits—is equally accessible to us through the capacity to empathize.

The Torah states, "Moses grew up and he went out to his brethren and he saw their misery."[56] According to Rashi, that is why Moses went out—to see their woe.

NOTES

shemittah ("fallow-year") fruits: first, we lose our money, then we must sell our fields, and finally we sell ourselves into slavery, first to a Jew, and then to a non-Jew (*Kiddushin* 20a).

54. Rejecting the Torah is forfeiting life. We see this from the Gemara in *Shabbos* (88b): "*HaKadosh Baruch Hu* [The Holy One, Blessed be He] held the mountain over the Jewish people like a great overturned barrel and said: 'If you accept the Torah, fine; but if not, here you shall be buried!'" This teaches us that one who is overcome by his nature succumbs to a spiritual death that renders his physical life not just pointless but hazardous.

55. "Everything [except closeness to God] that people believe is good is nothing but emptiness" (*Mesillas Yesharim*, Ch. 1).

56. Exodus 2:11.

"He devoted his eyes and his heart to feel pain over them."[57] The *Midrash* teaches us that Moses saw how the enslaved people were suffering, and he wept for them, saying, "I feel so bad for you. If only I could help you, I would be willing to give my life in order to do so."[58] The Sages, likewise, advise us to keep our eyes wide open and to look on the less fortunate with all of the compassion we can muster.[59]

Herein lies the marked distinction between sympathy and empathy. The former means that we feel pity for a person's situation, but we are disinclined to exert ourselves to alleviate his plight.

A person may be very sensitive to the suffering of others, but if he merely *sympathizes*, he is consumed with his own pain and is therefore motivated primarily to reduce *his own suffering* — usually by means of escapism and indulgence — rather than help the person who is actually in pain. He often wishes he was unaware of the sorrow around him so that he would not suffer as a result.

The typical notion of the egocentric mentality is one of arrogance and bravado, but even a highly sensitive person who is seemingly void of ego can also be self-centered and selfish — (this is the previously referenced doormat personality in Chapter 5). He is absorbed in his own pain, making him literally self-absorbed, and he cannot feel anyone else's pain when he is drowning in his own.[60] There is no real connection to anyone outside of himself, in spite of his seemingly noble nature. Without genuine humility, he will not — cannot — burden himself, unless there is a larger payout in the form of acceptance or approval.[61]

Empathy, by comparison, is the capacity to share another's emotions, to feel his pain, rather than to merely feel sorry for him. The person who has empathy is grateful for the knowledge of others' troubles because he genuinely wants to alleviate their suffering. Moral development, rather than just moral thinking, is what moves a person to altruistic behavior. In fact, sociopaths have been shown

---

NOTES

57. See *Shemos Rabbah* 1:27.

58. Ibid., 1:20.

59. See *Tomer Devorah* 2.

60. Even though a person may be overly consumed with the welfare of another—one's own child, perhaps—we cannot say that this person exhibits empathy. It is "my child," who is in pain, and while it causes distress, it is borne out of an ego-identification. The Torah recounts, "Hagar became lost in the desert ..." (Genesis 21:19). She placed Ishmael under a dried-up shrub and then sat in the distance and wept, "Let me not see the child die" (ibid., 21:16). Her focus was not on comforting her dying son, but on her own pain from having to watch him suffer. When push came to shove, easing her own pain trumped comforting her child and easing his pain.

61. He may also be motivated by the need to assuage feelings of guilt or inadequacy, but still, his aim is to reduce his own suffering, not someone else's.

to possess excellent moral reasoning but feel no need to act morally — this requires empathy.[62]

Parenthetically, the ease to which we rise above our own problems and shift attention to the welfare of another is a reliable marker of emotional health. While we all are, to some extent, self-absorbed — particularly when we are struggling with personal challenges — the intensity and duration are revealing.[63] Almost anyone can be warm, kind, and generous when he is in a positive mood. However, a true indicator of emotional health is when a person can respond to negative situations with patience and tolerance even when he is in a low emotional state or under physical distress.

DIVIDE AND BE CONQUERED

The self-absorbed person is trapped in the tomb of his own suffering, because he is incapable of empathizing with others. In contrast, where there is no ego, there is humility; a connection to others is born, and the barrier of "I am me and he is he" is broken down. Empathy awakens, and the trait of *chesed* ("lovingkindness") emerges.

As our ego recoils, we behold the suffering of the world around us, we concede the finite, temporary nature of the world and want to attach ourselves to something more, something real: God. This fosters growth but without the same growing pains.[64]

It should come as no surprise that both empathy and pain activate the same regions of the brain — the anterior insula and anterior cingulate. Knowing our loved one is in pain, for instance, automatically triggers the subjective pain-processing regions of our brain, which leads to empathy.[65] When someone whom we love is

---

NOTES

62. See Martin L. Hoffman, "Toward a Comprehensive Empathy-Based Theory of Prosocial Moral Development" (2001), in Arthur C. Bohart and D. J. Stipek, eds., *Constructive and Destructive Behavior: Implications for Family, School, and Society.*

63. Why is it so easy to dislike those who are "full of themselves"? Intense self-focus inhibits close relationships by precluding empathy, caring, and commitment. W. Keith Campbell, Eric A. Rudich, and Constantine Sedikides, "Narcissism, Self-Esteem, and the Positivity of Self-Views: Two Portraits of Self-Love," *Personality and Social Psychology Bulletin* 28 (2002): 358–368.

64. The Mishnah instructs us to "bear the yoke of others" (Ethics of the Fathers 6:6) for several reasons, including what we will discuss: A person who has mercy on another receives mercy from Above. The reason is that the pain that empathy causes us provides a measure of atonement for our sins and may thus prevent previously pending hardships. (See Chapter 40, footnote #114 for insight into how this works.)

65. Suzanne Keen, "A Theory of Narrative Empathy," *Narrative* 14, no. 3 (2006): 207–236.

in pain, we are in pain as well.[66] But again, to the degree that we do not love ourselves, we cannot love another, and our faculty to feel empathy becomes polluted. Prospects for growth, then, are confined to a narrow range of our own increasingly painful experiences.

The unambiguous outcome: The more self-consumed we are, the more we will suffer subjectively with whatever challenges we objectively face. This is certain. In some instances, greater difficulties—tangibly speaking—may be heaped on us, as well.[67]

The more responsible our choices, the greater our self-esteem; the ego shrinks and perspective widens. We then gain context and meaning, which in turn give us pleasure (and reduces suffering), as well as the ability to feel empathy for others. Alas, even with intense emotional pain, we still have the choice to deny it and distract ourselves, but our efforts will be in vain. If we fail to act responsibly, all pain swells into suffering. We sink lower and destroy ourselves from the inside out until we allow for the self-correcting mechanism of pain to penetrate our shell and steer us in a healthier and more responsible direction.

66. An oft-quoted anecdote is told about Reb Aryeh Levin (*A Tzaddik in Our Time*). He is said to have accompanied his wife to the doctor for a problem with her foot. When the doctor asked what they had come for, the Rabbi answered, "My wife's foot hurts us." The pain was as much his as it was hers. If she was in pain, so was he.

67. See Chapter 22, "Mazal: The Fine Print" and Chapter 29, "Extinguishing the Flames" for further discussion.

THE
FOUNDATION
OF FAITH

10

When we make a poor choice, we are not acknowledging God, and to the degree that He is not "let into" our lives, we cannot have a relationship with Him, let alone trust in Him. The rift widens afterward when we justify our actions, thereby continuing to engage the ego and pushing God still further away.[68]

This distance is felt as a lack of faith. Yet we do not lose faith in God without first losing faith in ourselves. It is we who have changed. When we turn away from what is right, it is inevitable that all of our relationships suffer.

FAITH AND TRUST

The ability to exercise self-control eliminates anxiety because it moves us beyond *emunah* ("faith in God") and into *bitachon* ("trust in God").[69] The difference is profound. We can have *faith* that things will work out, but we may still be plagued by worry and moments of doubt. When we have *trust*, however, negative thoughts do not fill our mind. We do not dwell on, or worry about, the outcome. Trust is an intellectual process, a natural outgrowth of our positive choices, and exists independent of our mood or emotional state.[70]

NOTES

68. "If you neglect the Torah, you will face many excuses to neglect it" (Ethics of the Fathers 4:12).

69. The word *faith* is a watered-down translation. *Emunah* should not be construed as blind faith or an abandonment of reason. True *emunah* is steeped in logic and flows from a true, unshakable knowledge of God and belief in His Divine providence.

70. "Cast your burden upon the Lord and He will sustain you" (Psalms 55:23). "Blessed is the man who made God his trust and did not turn to the arrogant or those who stray after falsehood" (ibid., 40:5).

The Chazon Ish details that *bitachon* is borne out of *emunah*.[71] *Emunah* necessitates that one believe in the fundamental tenets about God, whereas *bitachon* is actively applying these beliefs to our lives—and making choices that reflect our conviction.[72]

Productive living is the heartiest expression of our trust in the future, in God, and in ourselves.[73] A person who is too afraid to make long-range plans and to invest in his life is sending a message to his subconscious that he does not have *bitachon*. Then imperceptibly, unintentionally, he seeks to validate his fears and becomes attuned to whatever in his world can offer him proof that he is right. Because his decision to avoid stress—and opt out of life—was ego-based, his ego must now prove him right.

In short, action is what converts faith into trust.[74] It is impossible to establish trust in God if we do not live our lives in a way that demonstrates our belief in God.[75] Abraham's ten trials nourished his relationship with God, each adding a strand of trust in a bond that culminated in complete and total submission to His will, without question or compunction.

With the first test, God sought to assure Abraham: "I will make of you a great nation; I will bless you, and make your name great and you shall be a blessing."[76] By the last test, such reassurance had become unnecessary, even though the command itself was exceedingly more difficult and overtly contradicted God's initial assurance. Such is the bond of trust.

NOTES

71. The Chazon Ish writes (*Emunah U'Bitachon*, Ch. 2:1) that *bitachon* means knowing in one's heart that there is no such thing as chance, and that all of our life experiences are under complete and total Divine supervision. Unlike *emunah*, *bitachon* is a direct reflection of our relationship with God. The closer we are to Him, the stronger is our trust in Him, and the greater our recognition that everything He does is directed towards our good, out of His love for us.

72. Chazon Ish, *Emunah U'Bitachon*, Chapter 2.

73. Whenever we demonstrate our belief in God, we reinforce our belief in ourselves and in our knowledge that God believes in us.

74. The *Nesivos Shalom* states there are two tracks of *bitachon*: inactive and proactive. Inactive *bitachon* comes into play when a person is in a situation where there is nothing for him to do. In such circumstances, his *avodah* ("spiritual task") is to trust that everything that happens is for our ultimate good. *Krias Yam Suf* ("Splitting of the Red Sea") is an example of proactive *bitachon*, where a person actively exercises his free will and demonstrates his trust in God (*Nesivos Shalom, Parshas Beshalach*). Noted by Rabbi Yehonasan Gefen, *Insights on the Weekly Torah Portion and Festivals*. Retrieved: http://rabbiygefen.blogspot.com.

75. This is true on all levels. God does not do anything without a purposeful, positive reason. Senseless movement, talk, and even extraneous thought create a distance between a person and his Creator.

76. Genesis 12:2–3. While God offered such assurances, at no point did Abraham ever doubt God or hesitate in carrying out His will.

SELF-CONTROL = PEACE OF MIND

Individuals with high life-change scores (that is, they are experiencing multiple life changes at one time) are more likely to fall ill. Yet most surprisingly, studies reveal that the illness correlates with *any type of change*.[77] Whether the event is positive or negative bears no consequence on the stress experienced; the circumstances are largely irrelevant, but the ability to feel in control is fundamental. This is exactly why we may find ourselves engaging in self-destructive behavior, even when things in our lives are going particularly well. It is not the situation that we find unsettling, it is we who feel unsettled because we are not in control of ourselves.[78]

The psychological mechanics are as follows: A lack of self-control reduces our self-esteem, which automatically inflates the ego; this leads to arrogance and the inability to trust in God. As a consequence, we mistakenly believe that we are in control of our circumstances and thus become anxious when our lives are in flux and angry when things do not go our way.[79]

In direct proportion to the quality of our choices is our ability to free ourselves from worry and to trust in the outcome. The path to peace of mind is paved not by circumstance but by choice.[80] Below is a commentary on the Ramban's famous letter:

> Peace of mind is the key to spiritual growth; serenity is the trademark of the person who is truly Godly. The person who has trust in the Almighty is calm and composed.... On the other hand, one who feels that he alone carries all his burdens on his own shoulders can be overwhelmed by the weight of those responsibilities; such an attitude leads to severe anxiety and tension.[81]

The words of *Chazal*, illuminate hidden strands within this model: "The beginning of wisdom is the fear of God... ."[82] When we fear God, we stop fearing man, because we recognize that human beings are not in control of the Universe—only

---

NOTES

77. Thomas Holmes and Richard Rahe, "Social Readjustment Rating Scale," *Journal of Psychosomatic Research* 11, no. 2 (1967): 213–221.

78. "The desire to control everything is a major manifestation of arrogance" (*Chovos HaLevavos, Shaar HaK'niah*, Introduction).

79. "Behold! God is my salvation. I shall trust and not fear, for God is my might" (*Yeshayah* 12:2).

80. See Lieberman, *Real Power*.

81. Rabbi Avrohom Chaim Feuer, *A Letter for the Ages* (New York: Mesorah Publications, 1989), 28–29.

82. Proverbs 1:7.

God is.[83] As a result, our behavior is more responsible, which broadens our perspective and opens our eyes to God in our lives. In fact, the word *yirah,* "fear," and the word *ro'eh,* "see," share the same root.[84] This brings us to a higher level of fear, or awe of God, which is derived from being aware of Him—seeing His providence in this world; and we come full circle: "Those who fear God will trust in God."[85]

Whatever the *middah* ("character trait"), if we do not possess it, we cannot see it in others or feel it in ourselves. As discussed earlier, a person who does not love himself cannot fully love others or feel their love, and a person who does not trust himself is distrusting of others and is often not trusted by others. Those who lack self-control have no concept of trust. How can they trust in God when in their world "trust" is a theoretical concept and not part of their inner reality? God is Infinite and nonchanging. If we want to see His hand in our lives, if we want to trust in Him, it is we who must change. We must make different choices. There is no alternate truth.

---

83. In the Introduction to the *Zohar,* R. Shimon bar Yochai writes, "*Yiras Shamayim* [fear of God] is the portal to *emunah.*"

84. "If there is no wisdom, there is no fear of God; if there is no fear of God there is no wisdom" (Ethics of the Fathers 3:21).

85. Rabbi Avigdor Miller, *Praise My Soul,* para. 502; Psalms 115:11.

PART 4

THE GLORY
OF GOD

Here we assess the multifaceted role of free will and why it was ultimately designed by God to prepare us for a world that is beyond our own. Indeed, the quality of our choices forges not only our character but our eternity, and our innate search for self-expression finds its roots not only in our soul, but in the purpose of creation itself.

11 | THE PURPOSE OF FREE WILL

The Talmud relates the dialogue between Moses and the *malachim* ("angels") when he ascended to heaven to receive the Torah. The angels turned to God and said, "The Torah is a Divine treasure, too precious to be given to man. Let it remain with us and we will honor and cherish it." God told Moses to refute the angels' argument. Moses replied with a series of rhetorical questions: "The Torah commands, 'Honor your parents.' Do you have a father and mother? The Torah commands, 'You shall not steal.' Are angels capable of stealing? The Torah commands, 'You shall not murder.' Do angels kill one another?" With this reasoning, Moses was triumphant, and the Jewish nation received the Torah.[1]

Angels do not have free will, nor are they tempted to sin. Yet we, too, could have been created like angels, where we would perform God's will automatically, without question or reservation.[2] But God created man for a different, higher purpose.[3]

In order to fully grasp *why* free will exists, we must look at the purpose of creation itself and the reason that God created *two* worlds—this world and the next. First things first. The Ramchal explains that the purpose of Creation was for God to bestow His good to others:

Since God desired to bestow good, a partial good would not be sufficient. The

1. *Shabbos* 88b–89a.
2. Rabbi Isaiah HaLevi Horovitz (a sixteenth-century rabbi and mystic known as the Shelah HaKadosh) writes (*Shnei Luchot HaBrit*) that angels do not have a *yetzer hara* and thus cannot deliberately contravene the will of God. Nevertheless, angels are not perfect—they, like human beings, have their own perception of holiness and reality and, even with the purest intentions, are still capable of erring.
3. See Zechariah 3:7; Vayikra 26:3.

good that He bestows would have to be the ultimate good that His handiwork could accept. God alone, however, is the only true good, and therefore His beneficent desire would not be satisfied unless it could bestow that very good, namely the true perfect good that exists in His intrinsic essence. True good exists only in God. His wisdom therefore decreed that the nature of this true benefaction be His giving things the opportunity to attach themselves to Him to the greatest degree possible for them.[4]

How does a person attach himself to God? The Talmud states, "We bind ourselves to God by imitating His attributes."[5] As we mentioned, in the physical world, when we want to be closer to someone or something, we move toward it through space. In the nonphysical world, closeness is not measured in terms of physical space, but rather through similarities that manifest in levels of awareness.[6]

The more we resemble our Creator, the closer we are to him and the greater is our awareness and recognition of Him.[7] As a consequence, our love for Him grows, because the beginning of love is knowledge. In the words of the Rambam: "A person can only love God to the degree of a person's knowledge that he has of Him. According to the person's knowledge so will be his love."[8]

BECOMING LIKE GOD

Emulating the attributes of God is no easy task. God and man are conceptual opposites. "God is the Giver and man is the receiver."[9] This is true for two reasons. First, at the moment of Creation, God created man and gave him life and sustenance. Second, at the end of time, God will grant man His ultimate

---

NOTES

4. Ramchal, *The Way of God*, Rabbi Aryeh Kaplan, trans. (New York: Feldheim Publishers, 1981), 37.

5. *Sotah* 14a. Resonating with God-like qualities gives us "knowledge" of God (or, more precisely, knowledge of the manifestation of His will) that moves us closer to Him. "Knowing" or having knowledge of, is also a term for "closeness" (Rashi to Genesis 18:19).

6. To some extent, this is true in the physical world as well. Cross-race effect is a neural phenomenon whereby people are more able to recognize faces and emotional expressions of people of their own race, in comparison to other races. The greater the similarity, the greater is one's ability to discern features that look the same to others.

7. "The secret of God goes to those who fear Him" (Psalms 25:14).

8. Rambam, *Mishneh Torah, Hilchos Teshuvah*, Ch. 10.

9. Rabbi Aryeh Kaplan, *If You Were God* (New York: NCSY/Orthodox Union, 1983), 59.

goodness.[10] In this chapter we will deal with the former reason, and in the following two chapters, the latter.

The Sages declare, "God created the world with *chesed*."[11] *Chesed* is translated as "kindness" or "lovingkindness" and denotes an act of giving that has no prior cause. While human beings cannot know God, we do know that He operates without constraint.[12] To distend our finite minds with clumsy language, we can say that God chooses to be good.[13] The Ramchal thus qualifies that free will is a prerequisite to attain the "true perfect good that exists in God's intrinsic essence." He writes, "In [God's] sublime wisdom He knew that for His bestowal of good to be perfect, those who receive it, must earn it. Only then will they be masters of that good."[14] In other words, if we were compelled to choose goodness, then our similarity to God's goodness would be incomplete and God's purpose—to bestow ultimate good—would not be fulfilled.[15] The culmination of character development, the essence of what it means to be God-like, is to be a giver by choice.[16] Rabbi Dessler writes,

> While there is a limit to our intellectual understanding of God, there are no limits as to how refined our character traits can become. In this way, we can achieve more of an understanding of God's perfection than through our intellect … especially in the trait of lovingkindness, through which we resemble God.[17]

Essentially, only by applying free will, through which we choose to be givers instead of takers, do we move closer to our Creator and enjoy the greatest good.[18] In the previous chapter, we learned that fear of God brings us to trust in Him. Fear

---

NOTES

10. Ibid., 72–73.

11. Psalms 89:3.

12. According to many commentators, this is one meaning of man having been created in the "image of God." Cf. Rambam, *Yad Teshuvah* 5:1.

13. "The way one follows in the path of God is by following in His ways …" (*Shabbos* 133b. See also Rambam, *Hilchos De'os* 1:6, and *Path of the Just*, Introduction).

14. *Derech Hashem* 1:3:1.

15. "Why did God create the world in such a way that it deludes man into thinking that things exist in and of themselves? It was so that man could overcome this illusion through the power of his free will, and thereby become master of his own reward" (*Teferet HaChinukhi, Parshas Vayeira*).

16. Having children is intended, in part, to help us to become givers. A child's nature is to take. He comes into the world and does nothing but cry, eat, and create waste, yet, as parents, we give, and the more we give, the more we love our children, and so we catch a glimpse of our relationship with God.

17. Rabbi Eliyahu Dessler, *Michtav Mei'Eliyahu*, Vol. IV, 49–50.

18. Numerous studies show that acts of kindness can result in significant health benefits and are even capable of lifting depression. This is because giving and gratitude (which is itself giving—giving thanks)

is also the path to loving God, because if we do not fear Him and instead become preoccupied with impressing the world and indulging our desires, then we move away from Him. Then love, which is a product of giving, becomes impossible because we are only taking.[19]

As we will discuss in the next chapter, being a giver like God allows for the deeper purpose of emulation and the ultimate in giving—that is, to create ourselves, which is the quintessential act of *chesed*. Indeed, it is the union of body and soul and the ensuing conflict that activate the gift of free will and make our potential greater than that of angels. And using our potential to create ourselves not only reveals our essence, but goes to the purpose of creation itself: to reveal the glory of God.

NOTES

redirect our attention away from ourselves and fill us with a sense of purpose. In the words of Ralph Waldo Emerson, "It is one of the most beautiful compensations of this life that no man can sincerely try to help another without helping himself."

19. As our love grows, feelings of joy emerge, which is why the Sages proclaim, "Happy is the one who is always fearful" (Proverbs 28:14).

12 | **FOREVER UNIQUE**

Each soul is a spark of the Divine, Who is One, but this does not mean that we are undifferentiated. The soul is the Divine representative found within each and every one of us and is the root of *ratzon* ("will").[20] Kabbalists explain, "People differ from each other in their actions because they differ in their *ratzon*, and this is because they differ in their souls."[21] Rabbi Tzadok HaCohen of Lublin writes,

> God desired to create distinct and different characters so while each soul has within it all of the forces of life, God arranged that the combinations of strengths should differ from soul to soul. While each soul has all of the forces of life within it, in each soul there is one aspect that is primary. Other souls will also have that force, yet it will be secondary within them.[22]

Our forefather Jacob blessed each son with a unique blessing geared toward maximizing his potential. Then he blessed them again, as a group. Rashi explains that with this closing *berachah* ("blessing"), Jacob included every son in the others' blessing, but, as the Maharal of Prague states, Jacob's final *berachah* did not make them equal in every area. Each one was potent in the area that he was blessed in; this last *berachah* simply gave all of them an aspect of one another's *berachos* in order that they should be grounded and well-rounded.[23]

NOTES

20. See *Introduction to Kabbalah (Yedid Nefesh)*, Rabbi Y. Bar Lev, Ph.D. (date unknown). Based on the Ramchal's *138 Openings to Wisdom*.
21. Ibid.
22. See *Sichas Malachei HaShareis*, 21, s.v. *Sibas Hevdel*.
23. Maharal, *Gur Aryeh* to Genesis 49:28. Noted by Rabbi Yehonasan Gefen, *Insights on the Weekly Torah*

Naturally, people have different leanings and inborn desires. We come into the world with a unique set of traits that, as the Sages tell us, are not inherently good or bad but can be channeled to be either constructive or destructive. Even the basest traits can be used for good.[24] The preeminent psychologist Carl Jung explains,

> Creative powers can just as easily turn out to be destructive. It rests solely with the moral personality whether they apply themselves to good things or to bad; and if this is lacking, no teacher can supply it or take its place.[25]

Similarly, the Torah recounts, "She went to inquire of God."[26] The Sages explain that Rebecca visited the *Yeshivah* ("Academy") of Shem and Ever. She was told she was carrying two sons, one who yearned for the spiritual and the other drawn toward darkness, but both with great potential. Rabbi Dessler writes,

> There is no doubt that Esau was given powers for good corresponding to his powers for evil. Had he summoned up all his powers for good, he could have conquered the evil … and approached the level of our Patriarch Isaac [the "good" twin].[27]

The Talmud states that if someone is born under the sign of Mars—meaning that he has an inclination toward bloodshed—he can choose to be either a doctor, a *shochet* ("ritual slaughterer"), or a *mohel* ("one who performs circumcision").[28] His propensity toward bloodshed will not be fulfilled as an accountant or chemist, and such a career choice would only frustrate him. Dr. Abraham Maslow, who established self-actualization as the pinnacle of human need, sums up the principle:

NOTES

Portion and Festivals. "Each according to his own blessing he blessed them" (Genesis 49:28). Why is there a change from the singular to the plural? To teach us that each of them was also linked to the blessings of the others (*Tanchumah Vayhi 16*).

24. The nature of each person's intelligence reflects the path the soul took on its way into this world and its *tikkun* for this world. This accounts for the varied forms of intellect classified by Howard Gardner of Harvard University in his *Theory of Multiple Intelligence*. He identifies nine distinct types of intelligence: (1) linguistic; (2) logic-mathematical; (3) musical; (4) spatial; (5) bodily; (6) kinesthetic; (7) naturalist; (8) interpersonal; and (9) intrapersonal.

25. Carl Gustav Jung, "The Symbolic Life," *Collected Works*, 18.

26. Genesis 25:2.

27. Rabbi Eliyahu Dessler, *Strive for Truth*, Vol. III, 128.

28. *Shabbos* 156a.

A musician must make music, an artist must paint, a poet must write if he is to be at peace with himself. What a man can be, he must be. This is the need we may call self-actualization ... it refers to man's desire for fulfillment, namely to the tendency for him to become actually in what he is potentially: to become everything that he is capable of becoming.[29]

Therefore, he should, and must, find a positive outlet for his inborn drives. Any and all tendencies must be directed toward the person's growth, and if he fails to capitalize on their positive use, he will ultimately surrender to his unbridled desires and be governed by them.

The Sages reveal for example, that both Esau and David were of red complexion, signifying blood. The difference, they note, is that Esau killed to satisfy his own cravings for violence and bloodshed, while David would kill only with permission from the *Sanhedrin*.[30] He killed only when it was justified, and his battles were acts geared toward ultimate peace and Godly service.[31]

Unquestionably, Judaism does not suggest that every decision is a product of one's free will capacity, but it rejects the notion that all of our behaviors are effectively a preprogrammed function of nature or conditioning.[32] Even when we are at a genetic disadvantage, each of us can decide whether we will succumb to temptation or rise to our potential.[33]

Notably, large-scale surveys of gene-environment interaction research suggest that approximately one-fourth of the variation between the mental health statuses of different individuals is heritable, which means that three-fourths is not.[34] Chemical imbalance or genetic predisposition will shorten the fuse, but it is

---

NOTES

29. Maslow, *Motivation and Personality*, 46.

30. The Great *Sanhedrin* was the supreme religious body in the Land of Israel during the time of the Holy Temple.

31. *Bereishis Rabbah* 63:8.

32. Proving the existence of free will is not this book's objective. We will simply quote from the Rambam who summarizes its obvious and necessary place in creation. "If man's actions were done under compulsion, the commandments and prohibitions of the Law would be nullified and they would all be absolutely in vain, since man would have no choice in what he does" (*Eight Chapters*, pp. 84-5).

33. While the choices we make throughout our lives have a strong impact on our emotional stability, severe mental illness may be the result of serious trauma or a genetic disposition that impacts so significantly on one's basic life-functioning that one's thoughts and behaviors fall outside the scope of *bechirah*. Just as some people are physically disabled, others are emotionally impaired through no fault of their own. They neither choose nor cause their sickness, and to label them lazy or selfish is not only reprehensible, but mistaken.

34. See K. S. Kendler and J. H. Baker, "Genetic Influences on Measures of the Environment: A Systematic Review," *Psychological Medicine* 37, no. 5 (2007): 615–626.

the internalized stress and strain of life—via our self-generated perspective—that create the spark.[35]

PLANES OF HUMANITY

The lowest level of our soul, *nefesh,* is referred to as our animal soul, because of its animating properties. (This is not to be confused with an animal's soul, which contains only an animating force and is neither physical nor spiritual.) Our *nefesh*—which is spiritual—also accounts for our basic thought processes and gives rise to a generic ego-identity (with previously examined ego-based defense mechanisms).[36]

When a person operates on this level, he responds to life more than he lives it. He exists with animal-like emotions and status. Poke him, and he turns angry; feed him, and he is calmed; compliment him, and he is encouraged; disrespect him, and he becomes enraged. His personality is resigned to a visceral interface. When we allow ourselves to be swallowed up by our base selves, our lives are reduced to nothing more than a conditioned response to stimuli.

Human beings have higher dimensions to their soul, counterbalanced by corresponding levels of the ego or *yetzer hara.* The dynamic interplay between these forces creates our unique, richer personality. Because God creates each person with a unique purpose in this world, our talents and strengths are perfectly made for our mission. Our *yetzer hara,* too, is fashioned to oppose us.[37] Hence, what is a struggle for some may not be for others. The Ramchal speaks of the difficulty in penetrating these layers:

> Though the evil inclination causes a man to commit all kinds of sins, there are some which a person's nature renders more desirable to him, and, consequently,

---

35. Genetic histories identify risk factors, but having a genetic risk for a disorder or a disease does not mean that its appearance is inevitable. "A great deal of mental illness—and even stress that falls short of mental illness—can be the result of a person's own misdeeds. He lives in such a reckless way that he led up to it gradually. Now, of course, it could happen sometimes that even people who are not under such strain can suddenly lose it. However, usually it does not happen that way. It usually happens as a result of mental strains—and mental strains happen as a result of buildups and buildups. Even if it's hereditary, heredity means that he has a certain weakness that will cause him to break under strain. However, if such a person is able to avoid strain or at least minimize strains, he could live his whole live in a state of normalcy." Rabbi Avigdor Miller, *On Emunah and Bitachon* (Judaica Press, 2012).

36. See Ramchal, *The Way of God,* 3:1:1, p. 183.

37. See *Kiddushin* 52b.

provides him with more rationalizations for. He therefore requires in relation to them additional strengthening to vanquish his evil inclination and be clean of sin.[38]

The struggles we face are sometimes universal and generic—in other words, overcoming anger and laziness—and other times unique to us, such as dealing with a specific physical limitation or emotional sensitivity, which is often a function of *tikkun* ("repair" or "rectification of the soul"), and encompassed within our genetics and/or upbringing.[39]

BECOMING EXTRAORDINARY

King Solomon tells us throughout Ecclesiastes that all suffering comes from trying to give permanence to the temporary. The soul seeks permanence through giving—investing in a commodity that will be forever ours; it recognizes that we keep whoever we become, and that is ultimately shaped by what we give, not by what we take.[40]

Our soul is drawn to reunite with Immortality, but the aberration of this quest is the ego's search for permanence through taking.[41] The ego lunges after longevity through money, power, and control, while the soul yearns for true independence—freedom over the self—which enables the apex in self-expression.[42]

The ego relishes creative acts in order to make its mark on the world—an illogical pursuit of monuments and awards, anything that will stand the test of time.[43]

NOTES

38. *Mesillas Yesharim (The Path of the Just)*, Ch. 1.

39. It becomes clear why envy is such a destructive trait and "causes the bones to rot" (Proverbs 14:30). We each receive exactly what we need in order to maximize our potential. To envy someone else is to neglect our own uniqueness and the very purpose for our existence.

40. "The more flesh, the more worms [will eventually consume him in the grave]; the more property, the more worry; the more wives, the more witchcraft; the more maidservants, the more lewdness; the more slaves, the more thievery. The more Torah, the more life; the more study, the more wisdom; the more advice, the more understanding; the more charity, the more peace. One who acquires a good name acquires it for himself; one who acquires words of Torah has acquired himself a share in the World to Come" (Ethics of the Fathers 2:7).

41. The psychological motivation is explained: "By continually taking and piling and computing interest and leaving to one's heirs, man contrives the illusion that he is in complete control of his destiny." Ernst Becker, *Escape from Evil* (New York: Free Press, 1985).

42. The Sages ask and answer: "Who is strong? One who controls his [natural] inclination" (Ethics of the Fathers 4:1).

43. We say illogical because even while he rejects a world beyond this one, he desires to be remembered. But why? If there is no existence for him beyond the physical world, why should he care that those who come

It thirsts to be special, desperately longing to set itself apart, even if it tears us apart. It does not care whether the end-goal is accomplished through productive or destructive means. It only seeks to make a big splash. Hence the proclamation of the Sages: "The construction of fools is destruction."[44]

Ironically, the ego chase leaves us a homogenized, blended existence that only blurs our uniqueness and further obscures God. When we seek to follow a destructive path in a futile attempt to be different, we end up as carbon copies of all other ego-oriented people and are confined to an automated existence and a generic personality. When our ego dominates, life is indeed programmed—but we are the unwitting programmers.

LETTING GOD SHINE THROUGH

The serpent sought to convince Eve to eat from the forbidden tree by arousing her most powerful instinct to become a creator: "Your eyes will be opened, and you will be like God knowing good and evil."[45] Not surprising, the opposite is true: Only suppression of the ego (aka "serpent") allows for our individuality to fully express itself. We are created in the image of God, a reflection of the manifestation of His will.[46] Our purpose is to reflect as much of God as we can, and the degree to which we nullify the "I," the more we bring God into the world via the display of Divine attributes that emerges within us.[47]

The Talmud teaches, "For the mind of each is different from that of the other, just as the face of each is different from that of the other."[48] Based on the origin of one's soul, every individual has a special blend of character traits essential for a distinct mission that we are both designed for and drawn to. In following the precepts of the Torah, we move toward perfecting ourselves, and we fulfill our

---

after him are aware of his accomplishments? What good does this do him? None, according to his own logic, but his soul knows differently. "We do not erect monuments for the *Tzaddikim*; their words are their deeds and their true enduing memorial" (*Yerushalmi Shekalim*).

44. *Megillah* 31b.

45. Genesis 3:4.

46. Ibid., 1:26.

47. Rearranging the Hebrew word for "I," *ani*, spells the word *ayin*, which denotes "nothingness." Noted by Aryeh Kaplan, *Jewish Meditation: A Practical Guide* (New York: Schocken Books, 1985), 87.

48. *Berachos* 58a. This teaching is in response to the often-asked question on the *Midrash* that states that the waters of the Red Sea were split into 600,000 paths—one for each family: "What is the need for multiple paths when a single path would have been sufficient?" See *Midrash* (*Shocher Tov*) 114.

purpose in bringing God's glory into the world, as only we can.[49] A brilliant spark of Divine light is then illuminated, radiating throughout creation.[50]

LET US MAKE MAN

Creating oneself is not just an act of independence but the ultimate act of *chesed*. We take what exists and then, through our own efforts, put something new—a revised self—back into creation. We cannot give what we do not own. Only by creating ourselves are we able to become a genuine source of giving, instead of a mere conduit for goodness. Rabbi Dovid Hofstedter writes,

> *Chazal* [our Sages] proclaimed of Eliezer, "He has mastered his master's Torah" (*Yoma* 28b). *Chazal* teach that he also had complete control over his *yetzer hara* (see *Bereishis Rabbah* 59:8). No slouch. In fact he was one of the few individuals who did not die but entered *Gan Eden* while he was still alive. Why then did Avraham seek out a wife for Yitzchak from those steeped in wicked behavior including *avodah zarah* [idol worship]? Eliezer was a descendent of Cham, a people cursed by Noah to forever be slaves.... It became part of their genetic makeup, so deeply entrenched in their souls that it cannot be extracted even through the sacred fire of Torah study. We see the results of this in Eliezer, Avraham Avinu's [Abraham, our forefather] faithful servant.[51]

Eliezer did not have the spiritual roots to go beyond what he was. He could never be a creator in the truest human sense. Such a person can reflect uniqueness, even radiate it—but he cannot generate it. He cannot be original. Thus, he could not produce offspring who could contribute anything new. In order for the Jewish people to bring forth the Final Redemption to reveal the Oneness of God, we each need to emit our own spark of individuality. This he did not have, and so Abraham could not allow Eliezer's daughter to marry his son.

When a person is busy building an image or succumbing to cravings and

NOTES

49. "If I am not for myself, who will be for me? But if I am only for myself, who am I? If not now, when?" (Ethics of the Fathers 1:14).

50. This is the primary lesson taught by the great Chafetz Chaim, who set out to change the world. Realizing that was impossible, he decided to change his community. Then realizing that, too, was a foregone dream, he aimed to change his family. Finally, he realized his real goal in life was to change himself. He accomplished just that and, in doing so, changed the world.

51. Rabbi Dovid Hofstedter, *Dorash Dovid* (Israel Bookshop, 2011), 101-102.

impulses, he never rises above reactionary living. He does not create anything—certainly not himself. When we are independent, we are partners in our own creation and in creation itself.

The wisest of men exhorts, "All of this is *hevel* [futility or vanity].... That which has been is that which shall be; and that which has been done is that which shall be done: there is nothing new under the sun."[52] The *Zohar* states that futility here refers to our actions that are done "under the sun"; it adds, however, that *chesed*—acts of righteousness and lovingkindness—are done "above the sun."[53]

Only He Who is beyond the sun can create. When we tap into God's will and learn our nature in His way, we exercise the height of free will and leave the finite nature of this world behind. We draw down the power to create ourselves and enjoy true permanence—who we become for all eternity.

The desire to create burns deep within each of us. We derive intense and unparalleled satisfaction from creative thought and action. It rivets our attention and expresses our individuality. We notice how much pleasure a small child receives from drawing a picture. We are driven to be unique, to express ourselves. God is the ultimate Creator. This is why we find self-expression and creativity so pleasurable—because being like God is the greatest pleasure, and when we create ourselves, we fulfill our role in the greater tapestry of creation.

NOTES

52. Ecclesiastes 1:2–9. *Hevel* literally means "breath" or "vapor" and is often translated into words such as "futile," "meaningless," and "fleeting," to connote something that exists and then dissipates without a trace.

53. See *Zohar* II:59a.

13 | A PERMANENT SHAPE

In Judaism, we speak of two worlds: *Olam Hazeh* ("this world") and *Olam Haba* ("the afterlife" or "the World to Come").[54] The Sages say that this world exists only as a corridor to the next and was created by God to give us the opportunity to earn our place, so that we can enjoy eternity without the heavy shame that would accompany a "spiritual handout."[55] "The good that man ultimately receives is therefore as much the result of his own efforts as it is a gift of God."[56]

Rabbi Aryeh Kaplan writes, "A person experiences shame when he is caught doing something that he should not or when he finds himself in an improper place. But for a mere receiver to be close to God is also an improper place."[57] In the next world, we cannot be where we do not belong. Not because we are chased away, but because we flee as one would from a burning building. The soul aches to be closer to the glory of God, but the blistering, intense pain of unrelenting shame—of being where it does not belong—does not permit the soul to remain there.[58]

This is described as *nehama d'kesufa* ("the bread of shame"): "One who eats

NOTES

54. *Olam Haba* is referred to as *Gan Eden* ("the Garden of Eden"), the World to Come, and the next world and is used interchangeably throughout this work.

55. Ethics of the Fathers 4:21. Ramchal, *The Way of God*, 39 (1:2:2).

56. Kaplan, *If You Were God*, 59.

57. Ibid., 56.

58. "If a person does not prepare on *Erev* Shabbos, what will he eat on Shabbos?" (*Avodah Zarah* 3a). This parable teaches us that we will be sustained in the next world through our efforts in this world.

another's bread is ashamed to look in his face."[59] In this world, we do not feel the full weight of shame because the ego protects us with a sense of entitlement. But neither our ego nor our physical self exists in the next world.[60]

Still, even in this world we are wired to derive more satisfaction from something we have worked for than from something that was merely handed to us. Our experience testifies to the wisdom of the Sages: "A person prefers one portion of what is his more than nine portions from someone else."[61]

WE CANNOT PRETEND

But why do we need to earn our place? Why doesn't God use some Divine hypnosis to allow us to feel the pleasure of His proximity without the feeling of shame? Or better still, perhaps He could install within us a fabricated memory of earning our reward?

We learned earlier that in the nonphysical world, closeness is measured in terms of similarities that manifest in levels of awareness. It is thus impossible for spiritual opposites to be close to each other. Imagine the words *true* and *false*. In conceptual space, where might we put them in a room—next to each other or far apart? Now think of *love* and *happiness*. These two words would be placed closer together.

Our Sages have said, "The seal of the Holy One Blessed be He is truth."[62] The essence of God is *emes* ("truth"), and His will is truth. Our ego can deceive us in this world, but our soul dwells in *Olam Haba*, the world of truth. In the next world, we cannot pretend to be something that we are not and convince ourselves otherwise. The concept of falsehood does not exist within the nature of oneness and ultimate

NOTES

59. *Yerushalmi Orlah* 1:3, cited by Ramchal, *Da'as Tevunos*, p. 168. *The Knowing Heart*, Shraga Silverstein trans. (Jerusalem / New York: Feldheim, 1982), 315.

60. This soul world is also temporary. "The true time and place of reward will therefore be after the resurrection in this renewed world. Man will then enjoy his reward with both body and soul. The body will be purified by the soul, and will therefore also be in a proper state to enjoy that good. People will not all be equal in this time of reward. They will attain different levels, depending on their work to attain perfection in this world" (cf. Ramchal, *The Way of God*, 3:10).

Rabbi Kaplan notes that authorities differ on "where *Olam Haba* 'is,'" and whether it refers to a spiritual dimension that the soul enters after leaving the body or is a completely new stage of earth life that will be ushered in only after the Messianic Age and the Resurrection of the Dead. Those who maintain the latter view refer to *Olam Haba* as *Olam HaNeshamos* ("World of Souls") an intermediate dimension where all souls pass through, are judged, and remain until the resurrection. The essential formula is the same: temporary judgment (with resultant feelings of shame) and a subsequent eternal form.

61. *Bava Metzia* 38a.

62. *Shabbos* 55a.

reality. We either earn our reward or we do not; we are either similar to God or we are not—there is no make-believe.

In a similar vein, *halachah* ("Jewish law") is bound up with spirituality here and in the next world. There is no division when it comes to the truth.[63] Judaism does not separate service to God from monetary laws or relationships. God does not permit us to deny any aspect of truth that we find inconvenient or uncomfortable. The Ramchal writes,

> The righteous hate a false thing. And it is in relation to this that we were warned (Exodus 23:7), "Keep far away from a false thing." Note that we do not have, "Guard yourself from falsehood," but "Withdraw from a false thing," to awaken us to the greatness of the extent to which one must withdraw himself and flee from falsehood.[64]

HEAVEN AND HELL

The conventional understanding of the afterlife is that two different places exist: heaven and hell. Heaven is for the good people, and hell for the bad. Judaism teaches that in reality there is really only one place, and that people have different experiences depending on where they are standing.

A wine connoisseur, for example, and an unsophisticated consumer will have different experiences even when sampling the same bottle of wine. The experience is determined by the refinement of the person's senses, the awareness of subtleties—texture, finish, body, and so on. The connoisseur's knowledge of wine changes his perception of it (reality), and so the taste of the flavor is richer and more refined (his interpretation). He will enjoy a different reality within the

---

NOTES

63. Cf. *Derech Hashem* 1:3:2. The Talmud states that after our death, God will ask us a number of questions— the first one: "Did you conduct your business affairs with honesty and integrity?" (*Shabbos* 31a). Of the Torah's 613 laws, more than 100 deal with business. (Meir Tamari, *With All Your Possessions: Jewish Ethics and Economic Life* [New York: The Free Press, 1987], 35.) True spirituality is not some vague feeling of transcendence, but the conscious application of Torah to every aspect of one's life. *Halachah* delineates precisely how we are to conduct ourselves in the service of God. *Chazal* exhorts that one who wishes to be a pious person should be scrupulous in matters of civil and tort law (*Bava Kamma* 30a).

The Ramban writes that the commandment to be holy, "*Kedoshim tihiyu*," means that it is not enough to follow the letter of the law but the spirit as well. He explains that a person can be completely observant, keeping all the *mitzvos*, and yet be called repulsive. Let us heed the advice of the poet Ralph Waldo Emerson: "Pay every debt as if God wrote the bill."

64. *Mesillas Yesharim (The Path of the Just)*, Ch. 11.

same reality. His perception hinges on his knowledge, which, in turn, alters the experience.

A linear representation comes to mind when we speak of the world "above" and the world "below," but these worlds are divided not by space, but by levels of awareness that either reveal or conceal the truth on a near-infinite continuum.

This world is a metaphor for the next, in which a person determines his own reality via the choices he has made. We are who we create ourselves to be, each behavior moving us closer to God or further away—for now and eternity.[65] The Rabbis say that we are all alone in the next world, meaning that our reality is the sum of our choices—just as it is in this world, each of us experiencing a different reality within the same reality.

A FINAL FORM

The Gemara states, "There is no *Gehinnom* [hell] in the next world."[66] Our Sages explain that while there is no eternal damnation or permanent designation called hell, we do have a transitory concept. Our transgressions are a barrier to the enjoyment of *Olam Haba*, so in His Infinite kindness God allows for a purification process.[67] The fire of *Gehinnom* is actually the burning shame we experience because of our sins (which include wasted potential).[68] Rabbi Aryeh Kaplan explains:

> The Sages tell us that God will show us our potential, who we could have become; coming face-to-face with what we could have been, of realizing we will remain stunted and deformed having forever lost the chance to achieve the majestic and noble form we could have attained, is nothing less than shame. That is why this suffering is compared to fire, and the place of this terrible suffering is aptly called hell.[69]

---

65. The *Midrash* states, "Woe to us from the Day of Judgment! Woe to us from the Day of Rebuke!" (*Bereishis Rabbah* 33:17). The vernacular rendered is, "*l'fi mah shehu*," "each one according to what he is."

66. *Nedarim* 8b.

67. "Fire below is one sixtieth of the fire of *Gehinnom*" (*Berachos* 57b).

68. See Kaplan, *If You Were God*, 31. We cannot move on to the next sentence without appreciating that this shame is through the lens of our unadorned soul. We glimpse the intensity of this pain by picturing the eyes of a loved one who is helplessly etched into place, unable to move, to even budge an inch—cycling between fear, self-pity, and profound sadness.

69. Ibid.

This process—the experience of intense temporary shame to scrub clean potential eternal shame—can only lift the stains from our *neshamah*; it cannot change a soul's essence or remove what it has become enmeshed with.[70] Death brings no fundamental change to our personality. Basic character traits and tendencies acquired during our lifetime remain the basis of our future experiences in the spiritual world.[71]

This period of suffering lasts only as long as the purification process, because it *is* the purification process—which, according to most sources, does not exceed twelve months. The suffering ends here. Afterward, we "go to" "whoever we are." Our reality—perception as a result of potential minus actualization—is our experience.

For example, on a scale from 1 to 10, let us say that a soul's potential is a 7. In its lifetime, it actualized itself to a 4. In the next world, it will enjoy pleasure that is a "3" away from God. Another soul has a potential of a 5 and also actualized itself to a 4. In the next world, it will enjoy being just a "1" away from God.[72]

A person is not in a perpetual state of suffering because of his sins, and *mitzvos* are not canceled by his transgressions. After the cleansing process, the pain of the liabilities on the balance sheet is erased, and we are left to enjoy the net sum of our assets.

NO PLACE FOR EVIL

These above-stated calculations, however, do not apply to the purely evil soul. In *Olam Haba*, the concept of evil does not exist; therefore, the wicked cannot exist.

NOTES

70. See Rabbi Eliyahu Dessler, *Strive for Truth*, Vol. II, 26. The higher levels of the soul—*chayah* and *yechidah*—do not become blemished and remain forever pure. Some opinions say this applies to the second and third levels, *ruach* and *neshamah*, as well.

71. Ibid.

72. Even though a soul's capabilities max out at "7," this "7" represents a crude linear expression of potential in our world. In actuality, a "7" is this soul's "10," and we are thus rewarded based on our efforts, in contrast to our potential. Still, this is only part of the picture. *Tikkun* issues aside, the question we want to ask ourselves is, "What determines whether a soul comes into the world with a potential of a '7' or a '5' or whatever number?" The determination is representative of the soul's refinement and is based on a number of factors, ranging from deeds of our ancestors to our own soul's root and incarnations. Herein lies the application.

Who is on a spiritually higher level: One whose nature it is to become easily angered, but who has earnestly worked on himself to contain his rage? Or a person who is bothered by very little, yet freely expresses his anger, in spite of modest efforts to contain himself? Clearly, the second person's nature (not to feel anger) is more God-like, while the first person's conduct (in rising above his nature) is more praiseworthy. Hence, our intrinsic awareness of God (which is based on our soul's refinement) is fused with our self-earned status, which together establish our eternal closeness to God.

To continue with the above metaphor, there are no negative numbers in the world of truth.

Pain is distance from God, but, more deeply, it is separation from existence. God is everything. He is existence, reality itself. (The difference between everything and nothing is exactly this: existence—everything *is* and nothing *isn't*.)[73] Evil is incompatible with existence, and this is the worst suffering, the experience of nonexistence. In *Olam Haba*, we receive what we have created. What did the *rasha* shape himself into? Nothing. And this will be his experience: nothingness.[74]

We can catch a glimpse of this feeling through emotional suffering. Physical isolation—or even being ignored—is painful. In fact, studies show that feeling alone or loneliness, more than any other factor, causes more stress and an overall weakening of the immune system. This is not just a matter of speech. Functional magnetic resonance imaging (fMRI) scans reveal that brain activity in two areas where physical pain is processed—the dorsal anterior cingulate cortex and the anterior insula— become activated when a person has feelings of social rejection.[75] When we have no connection to anything real, we suffer, in this world and in the next.[76]

Jewish tradition teaches that God does not withhold His good from anyone;[77] hence, the wicked are compensated in this world (see the following chapter), and then the negativity that engulfs them becomes their permanent state.[78] Their suffering does not end.

MOVING ON

The transition itself from this world to the next also hinges on our deeds. A person who identifies with his body will be less prepared—and will suffer greatly as his whole identity ceases to exist—while one who knows that he is truly a *neshamah*

NOTES

73. This insight was framed by Rabbi Yitzchok Feldheim.

74. There is a dispute among the Sages regarding what happens to truly wicked souls at the end of the purification process. Some opinions hold that the wicked are utterly destroyed and cease to exist, while others believe in eternal suffering (Rambam, *Mishneh Torah, Hilchos Teshuvah*, 3:5–6). These views are perhaps marginally reconciled when we consider that the experience of nonexistence is the greatest form of suffering.

75. See Campbell, Rudich, and Sedikides, "Narcissism, Self-Esteem, and the Positivity of Self-Views," 358-368.

76. The concept of *Kares* is expressed throughout the Torah and refers to a "Divine separation" or "cutting off."

77. See *Bava Kamma* 38b, *Nazir* 23b, and *Pesachim* 118a.

78. The *Zohar* offers many additional insights regarding what constitutes evil, as well as the duration of punishment. Regarding our immediate discussion, it states that at the end of days, even utter evil will be saved from total annihilation, except for the nation of *Canaan*.

("soul") merely discards the garment of physicality and moves painlessly into a new reality.[79] Rabbi Nachman relates that for one who truly believes in God, the moment of death is a seamless shift from one life to another, akin to "removing a hair from a cup of milk."[80] The wisdom of the Sages is captured by the heart of a poet in "Death Is a Dialogue Between" by Emily Dickinson:

> *Death is a Dialogue between*
> *The Spirit and the Dust.*
> *"Dissolve" says Death—The Spirit "Sir*
> *I have another Trust"—*
> *Death doubts it—Argues from the Ground—*
> *The Spirit turns away*
> *Just laying off for evidence*
> *An Overcoat of Clay.*[81]

In the words of the nineteenth-century author Robert Louis Stevenson, "Everybody, sooner or later, sits down to a banquet of consequences." Our eternity is an inescapable reflection of the totality of our choices.[82] Measure for measure, our deeds are repaid, and just as one can easily smooth wet cement, once dried, the impression is permanent.[83] Our behavior becomes an everlasting imprint in which we dwell for perpetuity.[84]

NOTES

79. While the *neshamah* is, technically speaking, the third level of the soul, it represents the core of the soul and is thus used interchangeably with "soul."

80. *Moed Katan* 28a.

81. Emily Elizabeth Dickinson (1830 – 1886) was a prolific American poet.

82. "After death, this itself is a person's reward; all of his good cleaves together, uniting into one, and clothes him in the attire of Talmudic scholars" (*Ruach HaChayim* 2:1). "This garment consists of all of the deeds the person has performed day by day" (*Zohar, Vayechi*).

83. There are an infinite number of gradations within each whole number, and we will keep growing in *Olam Haba* in whatever fixed spectrum we have locked ourselves into: whether 10 percent or 95 percent. Humility hollows out a space for knowledge to exist within us, and from this point our knowledge grows— but cannot expand beyond the boundaries of our form. There are exceptions, as noted in the footnote below and in Chapter 25, "Unperceived Influences."

84. The *Midrash* states, "Man has three friends on whose company he relies. First, wealth, which goes with him only while good fortune lasts. Second, his relatives; they go only as far as the grave, and leave him there. The third friend, his good deeds go with him beyond the grave." The ongoing influence of our deeds continues long after we leave this world. This is why the righteous are called alive even in death, whereas the wicked are called dead even in life (*Berachos* 18a). The souls of the righteous enjoy perpetual development and "go from strength to strength" (Psalms 84:7).

PART 5

THE SYSTEM
OF MAZAL

We have thus learned that the quality of our lives—and of our after-life—hinges not on circumstance, but on choice. Here we discover something equally revealing: How to rise above a Heavenly decree to effect change in our *mazal*—the controlling force behind the direction of the entirety of our lives.

14 | AGENTS OF ADVERSITY

We do not know the ways of God, and we cannot presume to understand every cause of every hardship—much less grasp why bad things happen to good people. In general, though, many of life's challenges spring from one source, or a combination of nine sources, that we will assess. First, let us pose the often-paired question: Why do really good things sometimes happen to really bad people?

At times, God allows the wicked to prosper in order to reward them for whatever good deeds they have done. The Torah states, "God repays those who hate Him to their face, to cause them to perish; He will not delay the one who hates Him, He will repay him to his face."[1] The Rambam explains that God compensates him for any good he has done, because he will be lost from the World to Come.[2] The good that he speaks of does not consist of *mitzvos* (or ordeals as a result of a *tikkun*) because such deeds refine the soul and would allow him to receive a reward in the next world.[3] Rather, he means the good that is done through fostering the illusion of an independent natural world (which is detailed in Chapter 20, "The Nature of Chance").[4]

NOTES

1. Deuteronomy 7:9–10.

2. See Rashi on v. 10.

3. Other commentators hold the Rambam's view to mean that even good deeds which imprint onto the soul may be rewarded in this world. This happens when a soul is so completely encrusted by an iniquitous personality, that it is unable to appreciate any reward in the next world. A definitive understanding is elusive because, as the previous chapter explains, there are multiple opinions regarding the definition of absolute evil as well as its ultimate destination.

4. God may allow this person to be successful in the natural world, while a more righteous person may be unsuccessful, because his payment is possible in the next world. Furthermore, reward for the righteous may be withheld until the next world, in spite of their efforts in the natural world (*Berachos* 5a.). And in fact, they

All of the good that we help bring into existence benefits us in the next world to the extent that the soul grows from the experience. Therefore, even an otherwise good person may receive a *portion* of his reward in this world.[5]

We already know that there is no comparing the reward of this world to the next, so how does a just God orchestrate such a deal? The answer is that any facet of the soul that is not purified does not resonate with God and thus cannot bond with Him.

A person is paid in this world not with the intention of short-changing him, but because he cannot enjoy full dividends in the next world. The currency there is as valuable to him as play money is here, in this world. The logic is clear: He does not benefit because he has little appreciation for Truth (with respect to this facet); he has little appreciation for Truth because he has little recognition of Truth; and he has little recognition of Truth because he is too dissimilar from Truth. And for the truly evil, they must be fully paid out in this world, because in *Olam Haba*, they will be incompatible with existence.

DIFFICULT TIMES

Our Sages offer the insights above and below to help us grapple with the unknowable, but we are reminded, "It is not within our ability [to fully understand] either the tranquility of the wicked or the suffering of the righteous."[6] Now on to our original inquiry: the nine main categories or life challenges. To be clear, we are not speaking exclusively of *nisyonos* ("Heaven-sent tests to foster spiritual growth"), but also of troubles that result from self-inflicted wounds.

1. Awake and Atone

When a person transgresses—either willingly or unknowingly—his soul becomes tarnished, and God gives us the opportunity to cleanse ourselves of these spiritual blemishes. The Ramchal writes,

Good deeds incorporate an intrinsic quality of perfection and excellence in man's body and soul. Evil deeds, on the other hand, incorporate in

NOTES

may also experience additional challenges or *yissurim shel ahavah* ("tribulations of love") in order to maximize their reward in the next world. Certainly, the emotional laws of free will are always in effect, which allows the righteous to take extraordinary pleasure in their meaningful lives.

5. See Deuteronomy 7:10; Psalms 92; *Berachos* 55b; and Shabbos 32a.

6. Ethics of the Fathers 4:19.

him a quality of insensitivity and deficiency.... As long as [a person] still has this admixture, he is neither prepared nor suited to experience God. The Highest Mercy therefore decreed that some sort of purification exist. This is the general category of [affliction] ... to dispel the insensitivity in man, allowing him to become pure and clear ... prepared for the ultimate good at its appointed time.[7]

He explains that affliction may come to an individual in order to make him examine his deeds and motivate him to repent, or as atonement for sin. He writes, "Punishment was only created to exist in the absence of repentance. What God truly desires is that man not sin in the first place, and if he does sin, that he should repent."[8] *Teshuvah* ("repentance") removes the blemish, which refines the soul and creates change within us; as such, the growth potential is nearly limitless. If one does not repent he can still be purified through these punishments, but absent *teshuvah*, the suffering may be greater, quantitatively and qualitatively. Since a person can handle only so much, there is a limit to the damage that God can help us undo.[9] Whatever impurities remain need to be addressed after death.

But, as we recall, there are constraints here as well. The purification process we explained in the previous chapter—en route to the next world—cannot change a soul's essence. Referring to the World to Come, King Solomon writes, "If it is bent, it cannot be made straight, and if something is missing, it cannot be replaced."[10] The opportunity to make repairs is found in this world.[11]

2. Natural Consequence

We cannot assume that a challenge is a *kaparah* (the aforementioned "atonement for sin") when in actuality it may be an outgrowth of an irresponsible choice—which opened the door to a series of subsequent poor choices with unwelcome consequences. This category is different from outright negligence

7. Ramchal, *The Way of God*, 39 (1:2).

8. Ibid.

9. If we do not get the message, the challenge may continue longer (quantitatively enhancing the punishment), and our lack of awareness means that we have no context for the pain, so it is felt more intensely (qualitatively speaking).

10. Ecclesiastes 1:15.

11. Ethics of the Fathers 4:22.

(#4, below) because here, there is no direct and immediate correlation for having put ourselves into harm's way.

For instance, a person, out of arrogance, does something for which he feels guilty. As a result, he engages in self-destructive acts that over time injure his physical health. This is not an uncommon scenario. Failures at self-regulation are behind a wide range of poor health decisions, including obesity and addiction, to which an estimated 40 percent of deaths are attributable.[12]

Or let us consider a person who lacks *bitachon*. As a result, he suffers from anxiety and stress, which, as the Talmud states, weakens him physically.[13] This is not a cleansing process; it is a cause and delayed effect that ripples predictably.[14] Sometimes the association is more obscure. For example, Judaism advocates modesty, but when our ego gets the better of us, a desire to flaunt leads to dangerous consequences. The Gemara states that ninety-nine out of one hundred people die before their time due to *ayin hara* ("evil eye").[15]

3. Context and Consequence

While a person cannot expect that moving to a new place will automatically change his *mazal*, it may nonetheless affect his welfare. The Talmud states, "Once permission has been given to the Destroyer to destroy, he does not distinguish between the righteous and the wicked."[16] A person may find himself in the wrong place at the wrong time—facing a plague, tornado, earthquake, and the like—and when this force is unleashed, anything in its path is vulnerable.

In the Torah we learn that Lot is saved, but only because the angels insisted that he hurry before the destruction began. He did not have the merit to save himself from the midst of the upheaval.[17] As well, our standing may not warrant God to supersede on our behalf during a calamity, so we must

NOTES

12. See S. A. Schroeder, "We Can Do Better—Improving the Health of the American People," *New England Journal of Medicine* 357 (2007): 1221–1228. More people die from overeating than from hunger (*Shabbos* 33).

13. *Gittin* 70a. We cannot say that a person who suffers a physical ailment lacks *bitachon* or has a spiritual deficiency. A lack of *bitachon* or a spiritual deficiency may cause physical ailments, but there are other causes as well.

14. Medical research is equally unambiguous and confirms that up to 90 percent of all illness and disease is stress-related, according to the Centers for Disease Control and Prevention.

15. *Bava Metzia* 107b.

16. *Bava Kamma* 60a.

17. Genesis 19:15–26.

always take measures to protect ourselves. As such, the Torah commands us: "Take utmost care and guard yourself scrupulously."[18] A commentary on the Gemara expounds:

> Rashbash, the son of the Tashbetz, was asked: "How does it help to run away from a plague? If it was inscribed on Rosh Hashanah that one was to die from this plague, then the plague will find him no matter where he flees. And if he was not inscribed on Rosh Hashanah to die from this plague, then he has no need to run away!" Rashbash answered: "It is universally acknowledged in Jewish tradition that a man has an allotted life span. But years may be added to this allotment and years may be taken away. When years are added this is described as being written in the Book of the Living, and when years are taken away this is described as being written in the Book of the Dead. However, his original life span may never have been altered. Within this category, death is still possible before his time if he endangers himself. On the other hand, if a person takes the proper precautions, he may live out his full life span. Thus, when there is a plague in the city it is incumbent upon a person to avoid it, lest he cause himself to die before his time."[19]

4. Negligence

Unlike the person receiving atonement or one suffering the consequences of poor moral choices, this person willfully puts himself in harm's way. A person is responsible for his own personal safety, and our Sages warn us that whatever natural protection or decree was in place may be withdrawn or overridden by willful negligence.[20] The Ramchal writes,

> There is appropriate fear and there is foolish fear. On the other hand, there is confidence and there is recklessness. God has invested man with intelligence and judgment so that he may follow the right path and protect himself from the instruments of injury that have been created

NOTES

18. Deuteronomy 4:9

19. *Responsa* 195. Excerpted from Artscroll *Talmud Bavli*, Schottenstein Edition, 2008. Notes based on the passage, "The Rabbis taught in a Baraisa: If there is a plague in the city take your feet in to your house to avoid becoming infected" (*Bava Kamma* 60b).

20. *Kesubos* 30a.

to punish evildoers. One who chooses not to be guided by wisdom and exposes himself to dangers is displaying not trust, but recklessness.[21]

5. Soul's Root

This ordeal is not the result of a transgression but rather an inborn spiritual deficiency or capability. A character flaw must be corrected (and/or a hidden potential revealed) and only through a specific *nisayon* will necessary growth be achieved.[22]

Often these experiences are a *tikkun*—a fixing or repairing of damage from a previous incarnation, or *gilgul*.[23] The opportunity for rectification and soul-perfection through *gilgulim* arises when we make responsible choices in situations similar to those we had in previous incarnations but erred. The Chafetz Chaim says that most of our questions about hardships would be answered to our satisfaction if we fully understood the issue of reincarnation.[24]

6. Wake-Up Call

Here we face a particular challenge so that we can reassess our lives and change our trajectory to avoid unnecessary distress. In other words, our soul does not need what may ensue, and God gives us the opportunity to avoid this path—if we heed the warning. We need to be awakened spiritually, even if it means being shaken up, either physically or emotionally. We call this pain. God calls it love.[25]

We should note that at times these wake-up calls come as flashes of perspective—there is fear, but no lasting real-world impact. The purpose

---

NOTES

21. *Mesillas Yesharim* (*The Path of the Just*), Ch. 9.

22. See Rabbi Yeruchem Levovitz, *Da'as Torah*, ad loc.

23. *Gilgulim* refers to the revolving or recycling of souls through a succession of lives and is discussed at length in Kabbalistic works.

24. *Gilgulim* is the answer to another thoughtful question: What is the reason for the existence of severely mentally challenged or insane individuals? If the capacity for free will is gone, then what is the purpose of their lives? Such individuals might be here to teach others compassion, perspective, gratitude, or humility, but this cannot be the only reason. A person is never merely a *kli* ("vessel") for another's Divine service—unless he is already a perfected soul. His existence must also carry with it some benefit for himself. See Rabbi Eliyahu Dessler, *Strive for Truth*, Vol. 1, parts 1–2.

25. The challenges we face are in no way confined to personal experiences and most certainly extend to our loved ones. Even though a person may care little for his own well-being, these emotional soft spots remain a strong motivator for reflection and change.

is to help us realize that God has saved us from a potential heartache, and, filled with immense gratitude, we then move our lives in a more responsible direction, synchronized with our life's purpose.

7. Barriers and Barricades

Sometimes God sets up roadblocks, not to keep us from making a poor choice per se, but to prevent our putting ourselves into an unproductive or dangerous environment (as in category #3) from which we would not be saved. For instance, a broken foot may prevent a person from taking a trip that would put his life in jeopardy. To save us from a more devastating ordeal, God puts up signs and, when those are ignored, places guardrails and roadblocks should He deign to spare us.

8. Interdependency

The Sages teach us that when a *tzaddik* or an otherwise innocent person dies — God forbid a baby, for instance — it is a *kaparah* for *Klal Yisrael* ("the Jewish people"), and it has nothing to do with the person, the parents, the circumstances, or anyone's choices.[26]

Regardless of our spiritual standing, we are all connected and can thus be affected.[27] The extent to which others are dependent on us and how much our lives impact theirs play a dominant role in our heavenly judgment and status.[28] For this reason, there are some who advise that a person should be involved in helping as many people as possible, for if their *mazal* does not dictate that our help and support be withdrawn, then we have entwined another string in the rope to pull us out of any potential hazard.

NOTES

26. See *Kesubos* 8b. "There are also *tzaddikim* who die in their youth … because they have completed their fulfillment of their 613 *mitzvos* and other particulars" (Rabbi Chayyim Vital, *Sefer HaGilgulim*, 4). In such instances, we could not have prevented this tragedy. There is zero reason to feel a moment of guilt or regret, and there is no cause for blame. It has nothing to do with anyone's *aveiros* ("sins") or deeds. This was a pure *neshamah* that was tasked with a special mission and, as our Sages explain, goes straight to *Gan Eden*. For this reason, Rabbi Moshe Feinstein *paskened* ("ruled") that one shouldn't say *Kaddish* for infants because they do not need additional merit. Nonetheless, it is prudent to examine our actions and to do *teshuvah* should we find negligence on our part. "If one sees suffering coming upon him, he should investigate his deeds, as it says (*Eichah* 3:40), 'Let us search our ways and investigate and return to God'" (*Berachos* 5a). Still, even in such instances we are only a *shaliach*, and our behavior did not cause the finale to what was most certainly an unalterable destiny.

27. This is not to be confused with a seemingly similar Christian concept. In Judaism, our personal sins are not automatically forgiven through the death or suffering of another.

28. See Rabbi Eliezer Papo, *Pele Yoetz*.

9. Sign of the Times

We are living in *ikvos d'Meshichah* ("footsteps of the Messiah"). This unique period in history has brought not only the disintegration of morality, but a previously unbeknownst breakdown of the individual—emotionally and physically. Medical breakthroughs and technological advancements are ill-suited to counter the rapid and rising rate of illnesses in our generation. Travails and tragedies force us to reflect, to think—to decide what we are living for.

The era that is upon us leaves us no place to escape to and forces us to choose how we want to cope, how we want to live. Very few will be able to straddle the fence of indifference. The rest of us will have to decide whether we are going to turn toward God or away from Him. Such hardships are a sign of the times and not a reflection of individual failings. Even so, we are not without options. Our Sages tell us that one who engages in Torah study and acts of kindness will be spared the birth pangs of this period.[29] *"Chesed stands by man to the end of all generations as it is said: 'And the kindness of God endures forever and ever for those who fear Him.'"*[30]

After Moses petitions God to forgive the Jewish people for the sin of worshipping the Golden Calf, Moses asks of God, "Please show me Your glory." God responds, "You shall see My back, but no man can see My face and live."[31] The Talmud explains that Moses was plagued by the timeless question of why some righteous people prosper, while others suffer, and why some wicked people prosper, and others suffer.[32]

God was telling Moses that a finite mind cannot fathom an undifferentiated past, present, and future. Our limited perspective obscures the scope of His master plan and how it all coalesces into a single majestic image. While the full picture remains hidden, Rabbi Avigdor Miller reminds us that it is always signed with love by our Creator:

Whatever happens is being done by God for a kindly purpose. You may not

---

NOTES

29. *Sanhedrin* 98b. In as much as these times are a necessary condition to the coming Redemption, our *tikkun* is most certainly a factor because it is coordinated with *tikkun olam*.

30. *Yalkut Shimoni*, Psalms 103:17. See Chapter 17, "Reconfiguring Mazal—Part 2" for further elaboration.

31. Exodus 33:18–20.

32. *Berachos* 7a.

know what that purpose is; it might take years to discover; it might be necessary to go to the next world before you discover what happened—but someday you will realize the truth in this principle.[33]

The stated reasons for life's difficulties include those that are necessary for our growth and those that we bring upon ourselves. The former category is intuitively aligned with God's *chesed*. Acts of negligence, however, seem to disrupt the flow of His benevolence. How can we accept that all is for the good, when our very actions interrupt the good? We will shed light on this question in Chapter 21, "The Miracle of Nature."

NOTES

33. Rabbi Avigdor Miller, *On Emunah and Bitachon* (Judaica Press, 2012). "God is good to all, His love rests on all His deeds" (Psalms 145:9).

15 | MAZAL FUNDAMENTALS

The nine aforementioned categories in the previous chapter fall under the invisible umbrella of *mazal* and beg an obvious question. Yes, certain challenges inspire self-reflection and growth—but why is a particular flaw inherent in our *neshamah* in the first place? In other words, why would one person—or perhaps, one soul—through a succession of incarnations—be chosen by God to live a tranquil life, while another is decreed to live a more difficult life?

Questions of *gilgulim* aside, the Ramchal writes, "How [*mazal*] comes about that particular challenges are meted out to particular individuals depends on the spiritual roots of each person."[34] He explains,

> There may be a man who, in terms of his root purpose, is designated for a profusion of Divine providence [and resultant good fortune] which is one of the ways in which the universe is perfected ... as there may be another whose root purpose dictates for him the diminution of providence, the second means required for the perfection of creation. All of this relates not to the deeds of these men, but to the Blessed One's distribution of perfection of creation among the creations, each of them being perfected in its own way.[35]
>
> This knowledge is the greatest profundity, never having been perceived by any prophet or seer.... The generality of this ordinance, which is oriented not in respect to merit or guilt but in respect to what is required for the

NOTES

34. Ramchal, *The Way of God* (*Derech Hashem* 2:8:1).
35. Ramchal, *Da'as Tevunos*, 170.

perfection of the universe in terms of essence, our Sages referred to as *mazal*. For its nature is decreed and it is not dependent upon man's free will [or] upon his merits.[36]

Within the first man, Adam, God created 600,000 primordial souls that would include all of the souls that would ever exist in the world.[37] The point our soul originates from reflects the "place on Adam" where it originated. Each soul or spark continues to clothe itself into a human being until it corrects itself completely. When all of the souls complete their individual missions, we will once again merge (while maintaining a degree of individuality) into one collective soul, Adam.[38]

From a finite prism, the issue of fairness cannot be resolved, and while one may protest as to why he originates from one point over another, the inquiry is suspended when the true nature of reality is revealed. The Ramchal continues,

> The greatest good for Yisrael is the *sod* [secret thought] of removing jealousy and dimming the evil inclination. When each person recognizes his place within the hierarchy of ascension, although one will be higher and one lower, nevertheless, there is no jealousy or hatred, since this is the order according to designated levels [of spiritual development] … each person has his own place and no one oversteps his bounds, just like the spiritual luminaries.[39]

Even so, regardless of our roles and irrespective of whether they are earned or assigned, God rewards us in the next world for all of our efforts and struggles.[40] The Ramchal explains, "[Those] who were singled out by the Supreme ordinance for oppression and affliction are rewarded both for sufferings they underwent in this world and for all of their virtuous deeds."[41]

NOTES

36. Ibid., 313–314.

37. See Ramchal, ad loc.

38. Precisely speaking, the soul of Adam is indivisible and cannot be divided. Only its expression has been fragmented and will in time be re-expressed in its original state.

39. Ramchal, *Secrets of the Redemption*, trans. Rabbi Mordechai Nissim (Jerusalem / New York: Feldheim Publishers, 2011), 18.

40. Rashi (on Deuteronomy) with the statement, "Everything God does is just, there is no injustice."

41. Ramchal, *Da'as Tevunos*, 315. Recall from Chapter 14 that the soul experiences closeness to God to the degree that it refines itself. Therefore, reward for ordeals that the soul is unable to grow from are paid out in this world, and suffering from self-inflicted wounds is altogether forfeited unless they fall outside of one's *bechirah*.

TOOL KIT FOR LIFE

The word *mazal* is often translated as "luck," because from our perspective what happens to a person often appears to be random. What we fail to recognize is that in order for a person to complete his task in this world, he may enjoy undeserved riches or be faced with difficult challenges. This is why a person may seem to do all the right things, yet still not seem to "catch a break," while another person appears to effortlessly achieve success at every turn, often in spite of himself.

Mazal is more accurately defined as the confluence of attributes and circumstances that is required to complete humanity's dual raison d'être—perfection of oneself and of the world. A person's mission determines his *mazal*, and his mission is based on his spiritual roots. Rabbi Dessler explains,

> Before a person is created, the instruments which he will be given [to use in the service of God]—his *kelim*—are decided in Heaven in accordance with the task he will be called upon to perform in this world ... all his gifts, his physical and mental abilities as well as the material means at his disposal, are given to him to enable him to fulfill his portion.[42]

At specified times for reasons known only to, and directed by, God, our lives jump the track of reward and punishment and are governed instead by *mazal*. Below, the Ramchal expounds on this and then describes the two concurrent and coordinated systems of Divine influence:

> The Creator ... established two ordinances: reward and punishment and *mazal*. And He is the Decisor, resorting sometimes to one and sometimes to the other.... The Holy One, Blessed is He, combines these two ordinances so that even decrees of *mazal* materialize only though the agency of something which is attributable to reward and punishment.[43]

❑ *Hanhagas hayichud* ("guiding power of unity"): The unfolding revelation of God's glory (primary), where we have a set role to play in the master plan.

NOTES

42. Rabbi Eliyahu Dessler, *Strive for Truth*, Vol. IV, 40–46.
43. Ramchal, *Da'as Tevunos*, 317.

❑ *Hanhagas hamishpat* ("guiding power of justice"): The system of reward and punishment (secondary), where our choices dictate the consequences.[44]

In Kabbalistic language: The two main principles are: (1) the residue, which includes the guiding power of justice, reward and punishment, good and evil [*hanhagas hamishpat*]; and (2) the ray, which is the guiding power of unity [*hanhagas hayichud*]. Both of these work as one, though the guiding power of justice is revealed, and the guiding power of unity remains hidden until the guiding power of justice achieves its true purpose.[45]

Hanhagas hayichud is also referred to as *hanhagas hamazal* ("guiding power of *mazal*") because, as we will discuss, *mazal* protects our *tikkun*, which is synchronized to *tikkun olam* ("repairing this world"). Our *mazal* helps us advance the path we must travel and is not a reflection of our behavior or our merits—but rather of what is necessary for the perfection of the inner nature of Creation.[46]

An often difficult determination is how much of a given circumstance is our own doing via free will and how much of it is directed by God.[47] We can go through an experience that is a matter of our own doing, or it can be the result of a decree. Our physical health is a good example of this. A person can come down with an illness, if God wills it, but a person can also *make* himself sick through willful self-destructive behavior or with more subtle subconscious acts of self-sabotage. The percentage of our free will's contribution to the unfolding of a situation cannot always be discerned. The Ramchal writes,

> [W]ith respect to anything that befalls a man, there is no one who can determine whether it is an aspect of reward and punishment, based on his deeds, or on an aspect of *mazal*, decreed upon him. And in everything there is an aspect of both.[48]

NOTES

44. In actuality there are three types of *hanhagas hamishpat*: (a) *hanhagah* of lovingkindness; (b) *hanhagah* of judgment; and (c) *hanhagah* of mercy. However, "Kabbalists who received their wisdom from the prophet Elijah taught us that throughout the six thousand year period of the world's existence, human beings have not been worthy of these three types of *hanhagah* due to their low spiritual state.... During this period the Creator has emanated an integrated *hanhagah* [which we refer to as the guiding power of justice]." *Introduction to Kabbalah (Yedid Nefesh)*, Rabbi Y. Bar Lev.

45. Ibid.

46. Ramchal, *Da'as Tevunos*, 317.

47. Ibid., 146.

48. Ibid., 319.

FATE IS FLEXIBLE

In Chapter 22, "Mazal: The Fine Print" we will explore what makes one decree more malleable than another. For now, let us simply say that we cannot expect that fate will swerve to intercept us, and regardless of our efforts, fortune or crisis will simply materialize to reveal an unalterable destiny. We can trigger a fresh negative decree or thwart previously decreed blessings. Though God may have decreed good for a person, he often has to exert himself to obtain it.[49] Rabbi Kaplan explains,

> A person's days may be increased because of great merit, or decreased because of sin. It is thus written, "The fear of God prolongs one's days, but the years of the wicked shall be shortened" (Proverbs 10:27). A person can die before his time because of his wickedness or folly, as we are warned, "Do not be overly wicked or foolish; why should you die before your time?" (Ecclesiastes 7:17).[50]

A person can also unseal a *gezeira* ("Heavenly decree") and annul or minimize certain hardships. After Abraham and his descendants were chosen for a higher spiritual level—a direct relationship with God—active Divine providence began to operate in the world.[51]

God took Abraham outside and He said to him, "Look up, please, at the heavens and count the stars, if you can count them … so, too, will be your descendants."[52] God told Abraham to discount the effects of astrological influence.[53] "Even if there is a sign in the stars that you [Abraham] will not have children, you will rise above this and will merit having children." With this knowledge, the Talmud states, "There is no [stationary] *mazal* for the Jewish people."[54]

When we make a change, to the point that we recreate ourselves, our decree may be changed to reflect our newly revised selves. The portal between realms

---

49. "It is not the exertion itself that affects results; but still, the exertion is indispensable. Once a person has exerted himself, however, he has fulfilled his duty, and then there is room for Heaven's blessing to rest upon him" (*Mesillas Yesharim*, Ch. 21).

50. Rabbi Aryeh Kaplan, *The Handbook of Jewish Thought*, Vol. 2 (New York: Moznaim, 1992), 299.

51. See Rabbi Chaim Friedlander, *Faith and Divine Providence* (New York: Feldheim Publishers, 2008), 93.

52. Genesis 15:5.

53. Rashi, citing *Nedarim* 32a.

54. *Shabbos* 156a.

opens—and we exit the natural order—when we rise above our nature. Rabbi Dessler writes,

> A person can change his place in a spiritual [sense], and consequently his physical environment and instruments provided to him may also change correspondingly.... . A person may broaden his *mazal* and reach levels beyond those originally envisaged as his allotted portion.[55]

Mazal—the instrument of fate and fortune—is not fixed, meaning that we can acquire a different set of tools and conditions, should we evolve ourselves sufficiently. What we receive specifically in the physical world depends on what we need to actualize our potential. With expanded potential comes recalculated *mazal*. Different choices = different mission = different *mazal*.

55. Rabbi Eliyahu Dessler, *Strive for Truth*, Vol. IV, 40–46.

16 | RECONFIGURING MAZAL— PART 1: SPIRITUAL IMMUNE SYSTEM

Having observed that each person has a unique role in creation, we must ask what happens when one abdicates his responsibilities.[56] We do have free will, after all. The Sages explain that the spiritual slack is picked up by those whose desire is so great that it reconfigures their *mazal*. In the Purim narrative, the dramatic scene unfolds between Mordecai and Queen Esther, as he says to her:

> For if you will remain silent at this time, relief and salvation will come to the Jews from another source, and you and the house of your father will be lost. And who knows if it is not for just such a time that you reached this royal position.[57]

The dual message is clear: This is your job, but if you don't do it, God will assign it to someone else. Metaphorically speaking, imagine all of creation as a magnificent building, and a person chooses to forsake his unique contribution—a single brick. God will arrange that his efforts will now help others to complete the structure—including his brick. Rabbi Dessler writes,

> Individuals who are occupied with important matters on behalf of *Klal Yisrael* often receive an extraordinary—even miraculous—amount of Heavenly aid. Those that are truly humble are fully aware of their own unworthiness, and they are amazed at the success they are granted… . "How is it possible," they

---

NOTES

56. In the upcoming chapters, we will explain in greater detail the particular ramifications of defaulting on one's spiritual mission within the framework of Divine providence and *mazal*.
57. Esther 4:14.

think, "that we have the merit to accomplish great *mitzvos* such as these and with such an extraordinary amount of Heavenly aid?" The answer is that God in His great mercy bestows Heavenly aid on the person who steps forward to undertake a project needed by *Klal Yisrael* in spite of his personal unworthiness. God is prepared to make miracles happen for such a person.[58]

The Sages say, "In a place where there are no people [who are worthy of leadership], strive to be [a leader]."[59] This is not an option, but an obligation. After the sin of the Golden Calf, Moses, the humblest of men, was able to pray on behalf of the Jewish people and effect a tremendous change.[60] At that grave hour, he raised himself up to the supreme level at which he completely identified with the people of Israel.[61] His prayers had the potential to influence the entire world, creation itself.

Correspondingly, our Sages also teach that if someone prays for mercy on behalf of another, when he himself needs that very same thing, he is answered first.[62] Such a person cannot expect to be able to deceive God. We are speaking of one who, with true humility, genuinely feels the pain of another. We then morph into a *kli* ("vessel") that is now capable of accepting a great infusion of blessing and goodness.[63] The smaller our ego, the greater our expanded consciousness, and we effect greater change not just in ourselves but in our world.[64]

The power of blessing is also equally enhanced. The Malbim explains that our soul joins with the Source of all blessing, and the stronger our connection to God, the more potent our blessings.[65] "The closer a person is to God through Torah and *mitzvos*, the closer God approaches the person.... In fact, one's deeds affect not only

---

NOTES

58. Rabbi Eliyahu Dessler, *Strive for Truth*, Vol. 4, 207–208. A natural question arises regarding the person who works for the community, but whose motives are less than altruistic: Does that person receive Heavenly aid? The variables are too numerous to speak definitively in such instances, but we can say that the purer one's motivation, the more Heavenly aid he receives.

59. Ethics of the Fathers 2:6.

60. "One who is wise, humble, and fearful of sin may be promoted to serve as a community leader" (*Tosafos* on *Mishnah, Sanhedrin* 7:1).

61. Rabbi Eliyahu Dessler, *Strive for Truth*, Vol. 2, 153–154.

62. *Bava Kamma* 92a.

63. Expressed differently, we become a conduit through which this *berachah* is brought down and as the *berachah* "passes through" us, it affects us first.

64. "...when you reach the heights of *mochin d'galdus* [expanded consciousness], there you will attain the greatest humility and nullification of the ego" (Reb Nassan, *Likutei Halachos, Orach Chaim Hilchos Tefillas HaMinchah, halachah* 5).

65. The Malbim, on Genesis 27:3.

the *hanhagah* [guiding power] toward the individual [who acts] but even toward the whole creation."[66]

YIELDING TO A HIGHER WILL

Rabbi Samson Raphael Hirsch describes how our spiritual immune system becomes fortified, according us extra protection to advance our newly acquired mission.

People of integrity are aware of God's proximity, for He grants them both additional energy enabling them to carry out their good intentions and protection against their perils, which might keep them from striving to fulfill that duty.[67]

The Talmud states, "Whoever tries to manipulate fate will eventually be pushed aside; but whoever yields to God's Will, will overcome fate."[68] God will move heaven and earth, destinies and decrees, for those who make His will, their will. "Nullify your will before His will, so that He will nullify the will of others before your will."[69] This canon was poignantly expressed by James Allen:

A man has to learn that he cannot command things,
but that he can command himself;
that he cannot coerce the wills of others,
but that he can mold and master his own will:
and things serve him who serves Truth"[70]

When we transcend our base nature, we are granted not only additional energies and resources but we gain a real-world advantage over others.[71] (Recall: ego shrinks→perspective widens→see God=know God=love God→active Divine providence [to be explained].) Rabbi Chaim of Volozhin writes,

---

NOTES

66. *Faith and Divine Providence,* 163. If an ego-less state amplifies change in the world, how does an egocentric person affect change? The answer is that the ego attaches to, and energizes, negative forces that are granted powers to influence both the spiritual and physical realms.

67. Rabbi Samson Raphael Hirsch, *From the Wisdom of Mishlei,* Karin Paritzky, trans. (New York: Feldheim, 1976), 22.

68. *Berachos* 64a.

69. Ethics of the Fathers 2:4.

70. James Allen (1864–1912), British author, philosopher and pioneer of the self-help movement.

71. "Fortunate is he who is always in awe [of God]" (Proverbs 28:14).

There is a wondrous system by which a person can foil any evil designs of those who would harm him. If he follows these instructions, no harm will ever befall him. If he internalizes the concept that God is the One and only Power that exists in the Universe, and he devotes his entire being to Him, nothing else in the world can harm him in any way.[72]

He explains that when a person focuses his mind on the fact that God is the Source of all, and there is no other force or power whatsoever, God will help him by causing all other illusionary powers to be removed and nullified, and this is precisely our task in this world—to live with this awareness.[73] In terms of absolute reality, only God exists. As the Torah declares, "There is nothing beside Him."[74]

WHERE THERE'S A WILL

A person must have an unquenchable thirst for growth, to be closer to God—to do the will of God—in order to propel himself forward. "He who comes to be purified—he will be helped; he who comes to be defiled—a way is opened for him."[75] All of man's behaviors are predicated on will.[76] On this, Rabbi Shlomo Wolbe writes,

A person that succeeds in entering a desire to come near to God … so that this *ratzon* will fill him totally and unify on this [desire] … [it] will pull after him all of the powers of the body and the soul, and all of them will be joined to this aspiration.[77]

The Torah recounts, "Every man whose heart inspired him came."[78] The Ramban comments that none of the Israelites had the necessary skill to build the Sanctuary and prepare the vestments. However, because they so intensely desired to do God's will, they discovered a reservoir of talent within.

NOTES

72. *Nefesh HaChaim* 3:12 trans. R. Avraham Yaakov Finkel (New York: Judaica Press, 2009).

73. Ibid.

74. Numbers 4:35.

75. *Yoma* 38b.

76. "Whether love or hate, man does not know; all preceded him" (Ecclesiastes 9:1). "Man cannot even comprehend at times what inspires him to love or hate something" (*Metzudas David*).

77. R. Wolbe, *Alei Shor*, Book 1, Ch. 25, 120.

78. Exodus 35:21.

But more valuable than the power of human will, is the knowledge that we can change our will. And to do so, we must turn to God and ask Him not only for the *strength* to be better and greater—but for a greater *desire* to be better.[79] "The spiritual expression of *da'as* [knowledge] is *ratzon* and its physical expression is speech."[80] As we explained, the gateway between the spiritual and physical worlds opens when we rise above our nature—but we must take this first step. "Open for Me an opening the size of the eye of a needle, and I will open for you one the size of a hall."[81]

Will, or *ratzon*, is the source of all that materializes.[82] Since we cannot originate a cause—create something that does not exist—within us, we must go outside of ourselves. We must tap into the Infinite. Prayer—a yearning ache that bursts forth from us to God—is the sole means to change our will.[83] An essential dilution of ego occurs through heartfelt prayer.[84] The Ramchal writes,

> [P]art of the system set up by the Creator is that in order for people to receive ... from Heaven, they must first bring themselves near to the Source of that bounty and then request it. The amount and quality of that bounty they receive will depend on their efforts to attach themselves to its Source. If they do not make any such effort, they will not receive it. This is the essence of prayer.[85]

The will to change precedes a change in will. When we are fully devoted, heart, mind, and soul, human beings are endowed with the ability to draw to them the spiritual power and protection they need in order to manifest their highest reality—even beyond their allotted portion. "In hidden ways God grants energy. He is a shield to those with integrity."[86] "O Israel, trust in God—their help and their shield is He!"[87]

NOTES

79. "The one who sanctifies himself a little, Heaven will help to sanctify him much" (*Yoma* 39a).

80. *Mesillas Yesharim*, (*The Path of the Just*), Ch. 25.

81. *Shir HaShirim Rabbah* 5.

82. "'Will' which is [primordial] thought is the beginning of all things" (*Zohar* 1:200a).

83. "You open Your hand and satisfy the [deepest] desire of every living entity" (Psalms 145:16).

84. To maximize the prospect of having our prayers answered, it behooves us not to pray for selfish reasons, but to pray for what will allow us to better serve God and to come closer to Him.

85. Ramchal, *Way of God* (*Derech Hashem* 4:5:1).

86. Proverbs 2:7.

87. Psalms 115:1–11.

17 | RECONFIGURING MAZAL—PART 2: RISING ABOVE A HEAVENLY DECREE

At the time a person is suffering, the Heavenly court makes the angel of affliction swear not to leave that person until a specific date and hour and only through a designated messenger.[88] Yet a harsh decree may be reversed by *teshuvah* ("repentance"), *tefillah* ("prayer" and Psalms), and *tzedakah* ("charity," "good deeds"), even during that time period, thus annulling the decree of affliction.[89] What do all of these actions have in common? They all promote humility—the frequency to God.[90]

TESHUVAH

In Hebrew, *chet* ("shortcoming" or "sin") connotes "distance." *Teshuvah* means "to return," and when done properly, we instantly regain that distance and move closer to God.[91] In fact, our Sages tell us that when a person does *teshuvah* out of love, his intentional sin becomes a *mitzvah*. We understand this because a sin is something that moves us away from God, whereas a *mitzvah* is something that

---

NOTES

88. *Avodah Zarah* 55a.

89. "Charity saves one from death" (Proverbs 10:2). Prayer can change a *gezar din* ("verdict" or "Heavenly decree") (*Rosh Hashanah* 16b–18). On the *Yamim Noraim* (the ten days starting with Rosh Hashanah and ending with Yom Kippur and known as the Days of Awe or the Days of Repentance), we remind ourselves, "*Teshuvah, tefillah*, and *tzedakah* annul an evil decree."

90. "God gives favor to the humble" (Proverbs 3:34). "In the wake of humility comes fear of the Lord, even riches, honor, and life" (ibid., 22:4).

91. "Rabbi Levi said, 'Great is *teshuvah*, for it enables a person to reach the throne of God,' as it says 'Return, O Israel, to the Lord your God'" (Hosea 14:2) (*Yoma* 86a).

moves us closer toward Him. When a person does *teshuvah* out of love for God, the very deed that had moved him away becomes a vehicle for moving him closer.[92]

How is it possible to erase our past mistakes and even supernaturally transform them? The ability to do so defies the laws of human logic, yet is as real as gravity. Moving backward in time is unnatural. For that matter, emotional growth itself is unnatural.

Admitting that we did something wrong goes against our nature, but when we do so, God rises above nature for us, and He reverses the damage that has been done.[93]

Teshuvah springs from the well of humility, and when we release our egos and take responsibility, we free ourselves from the confines of time. While it is true that change in the physical world takes time, change happens instantaneously in nonphysical space.[94] The ego blinds us to reason and binds us to physicality.[95] Acceptance of responsibility dislodges the ego, and the rational aspect or the intellect—which is not locked in time and space—is freed. Instantly, we move closer to God and our destiny is reformulated.[96]

NOTES

92. The Four Stages of *teshuvah*:
   1. Feel remorseful. Genuine regret for our wrong actions is the first step toward releasing our guilt. We must be genuinely ashamed of our actions, or we cannot truly be sorry for them.
   2. Stop the behavior. If it was a one-time action, then there is nothing more to stop. However, if we are still engaging in the wrongful behavior, then we must stop it and resolve in our hearts never to commit the sin again. If we cannot change immediately, we should create a plan to gradually cease this behavior over a period of time and stick to it. We should also create deterrents for ourselves in order to avoid repeating the same transgression. In this way, we make a statement to ourselves and others that we have changed and that we are taking action to ensure that our improved selves thrive.
   3. Confess before God. By confessing before God, we offer aloud the commitments and sentiments that reside in our heart. We should say, "I have sinned with this behavior, I deeply regret my actions, and I declare before God, Who knows my innermost thoughts, that I will never do this sin again."
   4. Ask for forgiveness. If we wronged an individual, then we must first ask forgiveness from that person before asking forgiveness from God. We are not responsible for the other person's response, but we have to ask.

93. "By lovingkindness and truth shall sin be atoned" (Proverbs 15:6).

94. This can be compared to the concept of *kfitzas haderech*, "contracting of the path," as happened to Jacob (*Chullin* 91b). While this level is theoretical to our generation, we see that to the degree to which we reduce our ego, we create a vessel that cancels the natural order and clears the way to more rapidly grow and expand our spiritual dimension. The idea of folding space is found in scientific literature. A wormhole, also known as *abbreviated space*, is a theoretical shortcut or tunnel produced by a tear in the fabric of the space-time continuum.

95. Times of crises or special times of the year (e.g., Rosh Hashanah, Pesach) can facilitate *bechirah klalis*—the ability to make swift and substantial changes in a person's spiritual status" (Rabbi Eliyahu Dessler, *Strive for Truth*, Vol. 4, 93–95).

96. In Hebrew, the word *nisayon* means both "test" and "miracle." It is a miracle, or a breach of the natural order, when we rise above our nature.

Rabbi Kaplan explains that *teshuvah* comes from the level of *Keser* and, "It is only when [the *Sefirah* of] *Keser* is hidden and [the *Sefirah* of] *Da'as* manifests that God is bound by the laws and logic of creation.... Whenever man activates his free will [rises above his nature] God's *Da'as* disappears and *Keser* [which is beyond time and space] manifests in its place."[97] *Teshuvah* is not beholden to time since it preceded the creation of the world, and thus time itself.[98] A famed first-century Kabbalist explains that God gave repentance "its proper place before the creation of the world and if a person repents, God will have mercy on him and his evil star will be turned into a lucky star."[99]

TEFILLAH

Sincere and heartfelt prayer also has the power to annul a Heavenly decree.[100] When Jacob first met Leah and Rachel and their father, Laban, the Torah tells us that Leah's eyes were tender.[101] The commentaries explain this to mean that she wept constantly in prayer that she not have to marry Esau.

People of the town would say, "The elder daughter [Leah] will marry the elder son [Esau] and the younger daughter [Rachel] will marry the younger son [Jacob]." Moreover, the *Midrash* states that Leah looked at her *goral* ("fate") and confirmed that Esau was her intended. When Leah heard the description of the wicked Esau, she beseeched God with tears and prayers to change her destined mate. "May it be Your will I not fall into a lot of a wicked one."[102] Rabbi Huna said, "Prayer is strong; not only did it annul the decree, but Leah became the first to marry Jacob."[103] God heard Leah's prayers and orchestrated that she should become Jacob's wife.[104]

NOTES

97. *Inner Space*, 54. The *Sefirah Keser* is an alternate manifestation of the *Sefirah Da'as*. See Chapter 18, "A Quantum State."

98. "Great is *teshuvah*, that it preceded the creation of the world" (*Midrash Tehillim* 90:12). "One must know that before anything was created, when God stood alone, there was no such reality as time. Time, on its own, cannot exist" (Rabbi Yosef Irgas, *Shomer Emunim HaKadmon*, Debate II:17).

99. See *Introduction to Chachmuni*, Rabbi Shabsai Donnolo.

100. The Sages tell us that in *Kaddish* when a person answers, *Amen Yehei Shemei Raba* ("Amen, may His great Name be blessed") with full concentration, even a decree of seventy years is torn up (*Shabbos* 119b). Similarly, it is written in the *Zohar* (*Parshas Noach*) that whoever answers to *Kaddish* in a loud voice, "the Holy One, Blessed is He, becomes filled with compassion, and He has mercy upon all."

101. Genesis 29:17.

102. Rashi ad loc., *Bava Basra* 123a.

103. *Midrash, Bereishis Rabbah* 70:16.

104. The *Midrash* ends that God responded, "She davened so much, it is only fitting that she not fall to Esau, but rather to the *tzaddik*, Jacob" (*Rosh Hashanah* 16a).

The Gates of Tears are never closed to prayer.[105] The Gemara in *Rosh Hashanah* concludes: "Crying out is effective, whether before the decree or after it;"[106] and "If a person sees that his prayers go unanswered, he should pray again."[107]

However, if an experience is absolutely necessary for our growth, it would be destructive to override the decree.[108] Indeed, the Steipler Gaon teaches us that if God desires that a certain event (or sequence of events) take place, then it is essentially impossible for us to change that reality, despite sincere and great efforts.[109] Should we find ourselves unable to effect change, this does not mean that our efforts or prayers are ever wasted.[110] Rabbi Dessler writes,

> Not on bread alone does man live, but on all utterances of God, meaning that not on the utterance to create bread alone, but on all other seemingly unrelated utterances, do we get our bread. Even if there is no correlation in our minds between our *avodah* in, for instance, the area of *shmiras halashon* [proper speech] and the area of *parnasah* [livelihood], God may "use" it for *parnasah*.[111]

Furthermore, even if the decree cannot be annulled entirely, the consequences may be meted out in a more desirable way. Rashi writes, "If God decreed terrible torrential rains, they may come down hard as a staff and give powerful blows, but if they repent, God will bring these [torrential rains] on the mountains and hills, where no one lives."[112]

TZEDAKAH (AND TORAH LEARNING)

The Talmud relates that astrologers told the great Rabbi Akiva that his daughter would die on her wedding day. The cause: a bite from a poisonous snake. But on the

---

NOTES

105. *Bava Metzia* 59a.

106. *Chazal* tell us that everything is decided on Rosh Hashanah (*Beitza* 16a).

107. *Berachos* 32b.

108. For this reason, *Chazal* advise that if, after five years, we are not effective in making some headway, despite our best efforts, it is best to reevaluate our plans and consider a change in course (*Chullin* 24a).

109. *Birchas Peretz, Parshas Shemos*, 24.

110. On occasion, what we think is good turns out to be disastrous. Conversely, sometimes things happen that are difficult, but in hindsight we realize that it was all for the best. Life experience proves that we often don't know what is good for us. In addition to praying for a specific thing or circumstance, it is prudent to ask God that whatever happens, let it be a good that we can readily see—to pray for clarity as King Solomon did when he asked God to "Grant Your servant a listening heart to govern Your people and to distinguish between right and wrong" (II Kings 3:9).

111. Rabbi Eliyahu Dessler, *Strive for Truth,* Vol. 1, 277.

112. Rashi on *Ta'anis* (8b).

evening of this auspicious day, her bitter fate was thwarted. She removed a brooch from her hair and stuck it into the wall and unknowingly penetrated the eye of a serpent that was poised to strike.

Rabbi Akiva asked his daughter if she had performed any particular act of kindness that warranted such a miracle. His daughter explained that at the wedding, when all of the guests were busily celebrating, a poor man appeared in search of food. She took her own portion and gave it to him. On hearing this, Rabbi Akiva told her that in the merit of her charitable act, her own life had been saved. Thereupon he went out and lectured, "Charity delivers one from death, and not [only] from an unnatural death, but from death itself."[113]

In parallel, the *Zohar* states that the Torah is the remedy for all transgressions. Anyone who studies Torah, even if retribution was already decided for him in Heaven because of his transgressions, the punishment that was decreed is torn up, provided he studies Torah *lishma* ("for the sake of Heaven").[114]

The Gemara explains that the power of Torah learning in combination with *chesed* is the most effective way to alter an unpleasant destiny or to avoid suffering from any sin.[115] The reason is as follows: The Rambam observes that the nature of God and His knowledge are not two separate things. God's knowledge *is* Who He is, unlike human beings whose knowledge is separate from us. Therefore: (1) the more Torah we know, the more we come to know God and the closer we are to Him; and (2) all of the *mitzvos* relate to God's essence, so the more we learn, the more we can apply in our lives and integrate into our actions—particularly acts of kindness.[116] Both learning about God and emulating His ways move us closer to Him and further away from a harsh decree.

The logic is clear. Self-control allows us to rise above our nature and gain self-esteem; self-esteem automatically shrinks the ego (or "false self") and allows for humility to blossom; and humility is the portal to a reconfigured *mazal* and an altered decree. Hence, the apex of self-control—being Godlike—translates into a revised destiny.

NOTES

113. *Shabbos* 156b. The Talmud (*Bava Basra 9b*) teaches that when a person offers kind words, even without any financial aid, Heaven bestows eleven blessings upon him.

114. See *Shevet Mussar* 21:19.

115. Due to a decree, there was once a family in Yerushalayim whose sons all died at age eighteen, with the exception of those involved in Torah and good deeds. See *Rosh Hashanah* 18a. See also Vilna Gaon on Proverbs 16:6.

116. See *Toras Shalom*, 190. In a frequently-cited Talmudic discussion, the Rabbis conclude that "learning is great, for it leads to action" (Kiddushin 40b). See also *Megillah* 27a and *Bava Kama* 17a.

DIVINE INTERVENTION IN A FINITE WORLD

In loose language, God established three channels that run through the *Sefiros* and connect the physical and spiritual planes. *Chazal* explain that nothing in the physical universe exists that does not have a spiritual root above.[117] All of our thoughts, words, and deeds activate mechanisms in the nonphysical world, based on the power and parameters assigned to each. This is the first channel, which is inferior to the second channel that follows.

The Maharal explains that *mitzvos* are part of His Divine order and differentiate themselves from all other actions, be they good or bad.[118] With respect to this domain, there is a causal relationship—spiritual veins, so to speak, that interact directly with corresponding forces that are aligned with our *tikkun* and *tikkun olam*.

The third channel is the above-mentioned trio of *teshuvah*, *tefillah*, and *tzedakah*. Through this system, we effect change on a wholesale level—an override key, of sorts, that has the power to activate the frequency of *hanhagas hamazal* (also called *hanhagas hayichud*) to alter a decree. In such instances, it is not the behavior itself that produces a correlating effect in the nonphysical realm, but rather, as a result of our efforts, it is we who have changed, and it is this transformation within ourselves that initiates a change in the heavens and in our fate.

Here, God governs on the super-logical plane of *Keser*, and, as we noted earlier, He is not bound by the lower logic of creation.[119] *Keser*, Rabbi Kaplan explains, is referred to as "the world of mercy" and when God chooses to, "He overlooks any sin that might otherwise prevent Him from guiding the world toward its destined perfection."[120] The notion of super-logic is impossible for us to understand, so we will use a metaphor to give us a taste of the paradoxical method in which God intercedes in the finite world, without violating the very rules of justice that He set into motion.

Imagine a person's entire existence as a single dot. Without "touching" the dot, we can change it into something else. If we add a series of dots above it or below it, it becomes part of a line; should we extend the line at an angle, it becomes part

NOTES

117. See *Teferet HaChinukhi, Parshas Vayeira*.
118. Maharal, *Chiddushei Aggados, Kiddushin* 31a.
119. See *Inner Space*, 55.
120. Ibid.

of another shape; we can also reorient the dot to the top or to the bottom and make it a part, any part, of any shape. Put another way, the shape changes the context of the dot, and, as we explained elsewhere, it is context that gives meaning. With a new position or role, the rest of creation interacts with the dot, "us," differently. In the larger scheme—in absolute reality—the dot's entire world shifts, even as the preset rules of the "finite dot world" remain perfectly intact; and since creation is in a constant state of renewal and Infinity knows no bounds, this picture—"our lives"—can take on a new form, at any time God chooses.

As we observed, *teshuvah* comes from the level of *Keser* and is bequeathed with the power to change the larger picture because *teshuvah* operates outside of time and space.[121] *Tefillah* and *chesed* also tap into this realm.[122] We are reminded that prayer that originates from deepest recesses of *ratzon* can change a soul's essence, reformulating its *mazal* and its place in creation. Regarding *chesed*, we recall a passage in the Zohar that states that acts of righteousness and lovingkindness are done "above the sun," outside of time and space.[123]

RESHUFFLING THE DECK

Imagine a rocket ship heading to the moon. At takeoff, a minor course correction—a fraction of a degree—in the coordinates can save the craft from going hundreds of miles off course. At the beginning of its flight, minor adjustments affect significant changes. However, once the craft approaches its destination, even larger deviations—that is, efforts—prove less meaningful.

The longer an unpleasant situation is allowed to fester, the more effort it will take to repair the damage. Consider a person with an infection. He may eat better, get more rest, and quickly recover. But if he doesn't take care of himself, he might have to take medication. If he goes untreated, then the infection might damage his organs and he may need surgery. The earlier he takes action to stop the progression of the affliction, the easier it is to cure and the better chances he has of a complete recovery.

God works through nature; the more visible the reality, the greater the merit

---

NOTES

121. "He who covers up his sins shall not prosper, but he who confesses and forsakes them will experience the mercy of God" (Proverbs 28:13).

122. *Teshuvah* that is borne out of our love for God (rather than out of fear—to avoid punishment) is the tide that lifts the boats of *tefillah* and *chesed*. Proper *teshuvah* is the single most transformational act of free will and, as such, elevates all *mitzvos*, including our *tefillos* and acts of *chesed*.

123. See *Zohar* II:59a.

one needs for God to grant him a miracle that alters the natural unfolding of events. (See the following chapter where *Chazal* discuss that one who enters his granary to assess what he has accumulated should pray that his work receives blessing, but only before he starts to measure the grain.) When we rise above our nature, God supersedes nature in a concealed way. For those who are on an even higher spiritual level, God will alter nature to produce a miracle, even where it is an apparent violation of the natural order.[124] As *Chazal* explain, "God decrees but a *tzaddik* can revoke the decree," for such a person has the *zechus* ("spiritual merit") to do so.[125]

When reality has yet to emerge, less merit and effort are required to influence conditions. "Had you arranged your prayer before the onset of difficulty, then all would fortify your strength."[126] On this, our Sages teach, "Always pray before tragedy strikes."[127]

In times of crisis, it is common for people to make a *kabbalah* ("accepting something positive upon oneself"). We pray to God and perhaps we promise Him that we will do something specific should our prayers be answered, because intuitively we know what He wants from us and what we need to do—we just don't want to do it. The question we need to ask ourselves is, "What are we waiting for?"

God has given us an arsenal of weapons to wage war against our fate: *teshuvah*, *tefillah*, and *tzedakah*. Why wait until a painful reality has already begun to materialize before we are provoked into action? In the words of the familiar English axiom: "An ounce of prevention is worth a pound of cure."[128]

It is once again crucial to remind ourselves that even when we cannot annul a decree, we can make the bitter pill more palatable and perhaps, for the person

124. Some commentators maintain that for the truly righteous, God may shroud a miracle in nature to avoid any disruption to the *tzaddik*. See Shabbos 53b, which discusses the case of a newly widowed father and the miracle produced for his nursing infant.

125. *Moed Katan* 16b.

126. Job 36:19.

127. See *Sanhedrin* 44b.

128. Rashi quotes a parable from the *Midrash* (*Sifra*) to explain: "You shall strengthen him" (referring to a person who is in need). He writes, "Do not leave him alone so that he descend and fall, for it will be hard to raise him up. Rather, support him from the time his hand slips. To what might this be compared? To a burden on a donkey: While it is still on the donkey, one person can grab it and set it straight. But if it falls to the ground, even five people cannot put it back on."

who chooses to be extraordinary, turn it into a lavish feast. *Mazal* affects happenstance, but as we learned in Chapter 8, "Life in Context," we have the final say on our happiness. The emotional laws of free will—including, most important, life satisfaction—run on the track of reward and punishment (*hanhagas hamishpat*), which is always a function of choice. Life's challenges are not equally distributed, but the power of choice is the great equalizer.

PART 6

BEHIND THE CURTAIN OF DIVINE PROVIDENCE

Seeing the Oneness of God, being closer to Him, confers a host of benefits that have been explained. In the following chapters, we delve more deeply into how it affords us Divine protection, changing God's actual supervision of us. To best understand this, we explore how contrasting realities coexist without contradiction in a single framework and how our perspective influences our *objective* reality.

18 | A
QUANTUM
STATE

The Sages write, "All is foreseen, yet freedom of choice is granted."[1] From here, the classic question emerges: If God is Omniscient and knows what we're going to do, can it really be said that we have free will?" We cannot, of course, surprise God, Who is Infinite and All-Knowing.

Because we are locked into time and space, it is problematic for us to see how Divine knowledge does not preclude human free will, but let us consider an analogy. If we place a lollipop and a piece of baked tofu before a small child, we could easily predict which he will choose. Can we say that we denied him his free will? He is free to choose, and we reasonably assume what his choice will be.

Now, what happens if we put before this same small child a green lollipop and an orange one? Can we still guess which he will reach for? It would be harder to know, unless we happen to be aware that orange is his favorite flavor. Our ability to know what he will do is dependent on our knowledge of the child. Since God's knowledge of us is absolute and complete, the number of variables becomes irrelevant. Because He knows us, He knows what we will do. From our vantage, we face a decision; from His, the outcome is known.

While nothing is hidden from God, we should emphasize that it is not His knowledge of us that reveals our choice, but His knowledge, period. As we observed earlier, the Rambam explains that the nature of God and His knowledge are not two separate things. God's knowledge *is* Who He is, unlike human beings whose knowledge is separate from us.[2] God Himself proclaims, "The nature of My thoughts are not your thoughts."[3]

The Rambam explains five ways that God's knowledge is different from our own: (1) One idea encompasses all of the different ideas. (2) He can understand that which doesn't exist yet. (3) His knowledge encompasses the infinite. (4) God's knowledge of future events does not mean that He will make them happen. (5) God's knowledge does not change as new events develop, since He knew about them before they happened.[4] Elsewhere, he writes,

> The Holy One, Blessed Be He, knows everything that will happen before it has happened... . [T]he Holy One, Blessed Be He, does not have any temperaments and is outside such realms, unlike people, whose selves and temperaments are two separate things. God and His temperaments are one, and God's existence is beyond the comprehension of Man... . [Thus,] we do not have the capabilities to comprehend how the Holy One, Blessed Be He, knows all creations and events. [Nevertheless] know without doubt that people do what they want without the Holy One, Blessed Be He, forcing or decreeing upon them to do so... . It has been said because of this that a man is judged according to all his actions.[5]

A SPACE IN TIME FOR FREE WILL

Free will does not cease to exist because God has knowledge of what will happen. His foreknowledge of an event does not in any way impinge upon our freedom of choice. The paradox of God's knowledge and our free will exists only from a perspective inside time, while in true reality, God is outside of time. Past, present, and future are part of our reality, not His. Therefore a slightly modified position posits that free will events are actually unpredictable to God, but that His knowledge remains absolute for the same reason: Whatever occurs at any time

---

2. See Rambam, *Hilchos Yesodei HaTorah* 2:10.

3. Isaiah 55:8.

4. Rambam, *Guide for the Perplexed* (3:20).

5. Rambam, *Mishneh Torah, Teshuvah* 5:5 [32]. This approach is favored by the majority of early commentators, such as: (1) Rabbi Saadia Gaon who writes, "God knows in advance what human choices will be, but his knowledge is not the cause of those choices" (*Emunot v'Deot* 4:2); and (2) the Rivash (*Responsa* 118) who similarly writes the God's foreknowledge is not causative. Indeed, the following chapter introduces a compelling insight into the nature of time and causation.

during the existence of the universe is known to God at any other time, including a prior time.[6]

The distinction between these two positions is subtle but significant. The former opinion asserts that everything that will ever transpire is known to God, even before creation—because God, Who is Infinite, is not separate from His knowledge. Thus, His knowledge must be infinite—complete and absolute, and nothing can ever be unknown to Him. The latter opinion is slightly restrictive and maintains that God has knowledge of events because He is beyond time, and anything that happens inside of time becomes known to Him at any point in time. Accordingly, before creation or more precisely, before the creation of time, a free will event may actually have been unpredictable to Him, but the instant He created time, His knowledge of all future events—free will and otherwise—became known.

The unrestricted view represents the mainstream position, with a small branch adopting the time-sensitive model. An alternate approach to the paradox acknowledges God's omnipotence, but suggests that He chooses to withdraw from pockets of creation in order to allow free choice to emerge.[7] A dizzying array of nuanced opinions, disputes, and contradictions abound, none of which moves us closer to a consensus. Rather than parse each argument and counter-argument, we will highlight two of the early commentators (*Rishonim*) who favor this minority view.

The Ralbag adopts a radical solution by suggesting that free will can exist only if God holds back, as it were. He asserts that Divine foreknowledge precludes free will and thus God knows that certain states of affairs may or may not be actualized but He chooses to "not know" which of the alternatives will happen.[8] (This should not be confused with the above-stated view which holds that even though a particular choice may be unknown to God—before the creation of time—at no point *in time*, does He ever lack knowledge of what that choice is, or will be.)

The Raavad states that God does know the particular choices of man but that His foreknowledge is acquired through less-than-Divine means. He writes, "God has limited this power from His hand and given the power [of free will] to man, His knowledge is not a decree but rather like the knowledge of the astrologers who

---

6. See Avi Rabinowitz, "The Retroactive Universe," referencing a *Responsa* of Rabbi Hai Gaon, a medieval commentator. God's sacred name, the Tetragrammaton, YKVK, includes the past, present, and future tense of the Hebrew word "to be."

7. This position invokes a phenomenon referred to by the Kabbalists as *tzimtzum* ("contraction"), which is discussed in Chapter 36, "The Ladder of Harmony."

8. *Milchemes HaShem* (The Wars of the Lord) Book 3: Divine Knowledge.

know [from the constellations] what shall be the way of this person."[9] He then adds a Divine component to God's supervision. "God also gave man the power of reason to enable him to release himself from the power of the stars to be either good or bad. God knows the power of the stars and if the person has the will to extricate himself from its power or not, and this knowledge is not a decree." After he offers what he calls his "partial solution" to the question, he writes that even his own answer, "is hardly satisfactory to me."[10]

Naturally, any attempt to reconcile the paradox by limiting God's knowledge, in any way, has been met with fierce and vehement objection by other *Rishonim*. We must stress however, that there is complete agreement in both God's omnipotence and in human free will. The point of contention lays here: The majority hold that outside of time and space, foreknowledge does not interfere with free will, while the minority maintain that God voluntarily withdraws or constricts His "higher-knowledge"—which is synonymous with an irreversible decree—so that free will can exist. How much "lower-knowledge" God has of future events is a source of further dispute amongst those in the latter camp, while no such issue exists for those in the majority.

Following the mainstream view, we will now investigate how freedom of choice can exist within a known reality, and why this is so; not *in spite* of God being outside of time, but *because* He is.

DUELING REALITIES

Let us refine our inquiry. We need not address God's knowledge of our actions that lie above or below the point of *bechirah*, because these areas are not under the domain of free will. Free will emerges only where a person's awareness of the truth, that is, what is right, is not overwhelmed by a competing desire. Along the battlefront where free will exists, hovering in between truth and falsehood, the two outcomes are equally viable—with only our free will tipping the balance.[11]

In the physical universe, this very phenomenon occurs where two possible outcomes coexist. The overarching theme of wave-particle duality is that all subatomic

---

NOTES

9. *Hilchos Teshuvah*, 5:5.

10. Ibid.

11. See Dessler, *Strive for Truth*, Vol. 1, 111–120. To say that two choices are equally viable does not mean that they are equally balanced. See Chapter 24, "The Battlefield" for a more complete understanding of the free will battlefront.

matter appears as opposites—as both a particle and a wave.[12] (It is interesting to note that each of the *Sefiros*—the ten emanations through which God interacts with creation—can appear in both circular *iggulim,* and *yosher*, straight or upright, form.)[13] Research in quantum mechanics explains:

> The universe, or any subsystem of it, is capable of being in two (or more) mutually contradictory states simultaneously. Saying that the universe is uniquely in one state is just as invalid as saying that it is in the other state. Until the measurement [defined as observation by human consciousness] is made both views are only partially correct since the state is actually a combination. After the measurement only one becomes correct. However, this does not imply that it was always the correct one; there was no "correct" state until the measurement was made.[14]

At the quantum level, reality itself exists in a state of flux and materializes into one or the other form only *after* it is observed—and based on the perspective of the observer (this is called wave function collapse because it "collapses" potential realities into a single, unique reality). For this reason, the observer cannot observe anything without changing what he sees.

Chazal discuss that one who enters his granary to assess what he has accumulated should pray that his work receives blessing. "May it be Your will, O Lord our God, to send a blessing upon the work of our hands." Once the grain is visible and no longer hidden he should say, "Blessed is God Who sends blessing upon this store." Otherwise the blessing is in vain because our Sages explain that blessing rests only on that which is concealed from the eye.[15]

Measurement—by means of the subjective perception of a human observer—causes a collapse of the probability and effectively brings the object into a specific, quantifiable existence. Before that happens, reality is a supposition of possible outcomes (and, as noted, where prayer is most potent).

Yes, God has knowledge of all events–past, present, and future—so what does

---

NOTES

12. Light, too, can behave like a wave and be labeled with a wavelength, a frequency, and a velocity, but it also has a certain amount of energy and momentum. In those respects, it resembles a particle.

13. See Chapter 36, "The Ladder of Harmony" for further discussion of the *Sefiros*.

14. Avi Rabinowitz, "The Retroactive Universe: Quantum Kabbalistic Cosmology & the Meaning and Purpose of Life, Mind, Free Will & the Garden of Eden" (1993). Retrieved: https://files.nyu.edu/air1/public/RetroactiveUniverse.htm#_ftn294.

15. *Ta'anis* 8b. "God shall command the blessing upon you in your hidden things" (Deuteronomy 28:8).

it matter that physical reality is defined through human perspective? The answer is that perspective is a function of time and space, which God is beyond. Hence, His knowledge cannot be causative because perspective is the causative agent. God does not "interfere" through His observation. Perspective requires an observer and the observed. When they are One-and-the-Same, we shift beyond the definition of perspective to an all-encompassing reality. This is why He sees and knows all but does not hinder free choice. With man, it is different. Perspective does not make us see reality differently. On a quantum level, in a completely tangible way, it determines our reality.

Accordingly, our Sages explain that creation was not a "one-time event" but that God brings all of reality into existence each and every moment.[16] We therefore do not "undo" anything in creation, but rather facilitate its actual formation and revelation.

SLICES OF TRUTH

The basis of concurrent, even incompatible, realities existing within one reality is embedded into the building blocks of creation. Regarding the *Sefiros* the oldest and most influential Kabbalistic work reads, "Ten *Sefiros* of Nothingness; ten and not nine; ten and not eleven."[17] The *Sefirah* of *Keser* ("Crown") is not always counted, and when we include it, we omit the *Sefirah* of *Da'as* ("Knowledge"). If we were to preclude or include both simultaneously, we arrive at the erroneous conclusion of nine or eleven. The Sages emphasize that exactly ten *Sefiros* exist because in reality there are only ten—our perspective however, changes which ten come into existence at any one time.

Coexisting truths are also rooted in the Torah, which itself heralds multiple interpretations.[18] This teaches that valid observations and explanations of Torah can be dependent on the outlook of the scholar. For three years, there was a dispute between *Beis* Hillel ("the House of Hillel") and *Beis* Shammai ("the House of

NOTES

16. *Kedushat Levi*, Genesis. "The creative process did not cease at the end of the Six Days of Creation but continues at every moment, constantly renewing all existence." Rabbi Nissan Mangel, *Tanya*, Bi-Lingual Edition, (New York: Kehot Publication Society), 855.

17. *Sefer Yetzirah* 1:2.

18. The *Midrash* states that there are seventy "faces" or "facets" to the Torah (*Bamidbar Rabbah* 13:15). One verse may have several meanings (*te'amim*) (Sanhedrin 34a; cf. Shabbos 88b). Torah concepts themselves are revealed on four distinct levels: *Pshat, Remez, Drush*, and *Sod* (loosely translated: Simple, Hint, Exegetical, and Secret). Each interpretation is true, even though they may appear to contradict one another.

Shammai"), each asserting, "The law is in agreement with our views." Then a voice from heaven called out: *"Eilu v'eilu divrei Elokim Chayim,"* "These and those are the words of the Living God."[19] They are both right.[20]

The Talmud relates a famous debate regarding the *halachic* status of an oven that is cut into pieces.[21] All of the scholars agreed that it is susceptible to ritual impurity, except for the greatest amongst them: Rabbi Eliezer. He thus offered a succession of proofs to support his reasoning, but they were all refuted. Then things turned miraculous.

Rabbi Eliezer said to them, "If the law is as I say, may the carob tree prove it." The carob tree was uprooted from its place a distance of 100 cubits. Others say, 400 cubits. They said to him, "There is no proof from a carob tree." Rabbi Eliezer then said, "If the law is as I say, may the aqueduct prove it." The water in the aqueduct began to flow backwards. Once again, they were not swayed. "One cannot prove anything from an aqueduct." Finally, he said, "If the law is as I say, may the walls of the house of study prove it." The walls of the house of study began to fall in. Rabbi Yehoshua shouted at the walls, "If Torah scholars are debating a point of Jewish law, what are your qualifications to intervene?" The walls did not fall, in deference to Rabbi Yehoshua, nor did they straighten up, in deference to Rabbi Eliezer... . Rabbi Eliezer said, "If the law is as I say, may it be proven from heaven!" A heavenly then voice proclaimed: "What do you want of Rabbi Eliezer, the law is as he says..."

The passage concludes with Rabbi Yehoshua's bold response to the heavenly voice. He stood and proclaimed, "The Torah is not in the Heavens." He was referencing the verse, "For this commandment which I command you today is not hidden from you nor is it distant. It is not in heaven, for you to say, 'Who among us can go up to heaven and bring it to us so that we can listen to it and observe it? ... but it is very near to you, in your mouth and in your heart, to observe it.'"[22]

NOTES

19. *Eruvin* 13b, *Gittin* 6b.

20. At the quantum level, we can only calculate probabilities. The means to bring into existence a single, measurable outcome from the field of probabilities—or possibilities, for those on a higher plane of consciousness—is through human observation. The greater our consciousness (and thus the smaller the ego), the greater is our ability to affect an outcome outside of probability, beyond our natural efforts, and independent of cause and effect. See Chapter 37, "A World of Contrasts" for further elaboration and an explanation as to why we follow the reasoning of *Beis* Hillel.

21. *Bava Metzia* 59a-b.

22. Deuteronomy 30:11-14.

The Talmud explains that the very Torah that was given to man at *Har Sinai* instructs us to follow the majority opinion.[23] Therefore, Heaven has no "right" to intervene. It is we who define reality.[24] Elijah the Prophet said at that moment, God smiled and said: 'My children have triumphed over Me, My children have triumphed over Me.'"[25]

Our finite grasp is insufficient to gain more than a fleeting glimmer of how free will shapes our reality and intersects with an outcome that is already known to God. While many commentators speak of these two seemingly contradictory principles—the free will of man and the Omniscience of God—perhaps the Rambam offers the most candid assessment: "Know that the answer to this question is longer than the earth and wider than the seas… . A human being is not able to understand this issue completely, just as he is unable to perceive the true nature of God."[26]

23. While many stipulations exist, there is a general edict that "a case must be decided on the basis of the majority" (Exodus 23:2).

24. "God looked into the Torah and created the universe" (*Bereishis Rabbah* 1:1). The Torah not only is the blueprint *for* all of creation but the very instrument *of* creation.

25. *Bava Metzia* 59b.

26. Rambam, *Hilchos Teshuvah* 5:5. He adds, "[T]here are things of which the mind understands one part, but remains ignorant of the other; and when man is able to comprehend certain things, it does not follow that he must be able to comprehend everything" (ibid.). The Raavad is quite blunt, and admonishes the Rambam for bringing up the question itself. He writes, "He did not act wisely, for a person should not start something if he is unable to conclude" (ibid.).

19 | UNTYING
A
PARADOX

The Hebrew word for "providence" or "supervision" is *hashgachah*. God supervises all of creation in one or a combination of two ways:[27]

❑ **Hashgachah klalis** is general providence, also called *hashgachah minus* or group providence. This means that God has set into motion predetermined rules that facilitate the continued existence of every species—the laws of nature; the determination is based on the needs of the group so that it should fulfill its purpose to help man serve God (to bring forth the Final Redemption).[28]

❑ **Hashgachah pratis** refers to specific or individual providence, where God supervises an individual and either punishes or rewards him *middah k'neged middah* ("measure for measure") in accord with his deeds. It is further divided into two categories: (a) Divine providence over man to know

NOTES

27. Definitions are based on *Faith and Divine Providence*, which references the Ramchal (*Ma'amar Halkarin, On Providence*).

28. Rabbi Chaim Friedlander reminds us that these rules do not operate on their own, for it is God Who does everything; and this type of providence does not mean that any details are hidden to God or that His supervision is superficial. He writes, "It certainly makes no difference in His knowledge of events—either way He knows every single detail" (ibid., 195.) Rather, he explains, "general" means that, "the determination is based on the needs of the group so that it should fulfill its purpose—which is to help man serve God and to reveal God's glory... [However] when a particular animal or item belongs to a human, the deliberation over its existence is also influenced by the specific governance of its owner" (ibid., 43).

in full detail all of one's actions and innermost thoughts; and (b) Divine providence over man to save him from the influence of chance.[29]

The Ramchal explains that the human race was singled out to receive reward and punishment for its deeds, so its supervision is different from other species. *Hashgachah pratis* is reserved for human beings, while *hashgachah klalis* governs animals, plants, inanimate objects, and the like—although, it also extends to people. Even someone who is supervised mainly through specific providence is also partially supervised by general providence, because, as we explained, every person has a role in creating an environment that is conducive to the service of God.[30]

The percentage of supervision: *hashgachah pratis* versus *hashgachah klalis* is not the same for each person. The Rambam explains that "the amount of Divine providence that governs an individual is proportionate to the share of influence that he achieves through his inborn abilities and [spiritual efforts and] accomplishments."[31] Simply, the closer the distance between our behavior and our potential (with respect to our unique mission in life as well as our obligation to carry out the required *mitzvos*) the closer we are to God and to specific providence.[32]

The emotional and spiritual advantages of this relationship have been discussed, but now we see the inner workings of an incalculable benefit: special providence, Divine protection. Recall from Chapter 16, "Spiritual Immune System," that nothing can harm the person who devotes his entire being to the reality that God is the One and only Power that exists.[33] Such an individual moves with near impunity.

❑ "A man of honesty and integrity needs no atonement. Moreover, should a faithless man seek to kill him, he himself will fall victim in his stead, and the upright man will emerge safe."[34]

❑ "[T]he Divine providence to save one from the influence of chance is not with all individuals... . God does not forsake His righteous ones, and He does not remove His sight from them; rather His Divine providence governs the pious constantly."[35]

NOTES

29. See Rabbi Bachya, Genesis 18:19.

30. See Rabbi Chaim Friedlander, *Faith and Divine Providence*, 55.

31. Rambam, *Moreh Nevuchim* 3:18.

32. See ibid., Ch. 18. See also Rabbi Chaim Friedlander, *Faith and Divine Providence*, 48.

33. See *Nefesh HaChaim* 3:12.

34. Malbim, on Proverbs 21:19.

35. Rabbeinu Bachya, on Genesis 18:19.

❏ "To the point that the completely righteous person, who constantly clings to God, and never lets his thoughts be severed from Him by any worldly concern, will always be protected from all incidents—even those that occur naturally… . However, he who is distant from God in thought and deed, even if he isn't deserving of death due to his sins, is left to chance."[36]

The progression of the Ramban's position leads to a startling finale: To the extent that we fall short of our potential, we are left to the capricious winds of circumstance. While he is joined by a number of leading commentators, most compelling is that in the Torah, God Himself states, "I will conceal My face and they will become prey."[37] A representation of leading positions:

❏ If a person does not put his trust in [God] he places his trust in something other than [God]; and whoever trusts in something other than [God, He] removes His providence from him and leaves him in the hands of whatever he trusted in.[38]

❏ A lesser category of providence is the concealment of the face of [God], and, because of his sins, he is left to nature and chance … the person is supposed to protect himself from circumstances by using natural protective measures, and he cannot rely on trust.[39]

❏ As to fools who rebel [against Him] … their interests will be loathed and will be controlled by the [natural] order as are those of animals.[40]

Yet an enigmatic contradiction exists because contrasting sources assert: "No one strikes his finger down below unless it is decreed upon him above."[41] The Chassidic view further advances this position with the Baal Shem Tov, who contends that not only does Divine providence involve every particular occurrence that affects man, but that it continually governs inanimate matter, plants, and animals.[42] The

NOTES

36. Ramban, on "He will not remove His eyes from a righteous man" (Job 36:7).

37. Deuteronomy 31:17.

38. *Chovos HaLevavos (Duties of the Heart), Shaar HaBitachon*, Introduction.

39. Ramak (*Shiur Koma*).

40. *Moreh Nevuchim*, loc. cit., Ch. 18.

41. *Chullin* 7b.

42. *Igros Kodesh* 1:94.

Kabbalistic stance can best be synopsized with "No person who believes should entertain the concept that any action, large or small, takes place by coincidence. Instead, everything is determined by Divine providence."[43]

To add to the confusion, some authorities seem to present self-contradictory viewpoints. The Ramban speaks of "naturally occurring incidents" (noted above), while simultaneously preserving the notion that there is no such thing as a chance occurrence, and that everything is Divinely ordained.[44]

REVEALING REALITY

The hidden form of God's providence is often referred to as nature (*teva*) because, to the individual, it appears to lack meaning and design.[45] The Mitteler Rebbe, Rabbi Dovber of Lubavitch, explains that while God supervises and controls every aspect of every element of existence, the perceived manner in which His interaction unfolds is clothed within the workings of nature.[46] A meaningful pattern permeates the entirety of our experiences and circumstances, but the design is lost on those whose eyes are aimed at their own reflection.[47]

We discussed earlier that nature is devised to reveal God's Presence to those who have the ability to see it (leading to *he'aras panim*—"illumination of countenance"), and, at the same time, nature is designed to mask God's Presence from those who cannot see beyond themselves (triggering *hester panim*—"the concealing of God's ways").

The following passages are traditionally interpreted in this way. In the Torah, God states, "[If] you behave casually with Me, then I, too, will behave toward you with casualness."[48] And in the *Midrash* we read, "When you are My witnesses—declares the Lord—then I am God. But when you are not My witnesses, then I am, as it were, not God."[49]

NOTES

43. Rabbi Moshe Cordovoro (*Ein Kol Tamar 5*, Ch. 1).

44. See Ramban's commentary on Exodus (13:16).

45. Commentators observe that the word for "nature," *hateva*, has the same *gematria* ("numerical value") as *Elokim*—86—God the All-Powerful, which is the name that means "Master of all forces."

46. See *Derech Chayim, Shaar HaTeshuvah*, Ch. 9, pp. 13a-b.

47. "Men committed to evil do not understand the justice of providence, but they who seek God understand all things" (Proverbs 28:5).

48. Leviticus 26:23–24.

49. Isaiah 43:10.

SHIFTING REALITIES

Other authorities push past this view and explain that the inability to see the hand of God does more than obscure the meaning—it changes the meaning. Recall from the previous chapter that perspective endows reality. A deeper look at the phenomenon reveals a related principle called *retroactive causality*, where there is not only a blurring between cause and effect, but rather the effect can be—and thus can predate—the cause. This is nothing new. More than two thousand years earlier, the Gemara first taught us that God creates the cure before the disease.[50]

Returning to the field of quantum physics, Dr. John Wheeler, one of the world's leading theoretical physicists demonstrated that, an observation *now* can cause *retroactively* the emergence into reality of an event which occurred *in the past*—regardless of whether the outcome should logically have been determined long ago.[51] Another prominent researcher explains: "The precise nature of reality has to await the participation of a conscious observer. In this way, mind can be made responsible for the retroactive creation of reality."[52] The famous Nobel Laureate Dr. Richard Feynman writes that, "all the fundamental laws of physics are reversible."[53] This is because on the atomic and subatomic scales, cause and effect are interchangeable and time is completely mutable.[54]

Due to this phenomenon, the future can influence the past as the present influences the future. It may be correct to say, then, that events which do not appear unnecessary can become so. While in the desert, God fed the Jewish people "*manna* from heaven." But they decried it saying: "Who will feed us meat? We remember the fish that we ate in Egypt ... but now ... we have nothing ... but the *manna*."[55] Commentators note that the Jewish people could have survived without food or

---

50. *Megillah* 13b.

51. These findings were established using the delayed choice experiment, a variation on the standard "double-slit" experiment. See Avi Rabinowitz, "The Retroactive Universe: Quantum Kabbalistic Cosmology: the Meaning and Purpose of Life, Mind, Free Will & the Garden of Eden."

52. See P. C. Davies, *God and the New Physics* (New York: Simon and Schuster, 1983), 111. Cited in ibid.

53. Volume I: Lecture 46, "Ratchet and pawl"; section 46-1, "Order and entropy"; section 46-5.

54. This principle is significant to our discussion in the previous chapter. If a free will act in the present can redefine the past, then the paradox of man affecting change to a known future becomes slightly more digestible.

55. Numbers 11:4–6, 10. The *manna* itself is described differently in various places in the Talmud. Variances in description are due to the fact that it tasted different depending on who ate it, tasting like honey for small children, like bread for youths, and like oil for the elderly (*Yoma* 75b).

drink. They complained about the food and *then* they were hungry. If they hadn't voiced their objection, God would have suspended these physical needs (just as He did for Moses on *Har Sinai*). Their complaint was the cause of their affliction, not the other way around.[56]

Everything God does is for a purpose. If we cannot perceive the message, then there is no reason for it. The Artist does not make use of colors for the color blind. Therefore, if one's ego so distorts reality that, regardless of the circumstance, he will not discern the meaning, then the necessity for a clearly defined message becomes irrelevant. At the same time, though, we can never claim that anything in creation is arbitrary or haphazard. In the upcoming chapters, we will explore the intricate workings of providence within the context of randomness and negligence.

Suffice it to say, whether perspective determines our reality or our experience of reality, it is nonetheless our reality. When we fail to discern meaning within a situation, aspects of, or the entirety of, the occurrence may appear (or become) unnecessary. But if at any point we awaken from our spiritual slumber and accept responsibility—via proper *teshuvah*: (a) our ego shrinks and our perspective widens, and reality is revealed; or (b) due to *retroactive causality* the shift in our perspective gives rise to a new reality.

Albert Einstein famously said, "The distinction between the past, present and future is only a stubbornly persistent illusion." Both positions and realities—unceasing Divine providence and our being subject to circumstances—are simultaneous truths. Indeed, there is no word in *Lashon HaKodesh* for "history." The idea of a fixed, unchanging reality does not exist. The present gives shape to the past as the future gives meaning to the present. *Chazal* state that if the end is good, then all is good—spawning the common aphorism "All's well that ends well."

56. Rabbi Moshe Feinstein, ad loc.

20 | THE NATURE OF CHANCE

Even when a situation loses its rich surface design, the underlying purpose of life's travails is always and forever geared toward our greatest good, as will now be explained as we shift from the realm of nature to man versus man. In the Torah we find Joseph at the mercy of his brothers, who conspire to kill him, save for one brother who objects:[57]

"Let us slay him, and cast him into some pit, and we will say, 'An evil beast has devoured him'; and we shall see what will become of his dreams... ."[58] Reuben said to them, 'Shed no blood! Throw him into this pit in the wilderness, but lay no hand upon him.' [He said this] intending to rescue him from their hand and return him to his father... . Then they took him and cast him into the pit."[59]

Earlier in the *parsha* ("Torah portion"), Joseph said to his brothers, "'Listen to this dream I had: We were binding sheaves of grain out in the field when suddenly my sheaf rose and stood upright, while your sheaves gathered around mine and

57. Many commentators note that the brothers believed their actions to be *halachically* justified, in that they ate a meal, at peace with themselves and their decision. The Torah recounts (Genesis 37:25–27): "And they took him, and cast him into a pit.... And they sat down to eat bread." The Zohar (1:184a) further exonerates the brothers. It states that they would not have sold Joseph despite their feelings of animosity, if not for Divine intervention which guided their reasoning (so as to begin the fulfillment of God's covenant with Abraham).

58. Genesis 37:20.

59. Ibid., 37:22, 24.

bowed down to it.' His brothers said to him, 'Do you intend to reign over us? Will you actually rule us?'"[60]

The dreams exacerbated their animosity because they believed them to be the product of fantasy, not of prophecy. Hence: "…. and we shall see what will become of his dreams." In other words, killing Joseph would confirm that his dreams were not prophetic, because they would not be fulfilled—a dead man cannot rule over anyone. Reuben argued that this thinking was flawed because God may allow their free will to prevail—even if the dreams were prophetic and Joseph not deserving of death.[61] (The upcoming subchapter "Blood from a Stone" addresses the contrasting position: barring a Divine decree a person is unable to cause the death of another.)

Based on this exchange, the *Zohar* states, "If a man is righteous, the Holy One, blessed be He, will do a miracle for him or sometimes he is saved by the merit of his fathers; however, once a person is in the hands of his enemies there are very few who will escape."[62]

This is because every creature acts in accordance with its nature and the will of God, except for man. King David cries out, "Let us fall into God's hands for His mercies are abundant, but let me not fall into human hands."[63] Thus, there is quite a difference between an instance where we are "left to nature" and one where our own will lies in direct conflict with another person's will. Although man's free will cannot affect a completely righteous person, it does affect the rest of us—and this presents a quandary.

If we truly have free will, then we should be able to act against another person, even if it is not Divinely ordained, but in doing so, we might cause something to happen that is not "supposed to happen." Then perhaps we would say that regardless of our intent and efforts, we are not truly free to act and only believe ourselves to be. Both scenarios are troubling: either free will is an illusion or God is not in ultimate control. To understand what is really happening, let us recall the two systems with which God conducts the affairs of the world:

NOTES

60. Ibid., 37:5–8.

61. Rashi (ibid.) comments: "The pit was empty of water, but there were snakes and scorpions in it." *Chazal* draw a distinction between killing Joseph directly and causing his (seemingly inevitable) death through snakes and scorpions. See the *Mar'eh Kohen* in *Shabbos* 22a, quoting the *Zohar, Vayeishev* 185a.

62. On *Parshas Yayeishev*. Reuben reasoned that while Joseph might be killed unjustifiably at the hands of their brothers, snakes and scorpions, who are subject to God's will, would not kill Joseph if he was not deserving of death (*Igros Kodesh* 1:94., vol. 9). Alternatively, the Ramban (Genesis 37:22) writes that Reuben and his brothers thought that the pit was completely empty.

63. II Samuel 24:14.

❑ *Hanhagas hayichud*: The unfolding revelation of God's glory and total unity (primary), where we have a set role and part to play in the master plan.

❑ *Hanhagas hamishpat*: The system of reward and punishment (secondary), where our choices dictate the consequences.

The two systems operate in tandem because when we make proper use of our free will, we complete ourselves, as discussed, and help reveal God's Oneness. *Hanhagas hamishpat* is subordinate to *hanhagas hayichud*, because as a person proactively elevates and perfects himself, he fulfills his role in all of creation.

However, when we do not correctly use our free will, our role shifts to a *kli* (a "vehicle" or a "vessel"), and our lives are directed toward helping those who are fulfilling their primary and Divine purpose.[64] The foundation of creation itself utilizes the concept of primary and secondary purpose. Rabbi Kaplan explains,

> The primitive *Sefiros* represent the concept of something that God created that did not fulfill its purpose... . In a sense, however, since they were meant to shatter, they did fulfill their purpose. We can say therefore that they did not fulfill their primary purpose which was to hold light. They did fulfill their secondary purpose, however, which was to shatter.[65]

As we will discuss in Chapter 37, "A World of Contrasts," the Oneness of God will be revealed, and we will see that evil was merely an instrument used for this higher purpose. Rabbi Kaplan continues,

> Evil is like the peel of a fruit or the shell of a nut. In themselves, they are useless, but they serve the secondary purpose of preserving the fruit until it is ready to be eaten.[66] The same is true of evil. It does not serve God's primary purpose of bestowing good, but it does fulfill the secondary purpose of making it possible [by allowing for free will].[67]

NOTES

64. Rabbi Eliyahu Dessler, *Strive for Truth*, Vol. 2, 75–76. "From the perspective of *hashgachah pratis*, he has no right to exist in the world, since he has not completed his share.... [He] serves as tools for the *tzaddik* who is serving God" (*Sifsei Chayim, Pirkei Emunah Ve'hashgachah* 1:27–29).

65. Rabbi Aryeh Kaplan, *Inner Space* (New York: Moznaim, 1990), 83. Rabbi Kaplan explains that the first stage of creation is called the Universe of Chaos or *Tohu*. This is a state where the Vessels, which were the primitive Ten *Sefiros*, could not contain the "Light of God" and "shattered," giving us the concept of the "Breaking of Vessels."

66. *Sefer HaYashar* 1, ed. Rosenthal (Berlin, 1898).

67. Kaplan, *Inner Space*, 70.

One of the great paradoxes is how the trajectory for all of creation, God's master plan, ultimately reconciles with the collective free will of the individual.[68] On this point, the *Zohar* teaches that God can reorganize events so that His will is carried out through agents of free choice.[69] King Solomon likewise apprises us, "A man's legs are the guarantors to bring him to a place where God has ordained that he must be."[70]

A DEEPER LOOK

The Rambam brings the example of a wealthy person who builds a giant castle for his own enjoyment. God permitted, even choreographed, this, because one day a righteous man will stop and rest under the shade of the wall. All of the wealth of this person was Divinely routed so that one *tzaddik* would enjoy a respite from the heat. From the perspective of the traveler, the wall perfectly suits his needs—precisely and exactly. Yet how that wall came to be, the vicissitudes—twists and turns—that were required to build it, are largely insignificant. As long as the owner ignored any opportunity for growth, his primary—and perhaps sole—mission in life was reduced to building this castle.[71]

Providence has not been removed, but the above-referenced person moves from a state of independence—the active use of free will—to a state of dependency, where his actions no longer determine or encompass the entirety of his fate or circumstances, and he is largely dependent on how others use *their* free will. Like a generic puzzle piece, he is moved to where there is a space. This is, in part, what being left to chance means. We no longer take our place as free-willed beings whose unique essence bursts forth, but rather are corralled into an opening, to complete the larger picture.

As we discussed, the Chazon Ish explains that *bitachon* is the belief that nothing is accidental, and everything that happens is ordained by God, directed toward

---

68. This also applies in matters of Divine justice. See Rashi on the passage, "If a man did not lie in wait [to kill], but God caused it to come to his hand, I will appoint for you a place to which he shall flee" (Exodus 21:13).

69. *Parahas Vayeira.*

70. *Succah 53a.* World affairs will conclude according to God's plan, independent of our actions. What is directly determined by our conduct, however, is whether we receive reward or punishment, as well as whom we lift up and whom we drag down.

71. Even if a person is a *kli*, there is always the opportunity for *teshuvah*. We are rarely used for the benefit of anyone or anything without the prospect to discern some meaning for us in our own lives. Many of life's challenges are innately intended to foster humility, the master key to growth, which in turn, is the direct gateway to *teshuvah.*

our highest good. This does not mean, though, that it *had to happen*. Our highest good does not operate independently of our own efforts and choices—which to an indeterminable degree determine whether or not the experience is required. In short, the fact that a challenge may have been unnecessary does not mean that it was random.[72] Kabbalistic writings explain:

> Nothing occurs by accident, without intention and Divine providence, as it is written [Leviticus 21:24]: "Then I will also walk with you in chance." You see that even the state of "chance" is attributed to God, for everything proceeds from Him by reason of special providence.[73]

Divine wisdom ensures that circumstances are not arbitrary—on the contrary, it is precisely God's supervision that allows for events to unfold according to His will. However, to say that man is governed by ceaseless providence is not to say that every challenge we face is unavoidable. So, can a person strike his finger down below unless it is decreed upon him above? No. Providence dictates that he cannot—and will not, but when we are left to circumstances, we may strike our finger under the watchful eye of providence. Not because it was necessary, but based on our choices it became necessary—for our reluctant good.

NOTHING SPECIAL

If we are non-distinct puzzle pieces, God can move us into any number of positions, and the narrower our perspective, the wider the net of situations that can produce the same outcome—that is, what we gain. The circumstance that we find ourselves in is only a backdrop to our growth, so as we become more attuned to our world, our ability to discern meaning requires experiences that are tailored to our perception.

We will explain with a metaphor. Let us assume that God wants two adults to "read a book" (substitute any positive behavior that leads to refinement of one's soul/character), each for his own good, as well as for the benefit of humanity. Yet only one will actually read it, and the other will instead use it as a paperweight—which

72. Because the outcome of this scenario maximizes his contribution to creation, his purpose shifts, but again, because he moves in the realm of nature, this shift did not need to occur, at this time and in this way, had the situation not presented itself.

73. *Shomer Emunim* (cited in *Shoresh Mitzvas HaTefillah*, Sec. 34).

the world also needs. This is the most the second person will do with it, and because it will serve a purpose, God allows it, even facilitates it. In this way, God empowers us to actualize our potential, in spite of ourselves.

Returning to our metaphor, it is obvious that it does not matter what genre the book is, and, for that matter, any finer details—the font, the paper stock, the layout—are irrelevant. In this respect, reality is blunted, not because he is cast to nature, but because these variables become superfluous.[74] When we do not measure our actions toward God, then He does not measure His actions toward us. Where our perception is blurred, the precision to which God manifests circumstances is equally calibrated.

A PERFECT ECOSYSTEM

When we state that God does not measure His actions toward us, we are not stating that His actions go unmeasured. Rather, where our awareness ends, chunks, slices, or slivers of our lives are no longer for our direct good. While the font, the paper stock, and the layout may be irrelevant to us, they are perfectly meaningful and relevant within the larger context of creation.

The famous "faces–vase" drawing offers a fitting allegory to demonstrate this precept. Let us imagine that our purpose in life is to become a beautiful

black rectangle, but we fail to progress toward this form. Aspects of our life, or perhaps the entirety of our life, are used to serve others who are determined to actualize their forms. From our vantage, we are left misshapen and deformed. Our cuts—our difficult life experiences—seem haphazard and unfair. Yet every cut from our life is perfectly measured to become part of other shapes that we cannot see—in our example, the two white faces surrounding the vase.[75] In this way, we live in a world that is both simultaneously precision-orchestrated and yet seemingly random.

74. When writing to a person whose command of the language is poor, the perfect use of syntax and grammar is not altogether necessary. While our words are not random, our message may lack a degree of precision. Even if we wanted to convey a well-worded nuance, it would not be possible—not because of our writing skills, but because of the recipient's reading skills. Furthermore, if our note will go unread altogether, it makes no difference to *this person* whether or not the note is written in the first place.

75. At the risk of a too-dense metaphor, these cuts create us into a vase which then becomes our secondary use. As a result, we serve a purpose similar to the person who, in our previous example, chose to use a book as a paperweight.

Our lives do not exist in a vacuum, as evidenced by "the butterfly effect."[76] This phenomenon is born from the prospect that a hurricane's formation, path, and intensity may be subject to whether a butterfly had previously flapped its wings somewhere else in the world. The model is used to explain how a small change in the initial condition of a system sets off a chain of events leading to a large-scale cascade of events. The Torah alludes to this concept:

[Moses] saw an Egyptian man strike a Hebrew man, [one] of his brethren. [Moses] turned this way and that way and when he saw that no man [was watching], he smote the Egyptian and hid him in the sand.[77]

Rashi explains that "turning this way and that way," means that Moses was looking into the future to see what, if any, ripple effect would come and saw that nobody would descend from this person who would "fulfill a special purpose."[78] In this instance, there was no meaningful good that would come from this person, and as a result, he could be killed for the immediate benefit. With no direct connection to the will of God, this person became a total instrument of fate.[79] His utter and complete lack of awareness, in combination with the circumstances, made him more useful dead than alive—the consummate *kli*.

Everything God does is orchestrated for our ultimate good. He allows us to gain—even when we do not grow—indirectly, by making us a *kli* so that good can come through us and, when necessary, without us, to maximize our *s'char* ("reward in the next world"). This is not to say, however, that this Egyptian's death offered him next-world benefits equal to what he might have earned through the responsible use of his free will.[80] Let us explain.

NOTES

76. A term coined by Edward Lorenz, a mathematician and meteorologist at the famed Massachusetts Institute of Technology. Scientists explain that this effect is not simply a theoretical illustration of a mathematical principle, but a real-world occurrence. See E. J. Heller and S. Tomsovic, "Postmodern Quantum Mechanics," *Physics Today* (1993).

77. Exodus 2:11–12.

78. See Rashi on ibid.

79. This scenario should not be construed as anything other than a metaphor to explain that even seemingly small events can have dramatic consequences. It is obvious that an unfathomable number of variables leading to innumerable permutations wrinkle into the physical world, with the collective impact becoming part of a mind-numbing calculation that is beyond our comprehension.

80. The presumption is that his *mazal* did not dictate or design this path for his soul's rectification. If his fate was sealed by his *tikkun*, then he could not have avoided this destiny, and the cut would be deemed "scalpel," not "saw." In fact, the great Kabbalist the Ari (Rabbi Yitzchak Luria) writes that the Egyptian's

SCALPEL OR SAW

The potential we unknowingly squander is not lost, because providence makes use of us and we receive *s'char*.[81] In this regard, every cut from our lives is Divinely measured to become part of other shapes.[82] When there is negligence on our part, though, we are metaphorically disfigured by indiscriminate cuts via nature and man, but we are not credited or rewarded in kind; and the more negligent we are, the less bang we get for our existential buck. It must be this way. Where is the justice, let alone the significance of free will, if God allowed for negligent behavior to be offset by an equal gain elsewhere in creation? To reward everyone equally, regardless of their behavior, is spiritual socialism.

The question of indiscriminate cuts runs parallel to the issue of how a person can be harmed if no such decree exists, and clashes loudly with authorities who maintain that nothing happens by accident or happenstance. A careful analysis of the contested position reveals no contradiction, because all authorities agree that negligence can undermine any decree. We recall that a person is responsible for his own personal safety, and our Sages warn us that whatever natural protection or decree was in place may be withdrawn or overridden by willful negligence.[83] Thus, what befalls him is not outside of what "should" befall him. He lives in the natural world and is subject to the forces of nature, which God Himself has decreed.[84]

As long as we operate within our *madraigah*, our potential is preserved and accounted for, and whatever is, is as it should be.[85] Our purpose in life is coordinated

---

nefesh was in fact a *gilgul* of Cain, and his death—particularly in this way—was necessary for his *tikkun* (*Shaar HaPesukim, Chumash HaAri, Bereishis*).

81. This is an unavoidable oversimplification of God's administration, because numerous influences and exceptions come into play. Nonetheless, we can confidently draw a distinction between those behaviors that result from shifting circumstances, accidents, and interactions with other free-willed beings, and those that we bring upon ourselves, through willful negligence with wanton disregard for the truth.

82. While God maximizes our potential, this is a default potential. The reward we receive as a *kli* is not commensurate with the proactive use of free will. Failure to create ourselves comes at a cost, although it is mitigated by our secondary use.

83. *Kesubos* 30a.

84. These challenges should not be assumed to be the consequence of being thrust into nature, because in some instances they may be Divinely engineered. The troubles are unnecessary, in that we brought them upon ourselves, but in some instances there is a direct, causal relationship to help us get back on track. Further discussion can be found in Chapter 14, "Agents of Adversity."

85. *Madraigah* refers to a person's spiritual level, denoting where a free will choice is within the scope of one's capacity.

with the rest of creation (as explained in the following chapter). However, should a person fall below his *madraigah*, he is considered negligent, and whatever decree is in place may be withdrawn.[86]

The Ramban explains that this loss of protection is not a punishment but a natural outcome of cause and effect.[87] We see how this works with the Gemara that states, "Everything is in the hands of Heaven besides [illnesses related to] cold and heat, as the verse says, 'Cold and heat are in the path of a stubborn one, one who guards his soul will distance himself from them.'"[88] The Sages explain that failure to protect oneself from the natural elements defines negligence because it is preventable. And, as the Ramchal explains, the sin of negligence itself warrants one to be punished. He writes,

> One who wishes to act without wisdom and abandon himself to danger has not trust, but recklessness. And he is a sinner in that he acts against the will of the Creator, Who desires that man protect himself. So aside from the inherent danger of the matter which he is prone to because of carelessness, he openly calls punishment down upon himself because of this sin. Thus the sin of negligence itself leads him to be punished.[89]

It is no coincidence that *karcha* stems from the Hebrew word *kar* which means "cold" and has two connotations: "chance" and "spiritual impurity." The relationship is as follows: A person who irresponsibly exposes himself to the elements—for example, cold—leaves himself subject to chance because negligence attracts spiritual impurity, which then corrodes his bond with God.

BLOOD FROM A STONE

The negligence component is less of an exception to a precision-cut reality and more of an extension of it. When a person moves so far away from his purpose that he has no direct connection to God's will, then the good that can be accomplished with him is limited.

We will illustrate with an oversimplified and extreme scenario. Let us say

86. See *Kesubos* 30a.
87. See *Moreh Nevuchim*, Vol. III, Ch. 51.
88. *Kesubos* 30a.
89. *Mesillas Yesharim*, Ch. 9.

that Person A runs into person B, who wants to kill him. While an indeterminable number of factors come into play, not the least of which is *mazal* and active Divine providence, for illustrative purposes we will imagine that both people are operating without any protection, and all decrees that were in place have been withdrawn. This dynamic is radically different than a situation where one person becomes a *kli* to help another fulfill his primary purpose. Here, both people have opted out.

In such an instance, God allows both of them to serve as a *kli* for the expression of free will, which contributes to the collective coffers of revelation, because free will is the linchpin in God's revelation.[90] In other words, a person's total default position is to facilitate the open display of free will—which means that God allows for us to act freely (except where noted) with genuine real-world impact and consequences.

This hierarchy preserves the canon of God's complete providence while maintaining the integrity of free will, and allows God to stay hidden in nature—fostering the illusion of an independent natural world. In a situation that is rich with irony, those who abdicate their individual free choice allow for its very existence and emergence. In this respect, even challenges brought about through negligence are part of a larger cosmic order, but our lowly, self-determined place in this order makes a mockery of our lives.[91]

Practically speaking, should we live our lives completely antithetical to Torah values, thus forsaking all hope of the soul's refinement, the argument of whether or not providence exists becomes theoretically unnecessary—because the net reality to us is the same. Whether we want to say that a suit is poorly made (because nature is the craftsman) or tailor-made to fit poorly (because the Craftsman is God), we end up wearing a poor-fitting suit through nobody's fault but our own.

At this level of existence, there is no tangible difference between providence and randomness. When a person descends into absolute nature, his conduct brings no real value to his *neshamah* or to creation. Short of *teshuvah*, there is nothing he could do that would outrank the benefit of being used as a *kli* to openly demonstrate cause and effect in the physical world. God may still advocate for his good,

---

NOTES

90. See Chapter 36, "The Ladder of Harmony."

91. In addition to maintaining the spiritual infrastructure of good and evil, the Rambam (Introduction to *Zeraim*) explains that the majority of people—those who have no direct connection to the will of God—serve as necessary cogs in the wheel of society. They provide a physical framework for the righteous to sustain their spiritual endeavors.

but without any soul-oriented awareness or drive, the most providence can offer is to allow him to live—and die—in nature. (We should reiterate that "to die" in nature does not necessarily mean a physical death, and that success in the natural world may come with a steep spiritual price tag.)

When it comes to human beings the bottom line is this: When there is complete and total negligence, the ripple effect of one's actions is rarely significant enough to pull us out of the natural order, but the fact that this prospect is included in the equation is central to the legitimacy of a fully integrated system. Certainly, nature does not operate independent of God. He knows all and supervises every aspect in creation down to the tiniest detail, but He will not position this person for another use, or otherwise intervene, unless a greater good is achieved.

When a person fails to use his given strengths to maximize his potential and fulfill his mission, he becomes an instrument to help others who are making proper use of their free will. The ultimate goal of creation is to reveal God's glory. "All is from God, and serves to reveal His Godliness, wisdom and attributes."[92] Few will do this with proactive use of their free will, and the rest will assist those who do. In the words of Ralph Waldo Emerson, "All history is but the lengthened shadow of a great man."

92. Rabbi Menachem Mendel of Vitebsk, *Pri HaAretz* (*Bo*). Truly evil people become an unqualified *kli* in God's master plan, but in a narrow sense, they have greater reign than the sick or foolish. This is not an aberration in God's administration, but only appears so, because the rules are upside down from our perspective. Evil makes proper use of its free will when it maximizes its potential, which is to bring itself-—evil—into the world.

21 | # THE MIRACLE OF NATURE

God's intervention in the natural order is a matter of much discussion and more confusion. Before we continue our explanation of *when* God intervenes and what "the greater good" means, let us present a streamlined synopsis to explain *how* God intervenes.

Advancing one opinion is the Ramban, who holds that the natural order, which continues most of the time, uninterrupted via cause and effect, allows for periodic disruption—for example, miracles, by way of Divine providence. Nonetheless, because nature does not operate independently from God, he deems everything a miracle—some hidden in nature and others open and patently miraculous.

Others, led by the Rambam, contend that all events, even seemingly miraculous ones, are not just cloaked in reality but have been encoded into largely immutable laws set into motion by God.[93] So much so, that he also maintains that all of the miracles that were to occur—the parting waters of the *Yam Suf* ("Red Sea") the stalled sun of Yehoshua, and so forth—were built into the natural laws during the six days of Creation—or shortly thereafter, during dusk immediately prior to Shabbos.[94] Just as there are physical laws that are true, universal, and absolute, there are spiritual laws with clearly defined consequences. We simply

---

NOTES

93. We reemphasize that neither he nor any other authority suggest that God is ever on the sidelines. While the nonphysical universe has preset laws similar to those of the physical universe, nothing in creation operates independently of God. He knows all and interacts and intercedes as He chooses.

94. The Meiri (Menachem Meiri [1249–1310], a famous Catalan rabbi and Talmudist) tweaks this opinion by suggesting that these miracles were not actually embedded into creation but existed in potential—part of the flow-chart design but not programmed to be automatically enacted. This position is supported by an hypothesis in physics known as the *multiple world theory*.

activate them in ways that are not always clear to us—so they seem less constant or universal.

The disagreement narrows because the Rambam contends that Divine providence—which appears to interfere with the natural order—is itself a natural process. Simply, the natural order was created to allow for preplanned deviations—even miraculous ones—based on a person's conduct. The reasoning is thus: Miracles, which are a function of Divine providence, are set in motion by man's actions, via his free will. Such actions have designated, preexisting consequences (based on an established system of reward and punishment) that are enacted.

While the Rambam maintains that individual providence depends on the activity, not on the person, we can consider that cause and effect are not limited to the act, but also rely on the person—yet do not require direct providence. In other words, these laws apply to all in the same way, all things (people) being equal. But because each circumstance is unique, they are applied differently—not because they vary, but because we do.

For example, the laws of gravity are abundantly obvious when an apple falls from a tree. Can we say that the laws change because one apple falls slower or faster, or that one apple sinks into the ground, while another bounces, collides with other apples, and then rolls down a hill? The height of the tree, the texture of the apple, wind conditions, surrounding apples, moisture levels, and so on, all go into this computation. But the computation is fixed, while the variables are near-infinite. In our loose metaphor, providence (according to the Rambam) does not mean that God is intervening, but rather, such calculations are built into the laws of nature.

Since we are speaking of human beings, who have a unique mission, another dimension must be considered. That is, who the "apple" is. Therefore, one's spiritual DNA—specifically, *tikkun* and *mazal*—is integrated into this "gravity algorithm." The remaining sticking point in the calculation are free will choices—about which the Ramban maintains that Divine providence must come into the equation, while the Rambam would insist that no such intervention is required because the free will choice, too, is contained within the schemata. When we consider, though, that from God's perspective (outside of time and space), everything that will happen has already happened, we can, at least conceptually, bridge the two positions.

THE MAZAL OF NATURE

How natural is nature when it has nothing to do with man? Does a leaf fall from a tree with any wisdom or decree? Most authorities favor the view of the Rambam, who holds that the natural world—and its physical properties and laws—serves only as a backdrop for free will. He writes, "I do not believe that a particular leaf has fallen because of Divine providence; or that this spider has devoured this flea because God has now decreed.... For all this is in my opinion due to pure chance."[95]

Thus far, he would appear to have physics on his side because, as we discussed, quantum mechanics concedes a degree of unpredictability in the universe. However, a contrasting opinion—held mostly by the Kabbalists and Chassidim—maintains that nothing in creation is by chance—every blade of grass, every grain of sand, is where it is, because God wills it so. The early Chassidic master Rabbi Pinchas of Koretz observes that "...a man should believe that even a piece of straw that lies on the ground does so at the decree of God. He decrees that it should lie there with one end facing this way and the other end the other way." A later authority, Rabbi Hayyim Halberstam, similarly states,

> It is impossible for any creature to enjoy existence without the Creator of all worlds sustaining it and keeping it in being, and it is all through Divine providence. Although the Rambam has a different opinion in this matter, the truth is that not even a bird is snared without providence from above.[96]

Moreover, the *Midrash* tells us: "Even things which you may regard as completely superfluous to the creation of the world, such as fleas, gnats and flies, even they are included in the creation of the world and the Holy One carries out the Divine purpose through everything."[97] Our Sages also remind us, "Do not scorn any person and do not disdain anything; for there is no person who does not have his hour, and there is no thing that does not have its place."[98]

Enter another quantum mechanics theorem, the *Pauli Exclusion Principle*, which states that electrons cannot occupy the same quantum state simultaneously.[99] In simple terms, every electron, in every atom, everywhere in the universe is at a slightly different energy level and changing the energy of electrons in an object—even in

---

NOTES

95. *Moreh Nevuchim* 3:17.

96. *Divrei Hayyim* (New York: 1962), "Mikketz", 13d, Arabic no. 26.

97. *Bereishis Rabbah* 10:7.

98. Ethics of the Fathers, 4:3. "Nothing exists that isn't for some higher purpose, i.e., to reveal God's glory. The reason for this is that nothing exists that doesn't have a spiritual root above. This includes things that are covered by many layers of 'garments' and therefore seemingly totally removed from—and even antithetical—to Godliness" (*Teferet HaChinukhi, Parshas Vayeira*).

99. The principle applies to fermions (particles that obey the *Exclusion Principle*) which include protons, neutrons, and electrons—the three types of elementary particles that constitute matter.

a benign way, such as by warming it up—leads to changes in all electron energy levels in the universe.

Indeed, if a butterfly flapping its wings can stir the formation of a hurricane in another part of the world, is it so illogical that a falling leaf may be of greater consequence than we typically assume? Of course, reason informs us that some connections are more direct and stronger than others, and in the scheme of things, some things matter more than others, but a deep question emerges: When everything is connected to not just something else, but to everything else, does a concept of chance exist? Not only do we have competing rabbinic positions, but each seems to be supported by difficult-to-reconcile physics principles. To help answer this question, we will examine another set of contrasting sources:

- ❑ The *Midrash* states, "There is not a blade of grass that does not have a *mazal* [or constellation] in heaven that strikes it and says, 'grow!'"[100]
- ❑ The *Zohar* states, "There is not a blade of grass that does not have an angel who is appointed to look after it and strikes it and tells it to 'grow!'"[101]

Elsewhere, the *Zohar* illuminates the spiritual mechanics behind these two statements: "There is no blade of grass in the entire world that is not ruled by a star and constellation in heaven, and over that star there is one official appointed over it that serves before the Holy One. These are the angels."[102] God's providence works through the angels, and these angels, in turn, work through the stars and planets.[103] The Rambam echoes these sentiments.

Everything that comes into being in this lower world—namely, every "living soul" and every tree and every species of grass and every one of the species of minerals— the whole has the Deity as its maker, through a power coming from the spheres and the stars. And they are in accord that the power of the Creator flows first upon the spheres and the stars; from the spheres and the stars it flows and spreads through this (lower) world—everything that is, thereby coming into being.[104]

NOTES

100. *Bereishis Rabbah* 10:6.

101. *Zohar* 1:34a.

102. *Terumah* 171b.

103. Rabbi Aryeh Kaplan, Commentary on *Sefer Yetzirah*.

104. "Letter on Astrology." Cited by Isadore Twersky, *A Maimonides Reader* (New York: Behrman House, Inc., 1972), 463-47. Many themes swirl behind the scenes of Divine providence, such as the Land of Israel

Kabbalists explain it thusly: Divine energy flows through four worlds which terminate in the physical universe. *Atzilus* ("the world of emanation") is the plane of the ten *Sefiros; Beriyah* ("the world of creation") is the realm through which the influence of the *Sefiros* is directed down to *Yetzirah* ("the world of formation")—the domain of angels; they in turn influence the constellations in *Assiyah* ("the world of action"), which then affects everything in our world.

Crucial to our understanding is that the laws of nature and the course of nature are in accord with the will of God, because the natural world is synchronized with our *mazal.* (The Rambam's reference to "pure chance" does not include events that concern man, even though he and others hold that man, too, can be subject to chance—the definition of which, is open to much debate.) The extent of synchronization between the natural world and man is also in dispute—as is God's use of intermediaries and part and parcel, whether His will is actively or passively expressed, for whom, and how often. In broad strokes, the three major positions are as follows:

1. Significant events: (*tikkun*-related) with everything else subject to chance.

2. Major events and interactions: (*tikkun*-related plus soft *mazal*-related [see following chapter]) with everything else subject to chance.

3. All interactions: since all of creation impacts man, everything in creation—both animate and inanimate—is synched with humanity). Nothing is subject to chance.[105]

Following the common denominator of a synthesized approach, if we are living our lives in accord with our purpose in life, then *mazal* dictates that the bulk of our experiences and certainly pivotal episodes are perfectly necessary (fine-tuned to one's level of awareness). This is how life operates for most people, those who live within the margins of their *madraigah*. They have their role in God's plan, cloaked in the natural order of the universe, which itself is reflected in the stars—or *mazal.*[106]

NOTES

and God's use of angels in His supervision. While these areas are important to explore, our focus is limited to aspects that intersect directly with our free will. We should underscore, however, that God does not need intermediate mechanisms—angels, constellations, and the like—nor are they imbued with any authority that can ever deliberately contravene the will of God.

105. These authorities maintain that God creates the universe anew every moment, and nature, while governed by *mazal* is directed through active Divine Providence for all people and—according to a subset opinion—toward all of creation.

106. There is much written on the Torah view of astrology, the particulars of which, are beyond the scope of our discussion. However, the overriding *halachah* is most pertinent: It is forbidden to be superstitious, or to

The function of a decree is to assure the expression of a person's *mazal*, guaranteeing—to the extent that we do our part—those experiences that are necessary. Essentially, if we are "doing our jobs," then nothing of significance can happen to us that is not supposed to happen. In this way, the Talmud tells us, God has many messengers to carry out His will. This is what Joseph implied when he revealed himself to his brothers: "I am Joseph your brother. You sold me to Egypt. But don't worry or feel guilty because you sold me, for God has sent me ahead of you to save lives… . It is not you who sent me here, but God."[107]

If Person B is living in accordance with his purpose, then Person A cannot do to him what is not decreed—regardless of person A's spiritual station. *Mazal* assures this.[108] In addition, as long as Person A is acting within his *madraigah,* he also cannot do anything to Person B (no matter how deserving Person B may be) that is not within his own (Person A's) *mazal.* Generally speaking, we cannot act in any way to ourselves or to others that will render us incapable of fulfilling our purpose.[109]

Therefore, nature's incursion into humanity is not the issue; neither is its contact with those governed under active *hashgachah pratis.* God gives Divine permission for nature to "take its course" and to operate as is, unless and until it impedes on those governed under *hashgachah pratis;* because those operating within their *madraigah* are governed by *mazal,* which functions within the system of nature; and complete negligence deactivates our *mazal* and our purpose is absorbed into the natural world.

This explanation helps us to integrate the Chassidic view, which, as we will recall, maintains that even nonhumans operate under Divine providence. Inanimate matter, plants, and animals, of course, do not possess free will, and as such, their

---

engage in, or inquire of, a practitioner of sorcery, fortune-telling, astrology, and horoscopes (Leviticus 19:26; Deuteronomy 18:9-12). The Sages explain that we must place our trust in God, and not in any lesser force.

107. Genesis 45:1–11.

108. See Chapter 14, "Agents of Adversity" for two exceptions: (1) where we reference the Talmud (*Bava Kamma* 60a), "Once permission has been given to the Destroyer to destroy, he does not distinguish between the righteous and the wicked;" and (2) this unique period in history, referred to as *ikvos d'Meshichah* ("footsteps of the Messiah.") See also subchapter "Final Redemption" in Chapter 25 "Unperceived Influences," for a nuanced qualification.

109. We cannot resort to the pseudo-logic that says: Since a person who lives life above his *madraigah* is not subject to randomness, I am not responsible for whatever I do to him because all that befalls him is decreed. This mentality is ludicrous because we can never know where a person's *madraigah* rests. Furthermore, each person is responsible for his own actions, and we are held liable because we did not have to choose to be the messenger of fate. Regarding the period of Egyptian slavery, the Rambam says that while a decree on the Jewish people was enacted, each Egyptian citizen had the choice to not contribute to the oppression (*Hilchos Teshuvah* 6:5).

existence does not depend on their deeds; a system of reward and punishment requires the possibility of choice. Rather, the providence they receive is not unlike that of a human who is reduced to a *kli*, in how they affect all of creation.

When a particular animal or item belongs to—or affects—a human, its status is determined by the specific governance of the person. It is covered under an umbrella policy, in a manner of speaking. It is correct to conclude that a piece of straw will at times be given special providence, while God may permit a human being to be swept up by a force of nature.

PERFECTLY RANDOM

The above discussion is not meant to button up and an existential debate because the crux of the issue remains: How do we define *chance* and *nature* when it comes to human beings? It is indisputable that everything transpires according to the will of God. But does this mean that: (a) His precise will is carried out through nature, even when a person lacks awareness or is outright negligent (in which case we are left with the unsettling assumption that God not only permits the expression of evil but also directs it), or (b) His will is for man to be subject to the laws of nature. If the latter, is it conceivable or completely heretical to imagine that *chance* could mean more than the unpredictable—that something may truly happen randomly?

Re-examination of a fundamental concept acquaints us with a third option. We have established that reality is keyed into our level of awareness (our free will choices determine our perspective, and our perspective defines our reality). Although God presents a range of potential outcomes—within the bounds of nature and confined to our *mazal/tikkun* when applicable—it is *we*, not God, who bring definitive form to the world around us. This is His will—for us to complete, to perfect, creation.

By definition, a free will event is not based on any specific cause (explained further in Chapter 24, "The Battlefront"). If something were to compel us in one direction over another, the outcome would not be free but rather a function of factors which lead us to an inevitable conclusion. Free will shares a conspicuously similar definition to *chance* (the unknown and unpredictable element in happenings that seems to have no assignable cause) because what we call *chance* is none other than an unmeasured consequence of our free will choices; or possibly even a direct impression of these choices.

In short, blaming God for the unnecessary unpleasantries in our lives is like blaming the mirror for our reflection. Perspective (which is a function of choice) defines our reality from the platter of possibilities, but it also determines what is on the platter in the first place. Metaphorically speaking, our perspective determines:

- ❑ The selection of food that is on the menu. (Everything God does is for our good, so what is offered depends on what is good for us; and that depends on our ability to receive the good. The wider our perspective, the more God we see—receptive capacity expands—and the greater the field of possibilities.)
- ❑ Which of those foods we are actually served. (Perspective defines reality from the range of options.)
- ❑ How much pleasure we receive from what we eat. (As noted elsewhere, the qualitative experience of the circumstance is also based on our perspective.)

Since human consciousness is required to "collapse the wave probability," those who are completely unaware or spiritually unconscious, have to eat whatever is in front of them. They have no say in spiritual matters. Their world is entirely physically-based: cause and effect. However we define nature, this is it.

DRAWING ON PERFECTION

Perhaps the real difficulty in understanding the natural world lies not in our definition of *chance* but in our underestimating the sophistication of *chance*. In Kabbalah, *Tohu* ("randomness" or "chaos") originates at the level of the inscrutable *Sefirah* of *Keser*, which is above both nature and intellect.

It is highly relevant to note that human beings are incapable of duplicating true randomness, and a valid random number generator, for example, is impossible to create. We can only produce a stream of numbers that appear as if they were chosen randomly. It is obvious that our inability to fathom total perfection is matched only by our inability to fathom total imperfection. God is perfect, and everything He does is perfect. In absolute reality, there is no concept of *chance* as we understand it. But if a finite world can exist within the Infinite, if multiplicity can exist within unity, and if free will can coexist with Divine foreknowledge, then we will have to accept that disorder can exist within Divine order.

Still, the underlying flaw in our fixation is that everyone and everything must be in the "right" place and nothing can be "out of place" for perfection to be realized. Naturally, this would preclude the possibility of two or more legitimate outcomes or even routes—be it the position or path of a leaf or of a human being.

The presumption is that a given physical permutation will have an exacting spiritual outcome. This is not so. Fundamentally, *mitzvos* (which lead to perfection of oneself and the world) will have fluctuating spiritual impact based on one's awareness, intent, and effort. Whereas a poorly executed *mitzvah* carried out with extreme effort may generate greater spiritual perfection—and fixing of the world—than a *mitzvah* performed with technical precision and minimal effort; in fact, lacking proper intent (such as in the case of *Megillah* or blowing of the *shofar*) a *mitzvah* may be totally invalid.

The natural world awaits our contribution to move creation forward, but our awareness does more than infuse spirituality into physicality. We, as noted, give birth to a more perfect physical reality that is most profoundly, non-linear. The concept of *teshuvah* serves as a potent proof, whereby our heightened awareness (which shifts perspective) retroactively creates order out of disorder—sublimely so, a *mitzvah* can emerge from sin and make imperfection the very instrument of perfection.

On a macro level the core paradox—the harmonization of disorder and order—can be modestly grasped when we recall that in order to bring creation to its state of perfection—*tikkun olam*—we need to emit our own individuality, fulfill our own *tikkun*. Imperfection, or disorder, is thus a requisite for perfection, perfect order. We are about to see how this all plays out when we widen our focus to how God's perfect will expresses itself, in the system that manifests His goodness.

THE GREATER GOOD AND JUSTICE FOR ALL

We have noted a multitude of reasons for why there are challenges in our lives—all geared toward our good. But what if a situation exists where none of these reasons are in play? (a) We will not get the message; (b) it has nothing to do with our *tikkun* or *mazal*; (c) we are not a *kli* in this instance; (d) it will not lead to greater injury; (e) an open miracle is unnecessary; (f) there is no domino effect into anyone's life; and (g) the situation does not impose on anyone's free will, *tikkun*, or *mazal*.

Might an all-loving God choose to intervene to spare us from an unnecessarily painful ordeal—even when we are negligent? What is the harm? To answer this question, imagine our world as a giant cosmic game, with one Referee. If at any time He gives one player a single extra point outside of the rules, what happens to the game? It's rendered illegitimate. We would not have a game at all. In that instant, there is no longer a difference between that single unearned point and all of the rightly earned ones. All points become worthless.

We know, of course, that God does intercede in the game of life. Often, His wisdom does not make sense to us. Yet God is Truth. His system (comprised of *hanhagas hamishpat* and *hanhagas hayichud*) is unimpeachable—infinitely so. Our inability to grasp the rules of the game signifies a deficiency within ourselves, not in Truth.

Recall that *hanhagas hamishpat*, the system of justice, runs according to the rules God sets. It falls under the canopy of cause and effect and is to varying degrees observable. *Hanhagas hayichud*, which also runs according to a perfect order, is employed to bring the world to a state of perfection. When God governs along this trajectory, however, rules seem to bend arbitrarily, but only because they are part of a complete system that is further away from human understanding.

Broken laws do not exist. Should gravity fail even once, privately, and without harm to anyone or anything, no one would cry foul, but we would no longer have the laws of gravity. This is not about fairness. It's about reality.[110] Our world exists for us to earn our place in the next world. An unjust intervention to do "good" voids an entire system built on reward and punishment, because, as we noted elsewhere, the greatest good that God could bestow on us is that we should be like Him. This requires that we assume ownership over our status—who we create ourselves into.

We cannot discharge our *tikkun* and be brought closer to Truth, by breaching a system that is designed by, and defined by, Truth. Justice is not vengeance. It is an essential ingredient of *chesed*.[111] No matter how low a person sinks, he is always better off operating within a system that maintains the larger good—the unadulterated function of free will—so that in the next world, his soul can enjoy the benefits it has justly earned in this world, through its various incarnations.

110. Gravity is offered as a metaphor, not as an example. God created the laws of physics, and as such He is not bound by them. In fact, we know that He has performed miracles that suspend the natural order. Truth, however, is His essence and His essence is nonchanging.

111. *Gevurah*—the guiding force of justice—yields to mercy, via *chesed*, once the situation and every possible ramification is filtered through the Infinite lens of truth. This is because *chesed* is not truly *chesed* if a short-term gain comes at the expense of our long-term good; and it explains why "an abundance of truth" is considered one of the attributes of mercy (Exodus 34:6–7).

22 | MAZAL:
THE
FINE PRINT

We have learned that if reality is ignored, the purpose for specific experiences is rendered inert. There is an exception: the previously noted *tikkun*. In such instances, our soul needs to go through a transformative experience in order to grow, and neither awareness nor understanding is necessary.

Under parallel circumstances, a *middah* may be necessary for our growth. For example, a wealthy person who has become haughty may need to suffer a great financial loss, even abject poverty. Even if this person never once ponders the reason for his misfortune, it does not mean that the trait of haughtiness has not lessened. He may become angry at the world and envious of others and lust after the good old days—but haughty? Less so. Therefore, awareness itself is not the benchmark of whether or not something has a purpose—growth is. Without growth—voluntary or otherwise—the opportunity becomes meaningless.

That is indeed *mazal's* charter—to protect and promote our *tikkun*, the reason we are in this world in the first place. We now observe that not all *mazal* is created equal. Kabbalists describe two layers of *mazal*: *mazal elyon* ("upper *mazal*" or "hard *mazal*") which corresponds to our mission in life, and *mazal tachton* ("lower *mazal*" or "soft *mazal*") which corresponds to the conditions in our lives and our experience of those conditions. *Mazal elyon* is much more difficult to alter because it is bound to our *tikkun*, while *mazal tachton* relates to the ease or difficulty that we encounter while fulfilling our destiny.

LIMITS TO MAZAL

Hard *mazal* is like the skeleton of the body. It provides the overall structure and frame for our lives. Like physical bone, it does not break under normal circumstances.

Soft *mazal* is our spiritual skin; similar to its physical counterpart, it can become bruised by the natural elements.[112] What is the practical difference? Hard *mazal* safeguards certain critical experiences where growth can be realized without awareness, while soft *mazal* serves to facilitate growth opportunities that require effort and understanding (as such, altering our perspective and shaping the quality of those experiences).

The flow of soft *mazal* is more easily interrupted because the capacity to receive the spiritual cargo is only hardwired into hard *mazal*. Soft *mazal* requires our participation—there is no other way. For instance, a person who wishes to become stronger can be given weights and taught the proper exercises, but lifting the weights for him does not help; there is no growth, so there is no point.

Hard *mazal* is more durable but can be forfeited as well, because God set spiritual and physical laws into motion that are used by all of creation, and just as He does not suspend gravity to accommodate one's desire to fly, He does not upend reality as we choose to ignore it. Because *mazal* is integrated into the natural order, should a person move too far away from truth—in relation to his *madraigah*—then *mazal* simply ceases to operate in his world.[113]

Furthermore, the reason that we are granted a "Plan B" (to be used as a *kli*) is to make free will visible, and its integrity is undermined if *mazal* operates with obvious indifference to our behavior.

Imagine, for instance, a person whose *mazal* dictates great wealth, but he chooses to spend his time with trivial pursuits. As fate would have it, he is left an inheritance of one million dollars, which he promptly gambles at the racetrack. His *mazal* holds firm, and he wins. However, then he bets it all again, and again, and again. At some point, his

---

NOTES

112. *Chazal* observe that matters of life expectancy/health, children, and livelihood are not contingent on one's merit, but on one's *mazal* (*Moed Katan* 28a). Even though they are correctly identified as hard *mazal*, they are not necessarily immutable.

113. We walk straight into a question, which the principle of *Shomer Psayim Hashem* ("God protects the simple") answers. Because *hashgachah pratis* requires a bond that is based on an earned status, what happens to those who are not able to achieve this growth through no fault of their own? We learn (Psalms 116) that God protects the simple (the young or those of low IQ, who will always be like children). Therefore, those whose intellectual capabilities are limited or, in the case of children, whose *da'as* has not ripened, are protected from harm, even though they live in the natural world. This protection, however, extends only to ordinary behaviors and not to deliberate and flagrant recklessness. In addition, there is much discussion and dispute regarding for whom, how, and when this protection can be relied on.

We can further explain the welfare of these individuals in the following way: The Talmud states, "The righteous ones are judged to a hair's breadth" (*Yevamos* 121b). This means that God holds those of greater knowledge and perfection to a higher standard. The bond between man and God is not based on an objective standard, but rather on one's own capacity. Therefore, on their own level, "the simple" may have a stronger bond in contrast to those who tap into a smaller percentage of their greater potential.

mazal will run out. It needs to. Otherwise, he would reveal God's Presence—through a parade of open miracles—when he only merits to conceal His Presence.

This brings us to the following distinction: Hard *mazal* that keeps an undesirable decree in place cannot be broken by a person moving away from reality. For example, a preordained long life can be interrupted by reckless behavior, but a short life cannot be extended by such behavior. As we noted: "The fear of God prolongs one's days, but the years of the wicked shall be shortened."[114]

The reason is not punitive. Growth opportunities for a person whose life has so drastically deviated from his purpose are limited. Recall that the faculty to receive what hard *mazal* ensures is already inherent in our souls; therefore, God allows hard *mazal* to be preserved so that the soul can receive its *tikkun*. However, given the decision-making history of such an individual, hard *mazal* that facilitates good fortune is likely to be misused or abused, which would only serve to further distance this person from God—in this world and in the World to Come. Comparing *mazal* to a coat of armor is tempting but misleading; not because *mazal* does not protect us, but because its allegiance is to the real us—the soul.

Alas, we cannot completely oversimplify God's administration. The concept of *tzora'as habais* ("a type of spiritual fungus on the home") offers an illustration of how an irrevocable positive decree can materialize. The *Midrash* relates that the Canaanites hid their valuables in the walls of their homes before the Israelites conquered the Land, and that God would send a *nega* ("affliction") upon the home, which required the new Israelite owner to destroy the wall or even the entire house in order to eradicate it. In the process, he would find the hidden treasure. It was decreed long ago to give this man wealth, and God could have granted it to him in any number of ways. Why did this person have to suffer the destruction of his house to receive what was destined for him anyway? He did not. Our Sages tell us that *tzora'as* appears as a punishment for several sins, stemming from poor *middos*.[115] His wealth came to him in this way due to his own poor choices. Otherwise, he would have been granted his fortune in a pleasant way.

It would be wise to consider that we do not always know good fortune from bad. In the words of the Ramchal: "Great wealth in this world serves one of three purposes: either as a blessing granted by the Creator … or as a trial and test; or as a punishment and stumbling block."[116] Included in the "punishment" category is what

114. Proverbs 10:27.
115. *Arachin* 15a, 16b.
116. *Mesillas Yesharim*, (*The Path of the Just*), Ch. 4.

we have discussed: Good fortune in this world may constitute partial payment—for efforts and challenges that fail to refine the soul—and payment in full, for those who have no place in *Olam Haba*.

DESTINY OFF COURSE

Should a person sink below his *madraigah*, then his *mazal* is weakened or altogether shattered and no longer offers blanket protection against unnecessary challenges. While *mazal* exists to expedite needed growth for the soul, a person who is negligent is thus left unprotected—from others as well as from himself—and is subject to the aforementioned cuts.

Via *mazal*, God gives us exactly what we need to operate within our *madraigah*. Falling below our *madraigah* is the very definition of negligence because it means that we have proactively strayed from our purpose. As a person is cast lower and lower into nature, he encounters greater challenges and occasions to be harmed. As his *mazal* skin is ripped away and his spiritual bones become frailer and fracture, increasingly greater vigilance will be required to keep him emotionally, spiritually, and physically safe.[117]

Regarding our purpose in life, the Ramchal explains that God does not give us anything that we cannot handle.[118] Yet people commit suicide every day, which obviously renders the ordeal not only useless but destructive. Certainly, it is an indication that they were given more than they could handle, is it not?

The answer is that the above statement is true when we speak of *hanhaga hayichud* ("a person's role in creation") under strict *hashgachah pratis* (or under *mazal*, according to some definitions/opinions). Once a person deviates from his path and moves into *hashgachah klalis* ("general supervision"), then he is afforded no such guarantee or protection.[119] God does not test us in something that we cannot withstand, but self-inflicted wounds have nothing to do with being tested (unless they fall outside the scope of our *bechirah*.) Our Sages state, "[I]f someone wishes to kill himself by [jumping into] fire or a river, he can, even though there is no such decree [that he should die]."[120]

NOTES

117. "Those who are far from Him are prone to incidents, and have no one to protect them from harm; as one who walks in the dark is likely to fall unless he is careful to walk slowly." Ramban, on "He will not remove His eyes from a righteous man" (Job 36:7).

118. Ramchal, *Da'as Tevunos*, 170. See also *Avodah Zarah* 3a; and *Shemos Rabbah* 34.

119. The ways of *teshuvah* are always open and have the power to instantly realign us with our true path.

120. Tosafos, *Bava Basra* 144b.

IMPOSSIBLE ASSUMPTIONS

In total and complete arrogance, Pharaoh lost his free will. God said, "I will harden Pharaoh's heart, and I will increase My [miraculous] signs and wonders in the land of Egypt."[121] One might assume that being reduced to a full-blown *kli* would leave Pharaoh swaying in the precarious winds, yet even in the midst of the tenth plague—the death of the firstborn, of which he was one—God intervened to spare him. Such was his place in God's design.

Due to the hidden influences of providence, it should be understood that in any given situation, we are unable to identify "Person A" and "Person B." Just because Person A may injure Person B, we cannot assume that Person A is on a higher spiritual level. We are incapable of gauging what is in the overall best interest for each *neshamah* and the corresponding role each person is to play in God's master plan. Indeed, they may both have been caught in the net of a *kli* to advance the will of yet another person's agenda.

We can never say that a person who is injured or killed by a seemingly random event is a *kli* or has abdicated his role or responsibility, for many great people have met with tragic, untimely deaths. We can more confidently ascribe these instances to a *tikkun* or *kaparah* ("atonement") for the generation. A shared fate does not mean a shared spiritual level. We must never presume otherwise.

CAUTION TO THE RIGHTEOUS AND TO ALL

When a person rises above his nature, there are gradations of providence that become activated, based on his awareness of God. The apex of this relationship allows for enhanced abilities to succeed in his endeavors, protection from those who might thwart his efforts, and active intervention in a place of danger. Because a *tzaddik* lives above his nature, God does not allow the physical world—people, places, and things—to ensnare him.[122]

The righteous are protected because the world exists for them—they are bringing God into the world and are provided with the means to ensure their success. Yet attachment to God is not a stable system at fixed levels, and should a righteous

NOTES

121. Exodus 7:3.

122. It is frequently and wrongly assumed that Divine providence extends exclusively to one's physical safety. On the contrary, the spiritual mission of the *tzaddik* is the actual priority and his physical well-being may be preserved or sacrificed in order to aid him in his endeavors.

person's thoughts wander, such unreserved providence is temporarily suspended. The Rambam writes that this superseding level of providence is reserved for only when one's current conduct merits it.

> Providence is removed from him when he is involved in other matters... . [And] when one averts his attention from God, he is separated from God and God is therefore separated from him; then [this person] is exposed to any evil that might befall him.[123]

He then exists in the natural world without active Divine providence but not necessarily without the protection of *mazal*. As we explained, at what point God intervenes in the natural order is subject to dispute. Some opinions hold that the natural order is disrupted only for *tzaddikim*, and the protection of *mazal* is under the guise of nature, while others endorse a view where God actively intervenes in the natural order to maintain and preserve the flow of *mazal*. The end result to us is the same: we get what we have coming to us.

For those who live within the boundaries of their *madraigah*, this level of Divine providence (beyond the assurance of *mazal*) does not operate, and these people may not be saved from peril or aided in their efforts—through Divine intervention in the natural world.

This explains why the Talmud states, "It is prohibited for a man to walk under a dilapidated wall."[124] No one is immune. At times, even the righteous can find their special providence suspended;[125] those who live within their *madraigah* may not be afforded protection to begin with; and those who sink below their given *madraigah* are without active Divine providence, and the strength of *mazal* is diminished or altogether lost, leaving them without any nonphysical protection.[126] Finally, as a general rule, *mazal* does not govern every aspect of our lives or enter into every situation. Even with our *mazal* fully intact, we are susceptible to mishaps that will not interfere with our life's purpose.

In light of these insights, it would be foolish to assume that we can easily identify

---

NOTES

123. Rambam, *Moreh Nevuchim* (The Guide for the Perplexed) 3:51. "[T]he intensity of the calamity is commensurate with the length of time of the forgetfulness, and the baseness of the matter which he occupies himself" (ibid.).

124. *Ta'anis* 20b.

125. The Gemara in Shabbos (32a) gives us another reason. The miracles which are performed for us are deducted from our accumulated merits in the World to Come.

126. *Mazal* for the Jewish people as a whole is weaker during the Jewish month of *Av* (*Ta'anis* 29b).

what level of providence we are guided by. Not only are there degrees of providence, as well as fluctuations within these points based on our current conduct, but we can never be certain of our overall *madraigah*. The Rambam discusses the evaluation of iniquities and merits and concludes:

> This valuation takes into account not the number, but the magnitude [qualitatively speaking] of merits and iniquities. There may be a single merit that outweighs many iniquities ... and there may be one iniquity that offsets many merits... .[127] The whole world operates on this principle.... . This measuring system does not work on a one-for-one basis.... . Only God knows how to evaluate sins and merits in this respect.[128]

A NATURAL BORN SUCCESS

When a person loses his protection, it does not mean that the world collapses in on him. Rather, he does not maximize the opportunities for his soul's growth. For this reason, a person can sidestep *mazal* points, even when they are inherently challenging. For example, one can miss marrying his *bashert* ("destined spouse"), who, as it turns out, would have been difficult to live with but nonetheless necessary for his growth and integral to his spiritual mission—to say nothing of the children who were to come through this union. In a narrow sense, we might think that he was lucky, but the reality is quite different.

As noted earlier, God has many messengers to carry out His will, but when a person falls below his *madraigah*, no such messenger may come along because *mazal* is no longer operating at full capacity. By defaulting on his obligations, he pursues a different path and meets with "success"—not because *mazal* dictates, but because of his efforts in the natural world. Becoming a *kli* does not mean that we default to victim mode. Central to the workings of free will is that even when a person abdicates all personal responsibility, he may be, by all accounts, victorious in specific areas, but such prosperity is in appearance only.[129]

Recall the emotional laws of free will: A person who lives irresponsibly moves away from his purpose and potential and will de facto suffer from a range of emotional issues that will render him unable to enjoy what he has (whether achieved

127. Rambam, *Hilchos Teshuvah* 2:2.

128. Ibid., 3:1.

129. See Job 15:20–35. See Chapter 14, "Agents of Adversity" for an explanation as to why he may achieve success in this world.

through natural efforts or granted through unalterable decrees). A Heavenly blessing of long life to the depressed person becomes a self-imposed curse. The same is true for riches that are used to indulge in self-destructive vices or the loving family of one embroiled in self-promoted strife.

Being unable to appreciate the good is one thing, but, as we learned in an earlier chapter, such a person cannot easily endure any difficulties. Without perspective, his coping mechanism is disabled and it just feels as if the universe is relentless, heaping upon him trouble after trouble.

Compounding the consequences is that he is disposed to taking improper actions toward others and becoming a negative influence, causing them to sin, thus spreading viral-like consequences for which he is ultimately accountable.

Although our given *mazal* would not have permitted us to be used as a *kli* to cause damage or death to another, should we descend into absolute nature, not only are we not protected from others, but others may not be protected from us. We can cause injury to others regardless of how such an accident will affect our fate—because we have abandoned it. God may also position us as an ill-fated messenger (again, for our ultimate, though pitiful, good), forever altering our life, while ensuring the destiny of another.

Naturally, this is a two-sided proposition. To the extent that we are fulfilling our spiritual task, our lives are richly fulfilling and pleasurable. Our enhanced perspective further allows us to appreciate the good and to put the challenges into their proper context. As we rise above our nature, all of life's experiences become tailor-made for our good and direct growth—*direct* being the key word. As we move still higher, we are supervised with Divine providence and protected from unnecessary incidents and accidents—*unnecessary* being the key word. We live in a more beautiful world, objectively and subjectively, with the most treasured incentive yet to come, awaiting us in *Olam Haba*.

Metaphorically speaking, consider *mazal* to be a paved road, rather than a dirt road or no road at all. Although *mazal* makes it easier for us to get to our destination, a person can still choose to drive in the opposite direction. Even so, when all is said and done, the road of life is difficult—paved or not—and it's supposed to be, because there is no reward for a *mitzvah* in this world.[130] "Today is to perform; tomorrow is for reward."[131]

NOTES

130. *Kiddushin* 39.
131. *Eruvin* 22a, *Avodah Zarah* 50a.

Rashi explains that in this world, the fruit (reward) and the tree (*mitzvah*) are separate, and so *mitzvos* have no taste (relatively speaking, no comparison to the eternal pleasures) in this world.[132] While consequences are not intrinsic to the *mitzvah*, it should now be obvious that there is certainly cause and effect. Rabbi Avigdor Miller reminds us, "We have a right to hope for [pleasure] even in this world.... People who follow the dictates of the Torah are the ones who are happiest even in this world."[133]

NOTES

132. See Rashi on Genesis 2:25.
133. Rabbi Avigdor Miller, *On Emunah and Bitachon* (Judaica Press, 2012).

PART 7

FACETS
OF CHOICE

Although it is true that not all choices are created equal, the intention and expression of each choice also determine the full impact on our lives. Here we examine, through our finite lens, how God factors in the motivation behind our behavior, and how the decisions we make affect our lives and our world in ways we might never have expected.

23 | ANATOMY OF A CHOICE

A sin of any type damages our *neshamah*. However, if a person intends to act irresponsibly but does not follow through, he is not punished for the sin he thought to commit.[1] The Nefesh HaChaim writes,

> When it comes to sinning, the spirit of *tumah* [impurity] encircles the sinner only when he actually commits the sin, as opposed to when he does a *mitzvah*; the beneficial impact is made on the higher worlds the moment he intends on doing the *mitzvah*.[2]

There are limitations to this rule, for God disregards immoral intentions only if they remain completely in the realm of thought.[3] If any concrete steps are taken to actualize our intent, then we must seek forgiveness and atonement. Furthermore, if the sinner is a repeat offender (of the actual deed), then his future negative intentions will be counted as if he did them, even if he was unsuccessful in carrying them out this time. (Still, in such a case, the negative impact on his soul is not as severe as if he had actually carried out the sin.)

One exception where one's thoughts are as damaging as the behavior—regardless of whether or not he is a repeat offender—is the sin of *avodah zarah*

NOTES

1. *Kiddushin* 40a. The Gemara (*Yoma* 29a) explains that certain sinful thoughts are, in fact, considered even worse than actual sins.

2. Rabbi Chaim Volozhin, *Nefesh HaChaim*, 50–51.

3. The Rambam (*Hilchos Teshuvah*) discusses the complexities of sins that are entirely thought-based, such as: "Do not hate your brother in your heart" (Leviticus 19:17).

("idol worship"). Even the thought itself is a grave sin and carries with it its own consequences.[4]

THE RANKING

While we cannot say that one *mitzvah* is more vital to creation than another, God does give us a general hierarchy of commandments. As a rule, for example, transgressing a negative commandment is more severe than not fulfilling a positive commandment, and the sins of idolatry, adultery, and murder are indisputably more serious than other transgressions.[5] While there are innumerable nuances, exceptions, and combinations of motivation, the top three are presented to give the reader a sense of significance. We begin with the most damaging.

❑ One who leads others to sin. The gravest offense is when a person persuades others to engage in immoral activity. "Whoever leads the masses astray will not be able to repent for all the wrong he commits."[6] The iniquity that they commit through him is not erased, even if he himself repents.

❑ *Mumar l'hachis* ("a violator out of spite").[7] One who rejects a *mitzvah* out of arrogance, in order to anger God. Such a person transgresses openly and recklessly, without regard for collateral damage.

❑ *Mumar l'tayavon* ("one who rebels out of desire").[8] Such a person does not vigorously reject God's commandments but gives himself over to temptation, due to his inability to overcome his lusts or ego-leaning aspirations. This person wants to do what is proper, but he is unable to rise above his nature.

As we move all the way down the ladder of reckoning, we find that among the less severe is one who does wrong without knowing that it is wrong. This person

---

NOTES

4. The sin of *avodah zarah* consists of two parts: the act itself and the thoughts and satisfaction surrounding it. Each part of the sin is evaluated separately, and consequences are meted out separately (*Kiddushin* 40a). See *Tanya*, Ch. 1, for another important exception to this rule.

5. *Erchin* 15b. According to Jewish law, these sins are so serious that they are forbidden under any circumstances. The Sages also extrapolate a teaching that is too often overlooked—a fourth sin equal to these three combined: *lashon hara* ("slander"—lit., "evil tongue").

6. Ethics of the Fathers 5:18. The Rambam explains this to mean that it is more difficult, but not impossible, to repent. Elsewhere, we learn that one who causes the punishment of another is not accepted within the "inner circle" of God (lit., "cannot come close to"). See *Shabbos* 149b.

7. See *Avodah Zarah* 26b.

8. Ibid.

is a *tinok she'nishbah* ("a captured child"), a term that refers to a person who sins inadvertently as a result of having been raised without the necessary knowledge of proper conduct and one's Torah obligations.[9] Finally, and lowest on the scale of culpability, is an action through happenstance. When required, God makes us agents of negativity and we become the cause to bring about harm.[10]

ON THE PLUS SIDE

Our Sages teach us, "Greater is one who does something that he is commanded to do than one who does what he is not commanded to do."[11] A distinction, then, is drawn between doing what may be deemed proper, even pious, and an actual commandment or *mitzvah*. The former is praiseworthy, but we are not transgressing a commandment by failing to act.[12]

The very fact that a behavior is commanded by God makes it more vital to the relationship. With casual thought, we might assume that one who does something outside of what is required receives greater reward. This is not so. Any type of relationship will be healthier when we do what is asked of us rather than give only as we desire.[13] In regard to the spiritual plane, the Maharal writes,

> The fact that God commanded a certain *mitzvah* shows that it is part of His Divine order and one who is commanded and performs it enters God's realm. Conversely, if God did not obligate an individual in a *mitzvah*, this shows that

---

9. See *Shabbos* 68b.

10. Ibid., 32a. It cannot be assumed that this person is an instrument for negativity as a result of bad decisions and is thus used as a *kli*. The cause may be any one, or a combination, of the nine discussed reasons for life's challenges, or because God in His Infinite wisdom has chosen this person to be a *shaliach* ("emissary" or "messenger of God") for reasons that we cannot begin to fathom.

11. *Kiddushin* 31a. Tosafos explains this is so, because the ego desires to assert its independence, and complying with the will of God over our own will requires more effort. The name given to this is *reactance theory*, which is responsible for more stubborn thinking than anything else. It is so powerful that a person may do the opposite of what is asked of him if he feels that his freedom is being restricted. Astonishingly, this is true even if he actually *prefers* to do what is requested of him. See F. Rhodewalt and J. Davison, Jr., "Reactance and the Coronary-Prone Behavior Pattern: The Role of Self-Attribution in Response to Reduced Behavioral Freedom," *Journal of Personality and Social Psychology*, 44, (1983).

12. The Torah tells us that a person who desires to carry out his good deed but could not accomplish his objective still gets credit as if he had actually completed it (*Berachos* 6a). The Maharal, however, understands this to mean that we do not get all of the credit as if we had actually engaged in the behavior (*Shabbos* 63a, *Chiddushei Aggados Shabbos* 39).

13. "If someone is fulfilling all he must do and then goes beyond his obligations out of love, he is on a very high level and will be rewarded plentifully for his love and dedication" (*Mesillas Yesharim*, Ch. 18).

it is not part of the Divine order for that particular individual and doing that *mitzvah* will not uplift the person as much.[14]

THE MOTIVATION

One whose *mitzvos* are tainted with an ulterior motive does not capitalize on the opportunity for growth, nor does he elevate the world in the highest sense. On this, the Ramchal writes, "It is clear from their [the Sages] words that there are various kinds of "not for the sake of the *mitzvah* itself," the worst being the type in which one serves not for the purpose of Divine service at all, but in order to deceive people or to gain honor or wealth."[15]

Nonetheless, when we are the willful agents for good, we will be rewarded in kind.[16] Higher levels, of course, exist, and here too, gradations abound within two main categories: love and fear.[17]

One who does as he is commanded out of fear of God (and to gain reward and avoid negative consequences) is involved in Torah *lo lishma* ("not for the sake of Heaven"). The Talmud says what is known: "Greater is the one who acts out of love than one who acts out of fear." The Rambam writes,

A person should not say, "I will fulfill the *mitzvos* of the Torah, engrossing myself in its wisdom, to receive its blessings, thus meriting life in the World to Come." Nor should he say, "I will distance myself from all the sins the Torah cautions against, to be spared the curses listed in the Torah, so that my soul shall not be cut off from life in the World to Come."[18]

To perform God's will out of love is greater than to do it out of fear; to repent out of love is greater than to do so out of fear. It is important to note that even fear-based motivation is on a high level, because at least the position is rooted in reality: there is a Creator Who has set up a system of rewards and consequences.

NOTES

14. Maharal, *Chiddushei Aggados, Kiddushin* 31a.

15. *Mesillas Yesharim*, Ch. 16.

16. Rambam, *Hilchos Teshuvah*, Ch. 10.

17. The Gemara tells us that a person should perform *mitzvos* even for alternative reasons (*Pesachim* 7a). The expectation is that one will come to do what is right with pure motivation. The Rambam (*Hilchos Teshuvah*, 90) states that one should always engage in Torah, even *lo lishma* ("with ulterior motivation"), for out of *lo lishma* stems *lishma* ("for its own sake").

18. Rambam, *Hilchos Teshuvah* 10:1.

FOR HEAVEN'S SAKE

Our Sages write, "Be as careful with a light *mitzvah* as you are with a serious one. For you do not know the reward for the *mitzvos* ..."[19] In fact, the Torah barely discusses the reward that a person receives for each *mitzvah*, because even the smallest level of reward in *Olam Ḥaba* is unimaginable to us.[20] "One moment of pleasure in *Olam Haba* is greater than all the pleasure of *Olam Hazeh*."[21] It is therefore utterly impossible to communicate the qualitative nature of reward in the World to Come.

Knowing the reward of a *mitzvah* would also create a psychological hurdle that could stall our intrinsic motivation.[22] When clear compensation is introduced into the equation, we subconsciously disconnect from the innate satisfaction of the action, and our inner drive weakens. In the classic *Tom Sawyer*, the perennial observer of human behavior Mark Twain opines,

> There are wealthy gentlemen in England who drive four-horse passenger-coaches twenty or thirty miles on a daily line, in the summer, because the privilege costs them considerable money; but if they were offered wages for the service, that would turn it into work and then they would resign.

Nevertheless, there is a more profound reason God does not reveal our true reward: to allow us to act *l'sheim Shamayim* ("for the sake of Heaven"). For how can we expect to do a *mitzvah* out of love for God, if we can too easily calculate what is to be gained?

This brings into our discussion the oft-misunderstood concept of *mesirus nefesh* — which does not mean that we begrudgingly fulfill our obligation. *Mesirus nefesh* is where self-sacrifice (willful suffering — lit., "surrendering one's soul") gives us

---

19. Ethics of the Fathers 2:1.

20. Moreover, the intrinsic difficulty of a *mitzvah* is not the sole determinant of one's reward. "Someone whose nature is flawed, yet in spite of this constantly strives to overcome his evil inclination and to improve his ways, is rewarded by God according to the difficulty of the struggle" (Vilna Gaon, *Even Shleimah* 1:8).

21. Ethics of the Fathers 4:17.

22. Extrinsic rewards are often de-motivating. In one experiment, people who were paid $100 to perform a task rated it more difficult and stressful than did those being paid $25 to perform the same task under identical conditions, and as the size of the reward increases, one's desire and interest decline. See J. L. Freedman and S. C. Fraser, "Compliance without Pressure: The Foot-in-the-Door Technique," *Journal of Personality and Social Psychology* 4, no. 2 (1966): 195–202.

joy because our actions are pleasing—give pleasure, as we understand it, to God. Dwelling on the reward robs us of the opportunity to act purely *l'sheim Shamayim*— to eagerly give to God and not as a roundabout way to give to ourselves. We can only fully give of ourselves when we are focused on what we are giving and not on what we are receiving.

A similar dynamic exists in our everyday lives and relationships, where exerting ourselves to bring joy to a loved one gives us tremendous joy. We labor excitedly and enthusiastically—and so the giver becomes the receiver. This is evident from the verse "Jacob worked for seven years for Rachel, and they seemed to him as a few days, because of his love for her."[23] It was precisely these intense feelings that morphed the pain of the wait into an entirely different experience.

When we give out of love, we feel pleasure from what we give away—and we receive because we are part of the undiluted whole.[24] *Echad* ("one") and *ahavah* ("love") have the same *gematria* ("numerical value") of 13; love exists where we are able to shed our egos and connect with another and become one. Indeed, the root of *ahavah* is *hav*, which means "to give."[25] Even when our work is difficult, it can be transformed. In the moment of complete sacrifice, our pain has a purpose. It takes on new meaning, and meaning, as we know, brings pleasure.[26]

THE JOY OF GIVING

We can work tirelessly for someone we care about or for a cause we believe in and not feel the pain—on the contrary, we usually feel energized and invigorated. Similarly, to the degree that we love ourselves, we can invest in our long-term well-being (even beyond this world, toward *Olam Haba*) with maximum effort and enthusiasm.

To fulfill our obligations without joy quashes our spiritual vitality.[27] In much the same way that negative emotions—such as anxiety and anger—are tied into the ego, the more our behavior is an expression of our love, the more energy we

---

NOTES

23. Genesis 29:20.

24. In this way, we adopt the advice of the Sages to "love work" (See Ethics of the Fathers 1:10).

25. The *gematria* of *echad* and *ahavah* totals 26, which equals the *gematria* of the Tetragrammaton, God's sacred name.

26. Expressing our appreciation to God for the opportunity to do His will invigorates our motivation. In the words of C. S. Lewis: "We delight to praise what we enjoy because the praise not merely expresses but completes the enjoyment; it is its appointed consummation." (Clive Staples Lewis [1898–1963] known as C. S. Lewis, was a novelist, poet, and academic.)

27. Doing God's will, even without joy, is still a necessary and worthy endeavor, and our obligations do not cease simply because we do not yet connect with the pleasure of the *mitzvah*.

have, because those actions are an extension, an expression, of our *neshamah*—and derive from a source of limitless energy. One who lacks positive emotion needs to continually muster willpower because he labors under the incessant burden of woeful self-sacrifice.[28]

The Sages tell us, "The Divine Presence comes to rest upon a person only through his rejoicing in a *mitzvah*."[29] When we coat our actions with a layer of *simchah* ("joy"), we strengthen our love and bond to God's will. Rabbi Simcha Zissel Ziv writes,

> A strong desire within a person generates power, enhances thought processes, helps overcome laziness and propels him in the path of wisdom. For this reason, the Torah warned against not being happy, because lack of happiness is lack of strong desire; they are one and the same. And anything that enhances desire enhances success.[30]

In Chapter 11, "The Purpose of Free Will," we explained that the more we give, the more Godlike we become. Our similarity heightens our awareness of God, which then increases our love for Him. Yet qualitatively, acts of *mesirus nefesh* are in an entirely different category of giving, because God Himself is the addressee of our love.

The highest use of free will is to surrender it—each time out of love—and to give it back to God, with love. The Talmud teaches an important principle: "Whether one does more or whether one does less [he fulfills his obligation] as long as his intentions are directed toward God."[31] When we are filled with the awareness that we are performing His will, and our actions are not predicated on, or prompted by, any other cause, we arrive at the deepest level of *chesed*—almost.

While the pleasure we feel from doing God's will is not our motivation but a natural by-product, our giving is not complete, because it has a motivation. Namely, we desire to do His will. We noted earlier that: (1) *chesed* denotes an act of giving that has no prior cause; and (2) the act of creating oneself is the

---

28. "Because you did not serve the Lord, your God, amid gladness and goodness of heart, when everything was abundant" (Deuteronomy 28:47). This passage refers to the terrifying Chapter of Rebuke (*Tochachah*) that befalls a person who served God but without "gladness and goodness of heart."

29. *Shabbos* 30b.

30. Rabbi Simcha Zissel Ziv, *Chochmah U'Mussar*, Vol. 2, 224.

31. *Berachos* 5b and 17a.

quintessential purpose of *chesed*. These two criteria do not appear to be met until we appreciate that giving—*mesirus nefesh*—ultimately melds into our character and then into our nature. At this point, we give without cause because it is our essence, an essence that we helped create. It is now that we have unearthed the deepest level of *chesed*.

24 THE BATTLEFIELD

We have learned that a genuine free will choice has wide-ranging ramifications and affects us in unimaginable ways—in this world and into the next. Yet precisely what constitutes a free will choice and how it differentiates itself from other types of choices has not been fully clarified, for one reason.

We will not know until the next world what was within the scope of our *madraigah*, what lay just beyond our reach, and what was to be forever out of reach. Consequently, we must move through this world as if all of our decisions are free will–based. In fact, to some extent, all of our decisions do affect our free will, even though the choices themselves are not within the zone of free will. We will detail how this works once we flesh out the dynamics thus far.

THE NUCLEUS OF FREE WILL

We have observed that a free will choice exists only where there is an objective truth—a moral component in the decision-making process. Therefore, even the ego and the body can battle it out without entering the free will arena. Take, for instance, the example of a person who wants to get up early to rob a bank but is too sleepy to get out of bed; he hits the snooze button and goes back to sleep. Or our sleepy would-be thief can experience an intra-body conflict: as well as being sleepy, he is hungry. Does he opt to get out of bed for a snack or fall back to sleep? Even so, in the full absence of the soul's contribution to the equation, there is no basis to consider the process as a free will struggle, because there is no moral component—even though there are moral consequences to this course of action. Moreover, we cannot automatically assume that we are exercising free will, even when we stop to reflect on the virtue of our decision. There are times when our behavior is kept in check because we want to avoid the pangs of conscience. In effect, we have two competing desires. One is simply stronger than the other. The process is not dissimilar to an animal that decides to back away from its prey out of fear. Eating lunch and avoiding becoming lunch are opposing instincts—the animal merely chooses to stay alive.

What disqualifies the above as a free will choice is not necessarily our motive for doing what is right, but rather that one desire suppresses the other. As we explained, a free will choice exists when our awareness of the truth (via the soul) is in close balance with an opposing desire (ego or bodily-based)—giving us both the clarity and the capacity to act or not to act; and nothing other than our will tilts the equation.

This is not to say, however, that the decision is capricious, picked out of thin air. When we drill beneath the surface of free will, we find our essence, the root of the soul. Our deepest will emanates from this quintessential self.

Parenthetically, we recall from Chapter 16, "Reconfiguring Mazal—Part 1," that the means to change our will is through prayer. A burning desire that surges forth from us to God redefines the true "I," which then redirects our free will in a more perfect, God-aligned direction. Consequently, even if we do not care to pray, it

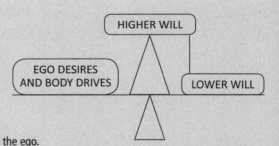

To fully appreciate the inner workings of human will, we need to know that there are two levels of *ratzon* ("will"): upper and lower. The upper will is a reflection of our quintessential selves, a level of the soul that is above intelligence and supersedes logic. Our upper will directs our conscious and rational soul, where the lower will is found. For instance, we do an act of kindness for someone because of the following:

1. We don't want him upset with us. This decision comes from the ego.

2. To avoid feeling guilt. This decision comes from the lower will.

3. Because it is the right thing to do. This decision comes from the higher will.

At the level in reason 3, we are not motivated by the pleasure of the act. But as a result of our actions, we experience the inherent pleasure found in truth—doing what is right, which in this example is an act of kindness. Here, will and pleasure are one because will is united with truth, and connection to truth is the highest sublime pleasure. The lower will, by contrast, is drawn to truth because we desire pleasure or want to avoid pain. It is an "I"-based desire as opposed to a truth-based or core soul desire. Put another way, the higher will finds pleasure in what is right, while the lower will does what is right to find pleasure. The more refined the soul is, the more leverage we have over our lower will, and in turn, the more leverage our lower will has over the forces of the body and ego.

Ego-based pleasures are entirely counterfeit, like salt water to the thirsty soul. The body is not good or bad. Physicality can be elevated and infused with holiness and, as such, genuine pleasure. But abuse and indulgence, of course, lead ultimately to pain and suffering.

behooves us to pray to care, because only the active use of our conscious will can shift the winds of free will.

We must also be aware of what is often misunderstood. While free will is rooted in our essence and regulated by our *madraigah*, a flash of perspective temporarily enhances our ability to see clearly and so it becomes easier, in that moment, to make a choice that would be otherwise beyond our grasp or *madraigah*. For example, after witnessing a serious accident, what happens? We do not feel like joking. We are quiet. We feel almost detached, separated from the illusion of the world. Our ego is temporarily blinded, and we have the ability to take an emotional/spiritual leap forward.[32]

Alas, the process works in reverse. In a burst of intense rage or despair, completely disconnected from reality, we can behave in a way that is far removed from what is good and true—and, as a result, fall fast and hard.

For this reason *bechirah* may be in effect even when opposing options hold disproportionate appeal. "Balance" does not mean that competing forces lie in fixed symmetry, poised on opposite sides of a proverbial razor thin line. The free will applecart is easily turned upside down—for better or worse—due to the force that we identify with in the moment—be it the body, ego, or soul. In this space, our *madraigah* momentarily oscillates, and as long as we are not overwhelmed by a competing desire, the choice can be legitimately labeled as free will.

A BATTLE WITHIN A BATTLE

Our *madraigah* is initially established by three main factors that are tethered to our *tikkun*: (a) the inherent refinement of the soul or how sensitized it is to truth, (b) the refinement of our emotional and cognitive faculties, and (c) our childhood environment and experiences, which shape our attitudes, beliefs, and values and orient our sense of right and wrong. These factors set the tone for our experiences *in* life, but they are largely irrelevant to our experience *of* life. As we learned, self-earned clarity via freedom of choice is the basis for life satisfaction.

Naturally, we are each on our own *madraigah*, so a choice for one person is not necessarily a choice for another. Using a spatial metaphor of a battlefield to portray a fluid process, Rabbi Dessler explains that the line shifts constantly. When two armies are locked in battle, fighting takes place only at the battlefront. Territory

32. See Lieberman, *Real Power.*

behind the lines of one army is under that army's control. If one side gains a victory at the front and forces the enemy back, the position—our *madraigah*—on the battlefield will have changed, and choices that had previously triggered an inner struggle—in the line of battle—have moved.[33]

POSITIVE ASPECTS OF OUR NATURE		
ZONE C+		
ZONE B+	POSITIVE BEHAVIORS	
ZONE A	MADRAIGAH	
ZONE B-	NEGATIVE BEHAVIORS	
ZONE C-		
NEGATIVE ASPECTS OF OUR NATURE		

Beyond Zone C, the behavior is not even on our radar as a matter of right or wrong. It is who we are. For better or worse, we do not wrestle with "Should I or shouldn't I?" At such times, we do not take pride because we have not injured an innocent person, nor are we consumed with guilt for not donating both of our kidneys to a complete stranger. Regarding Zone C+, if we are completely drawn to what is right that we are not tempted to deviate from the truth, then free will is not actuated. As we noted in Chapter 6, this is, in essence, wisdom—a clarity of reality so acute that it penetrates our hearts and rouses our souls (moral clarity is really an extension of intellectual clarity because intellect is the "seat of the soul" and drives our awareness—and interest in the truth—in the first place).

For this reason, Rabbi Dessler explains that a person who lives his life in this zone could be doing many *mitzvos* and learning much Torah and still not be encountering *bechirah*, because his conduct is only the result of his nature and nurture, without any self-generated growth.[34] Namely, he never conquered any aspect of his core self.

A behavior in Zone B does not qualify as a free will choice, but the soul is alert to the options and opportunities before us. By way of our conscience, our

33. Rabbi Eliyahu Dessler, *Strive for Truth*, Vol. 1, 111–120.
34. Ibid., 111–116.

behavior affects our emotional and physical well-being—even though we are not necessarily responsible.[35]

Regarding Zone B-, the question is: "How is it fair that we suffer for a choice that is not really a choice? It's how God made me!" The logic is sound but incomplete. In this zone, the pain associated with the behavior is meant to spur us on, to nudge us forward, so that our attitude and behavior move closer to the battlefront, where free will *does* exist. All of life's struggles are directed toward these epic battles.

While this may seem to be an extraordinary endeavor to bring a single decision over the free will threshold, the residual impact of one free will choice is life altering because it forks our entire reality into a new direction. Via something akin to the *butterfly effect* (see Chapter 20, "The Nature of Chance"), even if we were never to make another free will choice, we are now moving in a completely different world. Our thought process includes variables that we helped bring into existence because of that single previous free will choice, and whenever these additional elements tip our future decisions into a more responsible zone, we benefit in this world and are rewarded in the next.

Even when a person no longer struggles, and a positive behavior has become routine, there exists a qualitative component that does contain an element of free will. In Zone B+, we still choose the how—such as with proper intention and zeal. A layer of free will, then, still exists even when the behavior itself is no longer a question. The bandwidth of choice includes these micro-choices ("the how"), aspects that subtly affect our conduct, even though the larger behavior or macro-choice remains the same. Over time, the slightest changes can create the necessary momentum to integrate the behavior deeper into our personality.

Of course, the pleasure associated with the behavior encourages us to progress further into Zone B+ with the ultimate goal, to make what is right, natural: Zone C+. At which point we do good because that is who we are—like God.

PAYING INTEREST ON AN OLD DEBT

Rabbi Dessler explains that when a person has accustomed himself to a certain manner such that an improper behavior in question moves above his *madraigah,*

---

35. When good or bad is done through us—without any intent—it can still affect our emotional state. For example, a person who finds out that his car was stolen and then used to run down and kill an innocent person would feel awful. Why? It was not his doing, and yet, because it was his car that was used, he cannot help but feel somewhat responsible, even though intellectually he knows that he bears no blame. Conversely, if we were to learn that our car was parked in such a way that it prevented the injury or death of another, we would feel joyous, almost proud. It was "our" car, after all.

he will be liable for every indulgence, even though it no longer presents itself to him as a live choice. This is because it was he himself who was the cause of his dulled sensibilities.[36] In contrast, when a positive behavior moves below our *madraigah*, we receive a reward every time we perform a correlated *mitzvah*, even if it is seemingly part of our identity—because our free will efforts helped make it a part of our being.

Analogously, one who deposits money in the bank earns interest, even though he is no longer working for the money. In a manner of speaking, the money is now working for him. An area where we fall short to the point of habituation is similar to one who borrows money and must repay interest on the debt, even though the original sum borrowed has been long spent. The interest accumulated does not go away.

We must explain, however, what we mean when we say that a behavior has been absorbed into our nature. Not only is our *madraigah* fluid and often in flux, even when it presents itself as fixed, but the underlying tension is also integral to the calculation. For instance, we cannot simply observe the bar at a "5" and declare that if one rises to a "6," then he gets credit, and if one falls to a "4," then he will be punished. When a person swims against the tide—where both internal conflict (doubts and fears) and external forces (unforeseen circumstances and pressures) pull on his emotional resources, the ability to maintain his level (or even slip slightly) may be to his credit because the outward behavior does not reveal the true nature of the struggle. Where effort is required and energy expended to maintain the status quo, it cannot be said that we fully own the *middah*. It is not considered one's nature unless it would be a tremendous struggle to oppose it.[37]

UNINTENDED CONSEQUENCES

The above explains the consequences of an ingrained behavior, but what is the spiritual liability that stems from a single previous poor choice? Without proper consideration, a person decides to move to a town that proves harmful to his

36. See Rabbi Eliyahu Dessler, *Strive for Truth*, Vol. 2, 57–58.

37. Not only does our *madraigah* rise and fall, but our spiritual level should not be considered a straight horizontal line. It is more analogous to a line graph of a volatile stock. And, like a stock, there is a trend that shows our overall health, even though at each point—the highs and the lows—different *middos* are at different points. As a function of our *tikkun*, our struggles are not uniform. Moreover, a *middah* itself may not express itself evenly in all areas because some people and circumstances can be more trying than others.

spiritual growth. For how long will he bear responsibility? For example, if he asks a *shailah* ("a question of Torah law") of the local Rav and is given an incorrect answer, is he held accountable to the same degree as if he had purposely disregarded this *halachah*? Or perhaps he walks into his local kosher restaurant, with the full desire and intent to eat kosher food, but unbeknownst to him, this establishment does not have a reliable *hechsher* ("kosher certification").

The person's intentions were pure, but each situation produced a precarious outcome that stemmed from the first choice—which was careless. The Ramchal explains, "God judges each individual deed according to its circumstances, whether it is accidental or purposeful, whether it is forced or willful."[38]

The spiritual harm of a sin committed without premeditation is not as great as one committed knowingly and with foreknowledge. Hence, we are not liable to the same degree as one who consciously, willingly disregards what is proper. However, a lack of knowledge does not necessarily shield us against the consequence. We can leave home without an umbrella because we chose not to take one or because the forecaster wrongly predicted a sunny day. Either way, we will get wet.

We must be abundantly clear. A person who does not have *bechirah* is not held accountable for making a poor choice—because it was not truly a choice.[39] However, all of our experiences—positive and negative, even those that we did not seek out or choose—still etch themselves into our soul. Such instances are not a consequence of choice but of *mazal/tikkun*.[40]

Questions of culpability aside, proper *teshuvah* is the only way to halt the rolling impact from a self-instilled negative behavior and from future choices that originated from a previous poor choice. It is an escape hatch from even the harshest of consequences at the level of willful intent.[41] As noted, *teshuvah* is a process whereby

---

NOTES

38. Ramchal, *The Way of God*, 115 (3:4).

39. "The great [Jewish] philosophers established *bechirah* as the cornerstone for the whole Torah ... from this resulted a common misperception among the masses; that all people actively choose their every act and every decision. This is a grievous error" (Rabbi Shlomo Wolbe, *Alei Shur*, Vol. 1, 156). Indeed, we learn that someone who does not have control over his actions is not responsible for them (*Bava Kamma* 28b).

40. This assumes no contributory negligence. One's liability within a given situation is not easily discerned because the decision-making flowchart includes fluctuating junctures of awareness, effort, and intent. Therefore, even when we are a passive participant, the fact that God put us into a situation to serve as a conduit for negativity may necessitate us to do *teshuvah*.

41. Rambam (*Hilchos Teshuvah* 1:3) writes, "*Teshuvah* atones for all sins. Even a person who was wicked his whole life and repented in his final moments will not be reminded of any aspect of his wickedness." Later, he qualifies that *teshuvah* is not effective for someone who willfully sins with the intention of doing *teshuvah* afterward.

we ask God to forgive us for our transgressions, and we resolve never to commit them again. It is a proactive actualization of free will that resets the bar and wipes clean the spiritual slate.

The Rambam writes, "One should see the world, and see himself as a scale with an equal balance of good and evil. When he does one good deed, the scale is tipped to the good—he and the world are saved. When he does one evil deed, the scale is tipped to the bad—he and the world are destroyed."[42] When we stop to consider the consequences that stem from the smallest of choices, it fast becomes clear that there are no small choices.

NOTES

42. *Hilchos Teshuvah* 3:4.

25 | UNPERCEIVED INFLUENCES

Our choices do not have closed-ended consequences but go to the core of our being, our eternity, and pervade all of creation—impacting on areas beyond our assumption and straining our finite sense of fairness. We have discussed at length how our choices define the entirety of our lives and our after-life. The following highlights five additional areas of impact; before we turn our attention to strategies for rising above our nature, we must know what is at stake.[43]

FUTURE GENERATIONS

Adam was warned that should he disobey God's single commandment not to eat from the Tree of Knowledge, he would die and introduce the concept of death to all future generations. If Adam had resisted the temptation, the *Sifra* states, "[All] future generations would not have known of death." In the following parable, Rabbi Meir quotes, "The fathers eat unripe sour grapes and the teeth of the children are stumped."[44]

A fox was about to be devoured by a hungry lion. The shrewd fox said to his attacker, "How satisfied can you be by eating me? Come, let me show you a

---

NOTES

43. If we are married, our actions influence our spouse, and our spouse's actions influence us. Spiritually speaking, each spouse has "half of a soul," and together they complete each other. The Talmud states that God created Adam with two faces: one in each direction. God split them in two, and one half became Eve. The union of man and woman in marriage returns them to their unified state.

44. Quoted from the summary of a *shiur* given by Rabbi Avraham Kahn, based on Ezekiel 18:2. Retrieved: http://www.shemayisrael.com/parsha/kahn/archives/achrei66.htm.

person you can eat, who will surely satisfy your hunger." When the lion saw the person, it said, "I am afraid that this pious person will bring me down with his prayers." The fox put the lion at ease and said to him, "Don't worry. Nothing will happen to you or to your son. Your misdeed will not be punished until the time of your grandson. Now go and satisfy your hunger. It will be a long time before your grandson is born." The lion accepted the fox's reasoning and jumped to attack the innocent person. As it moved in for the kill, it fell into a deep pit that had been hidden by branches. As the fox caught up with the captured lion and looked down into the pit, the lion said, "Didn't you assure me that the punishment would not affect me and my son, but would only affect my grandson?" Answered the fox, "That's true. You were not captured because of your misdeed but because of the misdeed of your grandfather." The lion protested and said, "That's not fair. The fathers eat the unripe sour grapes and the teeth of the children are stumped." The fox smiled and said, "Why did you not consider that before?"[45]

The Torah states that the punishment of a sin committed today can be meted out to a person's children for up to four generations.[46] The following oft-quoted words of God bear repeating, for we do not always recall the full passage in the Torah. "I have put before you life and death, a blessing and a curse: so choose life for yourselves *and for your descendants.*"[47] Our choices today alter the future for our children and their children's children.[48] The Talmud reminds us that a wise person will think ahead:

One day as Choni Hama'agel ("the circle-drawer") was traveling along the road, he saw a man planting a carob tree. Choni asked him, "How long will

45. *Sanhedrin* 38b.

46. "He remembers the sins of the fathers upon children and grandchildren to the third and fourth generation" (Exodus 34:7). Our fate is not sealed because of the actions of previous generations. This sentence is in effect only as long as the children continue to pursue the sinful ways of the father (*Berachos* 7a).

47. Deuteronomy 30:19. The Thirteen Attributes of God include Preserver of Kindness for thousands of generations, which our Rabbis tell us speaks to how our good deeds bring benefit to our offspring well into the future.

48. In a spiritual sense, we pass down to our children our chief characteristics—those that are part of our essential being. Our children thus carry out our spiritual tasks (Rabbi Eliyahu Dessler, *Strive for Truth*, Vol. 5, 59). If we do not correct a *middah* that is within our level of *bechirah*, we put our children at a spiritual disadvantage, for they will find it easier to repeat our mistakes than to rise above them.

it take for this tree to bear fruit?" "Seventy years," the man replied. "Do you think that you will live another 70 years?" Choni asked. The man replied, "I found carob trees growing when I was born, because my forefathers planted them for me, so I, too, plant them for my children."[49]

PREVIOUS GENERATIONS

We are all connected—not just to one another but beyond the bounds of time: the past directing the present, and the present, the past. Since time and space are only a function of the physical world, not only do past generations affect us, but we affect them.

The Gemara teaches that the "inheritor is an heir as the legs of his father," that is, the actions of one's biological offspring and spiritual heirs in this world affect his soul's position in *Gan Eden*.[50] For instance, if we learned a lesson from a person prior to his death, and we are now able to do a *mitzvah* because of it, then his spiritual status is elevated. Hence, on Yom Kippur even the souls in Heaven are judged. The impact of what these souls did while alive brings about changes in their Heavenly status each year.

Chillingly so, the opposite is true. "Because of the sins of the living, the dead are disinterred from their graves."[51] The impact again reverberates back to us. The Gemara states, "It is also testified that the faithful departed pray for those who are alive, without which the latter would be unable to subsist for a single day or even part of a day."[52] Our actions in this world alter the spiritual status of those in the next world, which then puts those souls into a better or worse position to assist us in this world.[53]

NOTES

49. *Ta'anis* 23a.

50. *Eruvin* 70b. Rabbi Tzvi Hebel (*The Neshuma Should Have an Aliyah* [Judaica Press, 2009]) brings down other sources to explain that all of a child's meritorious deeds automatically benefit the departed parent, irrespective of the parent's contribution; unlike a spiritual heir who benefits the deceased through conduct that extends from the departed person's teachings. This process is not limited to these types of relationships—parent or mentor—and extend to anyone. The difference, authorities note, is that the one performing a deed (in merit of the deceased) has to stipulate this intent before fulfilling the *mitzvah* (ibid., 35).

51. *Yevamos* 63b.

52. *Shabbos* 89b.

53. The *Kaddish* that is said just before *Aleinu* (or right after *Aleinu* for Ashkenazim) is considered the "orphan's" *Kaddish*, and if the son recites it during the eleven months of his parents' passing, as well as on the anniversary of their passing (*Yahrzeit*) every year, it: (1) saves one's parents from judgment in *Gehinnom* and (2) helps raise them into *Gan Eden* and elevate their souls from one level to the next.

CHAPTER TWENTY-FIVE

THE UPPER WORLDS

God created a system wherein the waves of free will in *Olam Hazeh* crash on the shores of the spiritual realm. The *Zohar* reveals that when man accomplishes God's will below, he causes a parallel rectification above.[54] The Nefesh HaChaim explains,

> When God created man, He empowered him to control countless forces and worlds…. With his good deeds, words, and thoughts, man sustains and gives energy to countless forces and holy celestial worlds, increasing their holiness and light….[55] All of man's actions, words, and thoughts cause a reaction in the upper worlds, that is, in the root of all things.[56]

We are judged for both our positive and negative influences on others in this world and also for the impact of our actions on the higher worlds and powers.[57] The Nefesh HaChaim continues,

> [P]lease have pity and compassion on the precious higher worlds, which were created with wisdom, understanding, and knowledge. Be careful not to impair any of them through an improper thought. The upper worlds do not recover until the forces of pollution are eliminated when the sinners receive the punishment they deserve. When that happens, the worlds are healed from the blight and regain their original purity. Another way for the worlds to regain their wholeness is through the sincere *teshuvah* of the sinner.[58]

He adds that the amount of damage that is caused above is dependent upon the soul of the sinner. A small misdeed of a person with a lofty soul causes great damage in heaven, while a serious offence by an inferior soul makes less of an impact above.[59]

NOTES

54. *Zohar* I:35a.
55. Rabbi Chaim Volozhin, *Nefesh HaChaim* 1:3, 31.
56. Ibid., 1:4, trans., 34.
57. Rabbi Chaim Volozhin, *Nefesh HaChaim* 1:6.
58. Ibid., 50–51, 55,
59. Ibid., 85.

FINAL REDEMPTION

Because all Jewish souls are inexorably linked, the errors of the righteous may lead to the willful violations of the wicked. The converse is also true. The willful violations of the wicked may lead to the errors of the righteous.[60] Irrespective of our spiritual station, "All Jews are responsible for each other."[61] Our actions purify or pollute the collective pool and increase or decrease the traction of those around us and all over.[62]

When we fulfill our potential, we seal a crack in the vessel of humanity (and, to a larger extent, in creation itself) and allow for all of mankind to more easily align with its purpose. In doing so, we hasten the coming of the Messiah. God thus made the rectification and elevation of all creation dependent on the Jewish people.

ALL FOR GOD

According to the *Midrash*: "When Israel does the will of God, they add strength to the power Above, as it is written, 'Give strength to God.'"[63] But when Israel fails to do the will of God, they weaken the strength Above, so to speak, as it is written, "You have weakened the Rock that begot you."[64] Likewise, the *Zohar* states, "When the Jewish people are virtuous, they give God strength, as the verse says, 'Give strength to God.' How can one give strength to God? By performing good deeds."[65]

The Nefesh HaChaim tempers this statement by explaining that "… all the deeds of man, be they good or bad, do not affect [His essence]."[66] Nonetheless, it is a mind-bending notion that God arranged for our actions to touch Him, as it were.

NOTES

60. See *Sfas Emes, Nitzavim 5635.*

61. *Shavuos* 39a. The Torah states "… and a man will stumble over his brother" (Leviticus 26:37). Rashi (ibid.) explains that we can err in our own behavior because of the behavior of others. Most of us would be quite stunned if we fully comprehended how our seemingly minor deeds and misdeeds can become a life-and-death influence in the lives of so many people, especially those closest to us.

62. "A person should always imagine that the fate of the whole world depends upon his actions" (*Zohar* II: 42a).

63. *Midrash Rabbah Eichah* 1:33. Stated by R. Azariyah in the name of R. Yehudah, son of R. Simon (on Psalms 60:14).

64. Deuteronomy 32:18.

65. *Zohar*, 2:32b, quoted by *Nefesh HaChaim* (*Shaar* 1:3).

66. Ibid.

And this revelation is all the more marvelous in that this actuality exists because it is God's will.

Imagine two people in a small rowboat, as one begins to drill a hole into the hull beneath his seat. The other screams, "What are you doing?" and the man answers, "What are you getting so upset about? I'm making a hole under my seat, not yours."[67] We are never justified in believing that we alone bear the consequence of our sins. With supreme arrogance, we may think, *I know this is wrong, and I will probably be angry with myself afterward, but I will worry about that later.* With truncated foresight, we decide that the instant indulgence is worth the tradeoff. How wrong we are.

67. *Vayikra Rabbah* 4:6.

DREAMS INTO ACTION

We have learned that actualizing our free will consists of intertwining objectives. Moving closer toward God through character refinement (and resonating God-consciousness) is at the crux of our personal mandate, but we each have a unique purpose and destiny to fulfill, and we must actualize our God-given talents to perfect ourselves and, in the process, our world.

This section offers a range of Torah insights and psychological strategies to help us reach our goals, achieve mastery over ourselves, and enjoy success in our relationships. Many of the ideas presented in each of the following chapters can be applied to our overall strategy in other areas. Furthermore, success in one area also helps us maximize efficacy in others.

- ❏ Methods that we use to regulate our behavior in specific instances can be applied to help us stick to our long-term goals, and the benefits are mutual. The less frustrated we are with the direction of our lives, the easier it is to exercise self-control and to invest in our long-term well-being.

- ❏ The healthier our relationships, the healthier we are, and the more able we are to move responsibly toward our life's purpose without the need for ego-oriented approval or surrendering to the blinding fix of immediate gratification. Likewise, the happier we are with the direction and pace of our lives, the less frustrated we are with ourselves, and the more tolerant and patient we become with others.

- ❏ The more we give in to ourselves, the more we demand that the world accommodate us, setting the stage for unhealthy interactions and relationships. Equally true, the healthier our relationships, the better we feel about ourselves and our lives. And as such, we are less inclined toward anger-fueled self-destructive behaviors.

We cannot ignore an important aspect of our life and expect to be whole. Attempting to rid oneself of a negative character trait, for example, while disregarding a faltering relationship is akin to sticking wings on a caterpillar and expecting it to fly. In order to grow in a balanced, healthy direction, we must integrate critical aspects of our lives and character.

PART 8

REANIMATING FREE WILL

The God-given gift of free will bestowed on all human beings is secondary to the Divine gift of awareness. As the Talmud says, "A greater sign of our preciousness to God is that He told us we were created in His image."[1] This means that human beings have the freedom to forge their own reality, destiny, and eternity. But no amount of willpower can motivate us when we have abandoned genuine pleasure in favor of a comfortable numbness. In the following chapters, we will learn how to push off the dead weight of apathy and reignite our passion for life.

1. Ethics of the Fathers 3:18.

26 | SELF-IMPOSED CHAINS

"I am the Lord, Your God, Who took you out of the land of Egypt from being slaves."[2] God's introduction to the Jewish people at Sinai does not testify that He is the Creator of Heaven and Earth. The Sages explain that such a declaration might lead us to a grievous error—to think of God as Creator, but not as Sustainer, and mistakenly conclude that He does not desire a relationship with us or directly supervise the affairs of man.[3]

This prelude also cements the significance of bondage. Our relationship with God hinges on free will, and our enslavement, while an impingement to its expression, was also a prerequisite to its manifestation. The Jewish people needed the concept of oppression to become embedded in their spiritual DNA in order to fully comprehend and appreciate the beauty of freedom.[4]

ONWARD

The foundation of free will and our formation as a nation require that we be a free people, with the ability to serve God. "God said to Moses, 'Go to Pharaoh, and

---

NOTES

2. See Exodus 20:2.

3. *Kuzari* 1:1, 2. The message is, "You matter to Me." The entire mechanism of self-esteem is geared toward creating ourselves into a vessel that is capable of recognizing and receiving God's love for us. Only then do we live with the perpetual awareness that He takes an intimate and personal interest in every aspect of our lives, and that everything we do matters deeply to Him. Absent self-esteem we cannot help but feel that we do not matter to God, that we are irrelevant. Nothing is more painful or false.

4. See the discussion in Chapter 37, "A World of Contrasts." There are other explanations for the Egyptian exile regarding the *klipos* ("impure barriers" or "shells"). See Arizal, *Shaar Hagilgulim.*

say to him, "Thus says God: 'Let My people go so that they may serve Me.'"[5] After the tenth plague, Pharaoh yielded, and the Jews took leave. But let us back up a bit. When Moses readied the Jewish people, there wasn't necessarily a stampede for the exit.

Eighty percent of the Jews died in Egypt, because they chose to stay.[6] They suffered from a slave mentality. And even for those who did take leave, God took precautions. When Pharaoh finally relented to let the Jewish people leave, God led them on a longer, circuitous route out of Egypt, toward Israel. He knew that if He took them out on the direct course, they might be inclined to retreat—and God said, "Perhaps the people will have a change of heart if they encounter war, and they will return to Egypt."[7]

As much as the Jews suffered brutally at the hands of the Egyptians, life in Egypt offered an existence free of decision and self-doubt—the antithesis of free will. The allure of a life free from the burden of thinking was too tempting. Plunging to the forty-ninth level of impurity, the spark of the Jewish *neshamah* was all but extinguished.

Even for those whose trust in God propelled them toward the Promised Land, their choice for freedom was stained with regret. When the Jewish people faced a challenge in the Wilderness, they voiced their distress—ten times. "With ten trials did our ancestors test the Holy One, blessed be He, in the desert, as it is said, 'They have tested Me these ten times and did not hearken to My voice.'"[8] The Talmud chronicles the episodes, which include complaining for water at *Marah*, the sin of the Golden Calf, and leaving over *manna*.[9] Other incidents, in the people's own words:

❑ If only we had died by the hand of God in Egypt when we sat by the pot of meat, when we ate our fill of bread. For you have brought us out into this wilderness to kill the entire congregation by famine.[10]

❑ [T]he children of Israel also wept again, and said, Who shall give us flesh to eat? We remember the fish that we ate in Egypt for nothing; the cucumbers, and the melons, and the leeks, and the onions, and the garlic, but

5. Exodus 7:26.
6. Rashi, Exodus 13:18, from *Mechilta* and *Tanchumah* 1.
7. Exodus 13:17.
8. Ethics of the Fathers 5:6.
9. *Erchin* 15a; Exodus 15:24; ibid., 32:1–6; ibid., 16:20.
10. Ibid., 16:3.

now our soul is dried away; there is nothing at all save this *manna* to look forward to.[11]

❏ If only we had perished as our brethren perished before God! Why have you brought the congregation of God to this wilderness to die, we and our animals? And why did you have to have us ascend from Egypt to bring us to this evil place? Not a place of seed or fig or grape, or pomegranate, and there is no water to drink!"[12]

Their faculty to deal with uncertainty had been crushed, because their capacity to trust in God was handicapped, despite the succession of open miracles. The reason is, as we stated, that trust is a function of choice, and with the muscle of free will atrophied, the Jewish people struggled to trust in God, no matter how evident His Presence. Hence, the desire for familiarity displaced their innate yearning for self-expression and a relationship with God.[13]

When a climactic scene unfolds where the Jewish people are trapped between the Egyptian army and the Red Sea, they do not turn to fight—this generation was accustomed to the yoke of domination.[14] Without belief in themselves and without trust in God, how could the Israelites stand up for themselves, much less to their former oppressors?[15]

The desert offers no natural means of protection or sustenance. The years of wandering helped eradicate the slave mentality and allowed the Jewish people to reconnect with their humanity and reestablish their capacity to trust in God.[16] Yet this was not enough. The collective Jewish soul needed to shed itself of this crippling mindset. Without mentioning the years that had elapsed, the *parashah*

NOTES

11. Numbers 11:4–6.

12. Ibid., 14:22, 20:35.

13. King David writes, "I am Your servant, son of Your handmaid" (Psalms 116). Rashi explains this to mean that the slave who is born to a handmaid is considerably more submissive than one who was born free. Similarly, when zoos receive animals that have been bred in captivity, their instinct for freedom is largely absent. Their desire to escape pales in contrast to their born-in-the-wild counterparts, because when an animal is moved from its natural, free environment into captivity, most never settle down, even after many years.

14. *Gittin* 13a.

15. Ibn Ezra, Exodus 14:13.

16. The purpose of *mitzvos* is so that the People of Israel will put their trust in God (*Peirush HaGra*, Proverbs 22:19). As we explained, responsible action—i.e. doing God's will—is the surest and swiftest path to transform faith into trust. This entire section offers insights and strategies geared toward this primary objective.

("Torah portion") picks up approximately forty years later. The entire generation of Egyptian-born former slaves—anyone over the age of twenty—had died.[17]

THE IGNORANCE OF APATHY

The surest path to misery is to continue to put up with all of the things that do not work in our lives but are not quite bad enough to make us feel that we must change them. Human beings can become used to almost anything. That's both the good news and the bad.

> When the funeral procession accompanying Jacob's coffin arrived at his final resting place at *Meoras HaMachpelah*, Esau confronted the mourners, contesting the title to Jacob's plot.[18] The tribes argued that Esau had sold it to Jacob. A debate ensued in which each side claimed the right to this holy site. When Esau asked for Jacob's deed, certifying his purchase of the burial plot, the tribes decided to send Naftali back to Egypt to retrieve the deed. In the meantime, they would wait. Chushim ben Dan, who was deaf, was present during this dialogue and inquired regarding the cause of the delay. When he was told what was occurring, he exclaimed, "My grandfather will be compelled to lie in degradation until the deed is brought!" He immediately arose and struck Esau.[19] Why was it that Chushim was the only one who was so reactive? Was he more concerned about Jacob's honor than Jacob's own sons, who seemed to be negotiating with Esau?
>
> Rabbi Chaim Shmuelevitz, *z"l*, suggests that the Talmud implies the answer when it refers to Chushim's deafness. The brothers had slowly been drawn into a discussion with Esau. While the debate continued back and forth, they thought they were besting Esau. Although this might have been true, during this time period Jacob's body lay in shame. They did not realize what they were doing. Human nature causes one to adapt slowly to a given situation. The brothers' dispute with Esau dulled their sensitivity to their father's shame. Chushim was not a part of the debate because of his impairment.... His senses were not dulled... .

NOTES

17. "In this desert will fall all the bodies of all who were counted from the age of twenty and above ..." (Numbers 14:29). The only two adults who did not die were Joshua and Caleb.

18. Lit., "cave of the double tombs"—where Abraham and Sarah, Isaac and Leah were already buried.

19. *Sotah* 13a.

Rabbi Shmuelevitz explains that human beings are endowed with the gift of *histaglus*, "adaptability." We adapt to the conditions in which we are placed. We have seen people who had been exposed to the unspeakable horrors of the concentration camps, who experienced the most cruel and heinous torture, survive to rebuild their lives. As circumstances worsened, they found the ability to adapt to the situation, the courage and fortitude to go on. Indeed, one who has undergone a tragedy or has survived a horrifying incident will certainly be changed by the experience. The power to continue, to go on and start over again, is due to adaptability. This wonderful gift can, at times, be less beneficial. Like every attribute endowed to us by the Almighty, it all depends upon how we use it.[20]

The opposite of love is not hate. It is apathy. A relationship in which one does not have any feelings toward another is patently less viable than a relationship in which one, at times, becomes angry with the other. Similarly, a person who proclaims to hate his life is more in touch with his emotions than one who does not care to consider why he is alive.

The pleasure-pain mechanism is what keeps us moving in the right direction, but just as a person lying unconscious under anesthesia cannot feel the pain of a cut, it also fails us when we are numb to the pain. When neither inspiration nor desperation is sufficient to rouse our soul from its slumber, we are stuck in the torturous twilight of indifference.

The option of moving forward or living our lives in the relative comfort of the familiar and predictable exists for all of us—to escape from our own Egypt or to move to the Promised Land. Yet when we have accustomed ourselves to existing, rather than living, the real tragedy is not that we have lost our way, but that we do not care that there is a way.

NOTES

20. Rabbi A. Leib Scheinbaum of the Hebrew Academy of Cleveland. Quoted in *Peninim*, 54–55.

27 | A COMMITTED LIFE

We combat the slave mentality by constantly moving forward. "For a man is born to strive and toil."[21] Scattered or misdirected ambition, however, is as debilitating as inactivity itself. Movement is useless without a plan—we need a place to go and a path to get there.

We must not live our lives like the person who shoots an arrow at the side of a barn and then draws a circle around it after it embeds itself.[22] Caring little for what he aims for, he proudly convinces himself and the world that he is a success. Many people are indeed reluctant to plan their lives. They may have a vague idea of what they want to accomplish, yet they shy away from preparing for their future. This is true for two interlacing reasons.

What exactly does planning for the future involve? At the most elementary level, we must acknowledge where we are and then decide where we want to go. The challenge here exists as much in the first half of this process as in the second. Yes, the future is filled with many unknowns and uncertainties, but the hidden fear lies in not wanting to see where we are. We are afraid to examine our lives too closely and to come face-to-face with who we have become and with what has become of our finest intentions. The reluctance to set goals and plan for the future relieves us of the burden of self-examination. Yet another deep-seated incentive exists.

NOTES

21. Job 5:7.

22. The Dubno *Maggid* ("story teller") would create a story around the lesson and used this analogy to explain why his stories always hit home. (Born in Zateil, Lithuania in 1740, Rabbi Yaakov Krantz was a gifted orator and scholar who was known throughout Europe as the Dubno *Maggid*)

In order to move forward, we need to weigh different possibilities and directions that our lives can take. To do this, we must know what we are living for. In a word: commit. But we would rather get lost in the grand scheme of daydreaming than be forced to make choices that will forever define who we are.[23] We half-believe that if we never make a choice, we won't have to live with failure or regret.[24]

So rather than move our lives forward, we leave ourselves open to every possibility, with the misplaced hope that the perfect opportunity will present itself. But research shows what is self-evident: "Freedom of choice is a two-edged sword, for just on the other side of liberation sits chaos and paralysis."[25] Too many choices often overwhelm a person into inaction, and the more options available, the greater the likelihood that we will come to regret our decision, whatever it is.[26] The paradox of decision making shows us that when presented with an abundance of choices, people are most inclined to:[27]

- Opt for the same old choice as a way to avoid facing unlimited options.
- Rely on filters (i.e., society), rather than on themselves.
- Become more passive in their lives.

MORE CHOICE, LESS ACTION

In Numbers, the Torah discusses the five remarkably righteous daughters of Tzelafchad, who had not yet married. Their father died, leaving no son to inherit his portion of the Land. In the absence of a male heir, it was expected that the inheritance would fall to their uncle. The daughters of Tzelafchad did not want to lose the opportunity to take possession of a portion of the Holy Land, and they approached Moses for help. Their request was simple: Since there were no sons, let their father's portion fall to them, his daughters. Moses, in turn, posed the question to God, who

23. The English word *decide* has the same etymological root as *homicide*: the Latin word *cadre*, meaning "to cut down" or "to kill."

24. Functional magnetic resonance imaging (fMRI) has been used to show that the amygdala is stimulated when we make decisions couched in uncertainty. Our brain is literally afraid of being wrong. See Benedetto De Martino et al., "Frames, Biases, and Rational Decision-Making in the Human Brain," *Science 313* (2006): 684–687.

25. Barry Schwartz, "Self-Determination: The Tyranny of Freedom," *American Psychologist 55*, no. 1 (2000): 79–88.

26. "Can There Ever Be Too Many Flowers Blooming?" Barry Schwartz, to appear in W. Ivey and S. J. Tepper, eds., *Engaging Art: The Next Great Transformation of America's Cultural Life* (New York: Routledge).

27. Ibid.

commanded that the daughters of Tzelafchad be given their father's inheritance in the Land.[28] Later, God stipulated that the daughters marry within their father's tribe so that their inheritance would stay within the tribe and not eventually become part of another tribe's portion by virtue of their husbands' lineage.

Notably, as soon as these women were instructed to choose husbands from a specific tribe, the Torah tells us they were married.[29] Though there are surely other explanations, we can understand the connection in light of our discussion here.[30] God helped them fulfill their destiny by narrowing their choices to men from one out of twelve tribes.

In all areas of life, excessive choice is debilitating, not liberating. One such study found that the more choices that were offered for a retirement fund, the less likely employees were to enroll in any program at all.[31] What makes this all the more shocking is that by not participating, employees passed up as much as $5,000 a year in matching contributions from the employer.

In another revealing and perhaps relatable experiment, researchers set up a tasting table in a neighborhood supermarket. When a selection of jams was on display, shoppers showed more interest in the larger assortment (twenty-four varieties) than in the smaller assortment (six varieties). In fact, customers stopped 60 percent of the time for the wider selection, compared with just 40 percent for the smaller selection. Yet when it came time to actually make a purchase, of the consumers who stopped at the table with twenty-four varieties, only 3 percent bought jam. At the booth with a more limited selection, however, 30 percent made a purchase. In short, those presented with the smaller assortment were *ten times more likely* to take positive action.[32]

For effective decision making, Nobel Laureate Herb Simon, Ph.D., suggests the "satisfying" option: the first choice that fits our preference, as opposed to exhaustively scanning all options until finding the perfect or "maximizing" one.[33]

NOTES

28. Numbers 27:1–7.

29. Ibid., 36.

30. No doubt, in their righteousness, these women now felt an obligation to marry as quickly as possible to men of their tribe so as to fulfill the Divine command and perpetuate the inheritance of their tribe.

31. Sheena S. Iyengar, Gur Huberman, and Wei Jiang, "How Much Choice Is Too Much? Contributions to 401(k) Retirement Plans," *Pension Design and Structure: New Lessons from Behavioral Finance*. Specifically, for every 50 new funds added to the selection, the participation rate fell by 10 percent.

32. Ilan Brat, Ellen Byron, and Ann Zimmerman, "Retailers Cut Back on Variety, Once the Spice of Marketing," *Wall Street Journal* (2009).

33. In another industry, when Proctor & Gamble reduced the number of versions of its Head and Shoulders shampoo from 26 to 15, sales increased by 10 percent. See Sheena S. Iyengar and Mark R. Lepper, "When Choice Is Demotivating: Can One Desire Too Much of a Good Thing?" *Journal of Personality and Social Psychology* 79, no. 6 (2000): 995–1006.

Expressed differently: the energy expended on deciding between two or more viable options is always greater than any marginal advantage gained.

Perfection—the henchman of procrastination—is demoralizing. "God looked upon all that He made and, behold, it was very good."[34] Not perfect.[35] We should not let an irrational quest for perfection keep us from making decisions and moving ahead.[36] And lest we think otherwise, neither intelligence nor talent will shield us against the crime of procrastination. On the contrary, *Cheshbon HaNefesh* states:

> There are those people who are intelligent and quick in a certain field of learning or in a certain craft but who lack the ideas or experience in other fields. When faced with a situation they ponder, then they consult and think again interminably. This man's virtue is, in truth, his problem. Because he is intelligent, he can always find endless rationales that support different courses of action. Because of his inability to reach a final decision, opportunity passes him by or he delays an enterprise with his hesitation for days or years thus sacrificing their benefits for long periods of time.[37]

It is human nature to want to keep our options open, and as the ego looms larger, the fear of commitment is magnified—it cannot be wrong or feel restricted. It is always looking for a way out should we want to escape.[38] Yet this back door is built out of fear (aka a lack of *bitachon*), and indecision does not free us, it keeps us trapped—and it bends us into someone who is afraid to live. Because nothing will become of our lives—NOTHING—until we decide what we want out of life, and there's no enduring success without a profound commitment to that decision. Without recognition of this truth, we cannot go any further.

---

34. Genesis 1:31.

35. God is perfect, but we are not Him. Let us strive for excellence, not perfection.

36. "A good plan today is better than a perfect plan tomorrow" (George S. Patton, 1885–1945, American army general during World War II).

37. Rabbi Menachem Mendel Levin, *Cheshbon HaNefesh*, 137.

38. In *Think and Grow Rich*, Napoleon Hill recounts the true story of the Spanish general Hernan Cortez whose forces were outnumbered ten to one. "A long while ago, a great warrior faced a situation which made it necessary for him to make a decision which insured his success on the battlefield. He was about to send his armies against a powerful foe, whose men outnumbered his own. He loaded his soldiers into boats, sailed to the enemy's country, unloaded soldiers and equipment, then gave the order to burn the ships that had carried them. Addressing the men before the first battle, he said, 'You see the boats going up in smoke. That means that we cannot leave these shores unless we win! We now have no choice—we win—or we perish!' They won. Every person who wins in any undertaking must be willing to burn his ships and cut all sources of retreat. Only by so doing can one be sure of maintaining that state of mind known as a burning desire to win, essential to success" (New York: Fawcett Books, 1987).

A DEFINITIVE PURPOSE

The seminal work on personal development, *Mesillas Yesharim,* opens with the necessity for clarity of purpose: "The foundation of devotion and the root of service [to God] is to clarify ... what one's obligation is in the world, and what he must place his focus and direction on, all the days of his life."

We must know what we are living for, because to achieve anything worthwhile we are required to spend much of our time devoted to the arduous and the mundane. Only a strong sense of purpose can give our lives the meaning and inherent pleasure we need to endure the relentless onslaught of obstacles and distractions. Victory will not come in one sweeping burst of inspiration. Yes, there will be special, near-magical moments, but they are generated and sustained by our own will. It is a self-defeating myth that we should feel consistently inspired, and if we are not, then we are doing something wrong.

Emotion is a powerful ally, and we should mine the meaning within our goal, to infuse significance into our actions, but this does not mean that we should expect to enjoy every inch of our pursuit or that we should cease to press on when a span turns dull or tedious. The professional works when he does not feel like it, while the amateur dabbles only when he feels inspired. Success comes to those who are prepared to do the things that other people don't like to do and aren't willing to do.

Research supports what life experience confirms: commitment—an unswerving dedication—is the most powerful source of motivation and can lead us to persist, even in the face of daunting opposition.[39] In a former United States president's oft-quoted words:

Nothing in the world can take the place of persistence. Talent will not; nothing is more common than unsuccessful men with talent. Genius will not; unrewarded genius is almost a proverb. Education will not; the world is full of educated derelicts. Persistence and determination are [invincible].[40]

A great *mussar* teacher writes, "If a person has a commitment, all his senses

NOTES

39. John P. Meyer, Thomas E. Becker, and Christian Vandenberghe, "Employee Commitment and Motivation: A Conceptual Analysis and Integrative Model," *Journal of Applied Psychology* 89, no. 6 (2004): 991–1007
40. John Calvin Coolidge, Jr. (1872–1933), thirtieth president of the United States.

act as instruments which bring out his thoughts and commitments to action ... [because] after a commitment, nothing more is needed."[41]

A WILL TO WIN

Although our success is ultimately up to God, the amount of human effort required to bring us that success seems to be quantifiable. The 10,000 Hour Rule is based on a groundbreaking study that divided students into three groups based on skill (amateur, impressive, and expert or concert-level) at the Berlin Academy of Music and then correlated achievement with hours of practice.

Among these three groups, the difference came down to a single factor: the amount of time spent in solitary practice by the age of twenty. The amateur group averaged 4,000 hours of practice; the impressive musicians put in approximately 6,000 hours; and the group with concert-level potential totaled around 10,000 hours of practice.[42]

This rule was then applied to research in other disciplines—from the arts to the sciences—and indisputable results were found to support the hypothesis. A renowned neurologist and cognitive psychologist explains the findings:

> In study after study, of composers, basketball players, fiction writers, ice skaters, concert pianists, chess players, master criminals, and what have you, this number comes up again and again. Of course it doesn't address why some people get more out of their practice sessions than others do. But no one has yet found a case in which true world-class expertise was accomplished in less time. It seems that it takes the brain this long to assimilate all that it needs to know to achieve true mastery.[43]

More than thirty years of research into achievement have been culled and compiled in the *Cambridge Handbook of Expertise and Expert Performance*. Having examined a range of individuals from Mozart to Einstein, the conclusion is that genius is built, not born.

NOTES

41. Rabbi Dovid Bleicher, *Divrei Binah U'Mussar*, 141–142.

42. K. A. Ericsson and N. Charness, "Expert Performance: Its Structure and Acquisition," *American Psychologist*, 49 (1994): 725–747.

43. Daniel Levitin, *Foundations of Cognitive Psychology: Core Readings* (Massachusetts: M.I.T. Press, 2002).

[I]t isn't magic, and it isn't born. It happens because some critical things line up so that a person of good intelligence can put in the sustained, focused effort it takes to achieve extraordinary mastery…. . These people don't necessarily have an especially high IQ, but they almost always have very supportive environments, and they almost always have important mentors. And the one thing they always have is this incredible investment of effort.[44]

There will never be a perfect time for anything, and if we wait for all of the stars to align before taking action, we are, in blunt language, waiting for our death.[45] Great people across a wide range of fields and industries are identified by a pattern of conscience and conviction: they decide, commit, and persist. They know who they are and what they want, and they simply do not give up. Modern research is easily summed up with centuries-old wisdom of the Talmud: "In the way one is determined to go, he will be led."[46]

NOTES

44. Anders Ericsson, editor, *The Cambridge Handbook of Expertise and Expert Performance* (Cambridge, U.K.: Cambridge University Press, 2006).

45. "Generally, one must be content to rely on logic [and then] make his determination based on probability" Rabbi Menachem Mendel Levin, *Cheshbon HaNefesh*, 137.

46. *Makkos* 10b. More precisely translated: "The way a person wants to be led—they lead him." In his commentary on the Talmud (ibid.), Rabbi Shmuel Eliezer Eidels asks, who are "they" who lead the person where he wants to go? He answers that these are angels that a person creates with his own thoughts, speech, and actions. We might add that "they" also implies a supportive environment, as well as the forces of the world that become mobilized to help one to achieve success, should his desire be sufficient enough to garner it.

28 | FREEDOM FROM FEAR

Moving forward with a definitive purpose not only fortifies our resolve, but it enables a powerful emotional catalyst for responsible action: a relevance to death. The Baal HaTanya writes that a person has two ways open to him: the way of life (which is to see God via a reduction of ego), and the way of death.[47] Ethics of the Fathers resounds with themes that foster humility through the lens of mortality, such as: "Be exceedingly humble in spirit, for the anticipated end of mortal man is worms;"[48] and "Know from whence you come—from a putrid drop; and where you are going—to a place of dust, worms, and maggots."[49]

Death was a consequence of the first sin, because, in part, reflecting on death can purge us of the *yetzer hara*.[50] The prospect of death is not a punishment. It is the antidote to rid oneself of the ego.[51] The well-known *mussar sefer Chovos HaLevavos* states, "Our days are like pages in a book; inscribe in them that which you want to be remembered for."[52] It is imperative to note the passage of time in order to utilize it properly. Without the deadline of mortality, how much value would we place on life? [53]

NOTES

47. See Deuteronomy 30.

48. Ethics of the Fathers 4:4.

49. Ibid., 3:1.

50. Man had to be banished from the Garden of Eden so that he would not be able to eat from the Tree of Life and live forever (Rambam, *Sforno* on Genesis 2:8–17).

51. "Torah, prayer, and the contemplation of death will help you in your struggle against the Evil Inclination" (*Berachos* 5a).

52. *Chovos HaLevavos, Shaar Cheshbon HaNefesh, Cheshbon* 11.

53. Parkinson's law states, "Work expands to fill the time available." In other words, if something is allotted a week, it will take a week to accomplish it; if we have two weeks, it will take two weeks. Regardless of

Death prompts us to concede that we are not owners of anything other than our choices. While we all meet the same fate of the physicality, our eternal fate is uniquely our own—and of our own choosing. It is precisely death, and the reflection on this fragile and finite existence, that punctures the illusion of this world and deflates the ego.[54] It becomes clear, then, why the wisest of men counsels, "It is better to go to the house of mourning than to go to a house of feasting," because, he adds, "[death] is the end of all man, and the living should take it to heart."[55]

DATE WITH DESTINY

Although we should not preoccupy ourselves with thoughts of our demise, the only way to live with intellectual honesty is to acknowledge that one day it is an absolute certainty that the sun will rise and set without us in this world. If we find this depressing, rather than motivating, we are not alone. In fact, we belong to the overwhelming majority.

The approaching threat of death, as a positive motivator, has zero traction in the lives of those who have no life. On the contrary, thinking of death does not make us want to live, but, rather, we welcome our final exit, so that we can permanently escape. A Harvard professor and president of Preventive Medicine and Research Institute writes,

> People may initially get interested in changing their lifestyle because they are hurting, but what sustains these changes is not fear of dying, it's joy of living.... What often lies at the root of self-destructive behaviors is loneliness, depression, and isolation. The number-one epidemic in America is not obesity or heart disease, it is depression. The most commonly prescribed prescription drugs last year were antidepressants. We assume that people want to live longer, but telling somebody that they are going to live longer if they just quit smoking and change their diet is not very motivating if they are depressed, stressed out, and unhappy.[56]

NOTES

whether we have short Friday afternoons in the winter or long ones in the summer, people are always ready for Shabbos at sunset. Somehow, there's always "just enough time." The feeling that we have an entire lifetime to accomplish a goal can impede forward movement. With such an attitude, it is difficult to accomplish our goals, because there is no sense of necessity, much less urgency.

54. When the Talmud teaches that we should repent one day before our death, it is to encourage us to recognize the possibility that today may be our last day alive (Ethics of the Fathers 2:15, *Shabbos* 153a).

55. Ecclesiastes 7:2.

56. Dr. Dean Ornish, distinguished clinical professor of medicine at Harvard University and known for his lifestyle-driven approach to the control of coronary artery disease (CAD) and other chronic diseases.

We are trying to kill ourselves because we want to die, and being informed that our actions will hasten our death only incentivizes self-destructive behavior. In the Torah, God warns the Jewish nation: "Be careful that you do not go up the mountain or touch the edge of it; whoever touches the mountain shall surely die. Do not set your hand upon it, for he shall surely be stoned."[57]

First, God states the consequence for touching the mountain. Then, He issues a command against doing so, because the first warning was inconsequential to most of the people—they were willing to die in order to become closer to God. When death is not a deterrent, it does not stop behavior. Certainly, *Klal Yisrael* did not suffer from low self-esteem, but this event points to the above-mentioned truism that fear of death, when death is desired, only incites our insolence in regard to life.

THE KEY TO SELF-CONTROL

A well-lived life gives meaning to death, and in exchange, death gives renewed meaning to life.[58] Therefore, the constructive power behind the contemplation of death is only in force where there is an appreciation for life itself and for our lives in particular. Otherwise, there is no real shift in our mindset; we just slide along the spectrum to another shade of gray. Coupons have an expiration date to force action, but if we are not interested in the products, then the coupons are just as useless to us before the date as they are after the date.

Having purpose in our lives gives us perspective on life *and* on death. This is crucial because a pivotal factor in the ability to exercise self-control lies in how we manage our fears. *Terror management theory* explains that we deal with the fear of death and the resultant anxiety in one of two ways. When we are living a full and robust life, we tend to embrace our values and beliefs—that which brings meaning into our lives. This is known as the *mortality salience hypothesis* and promotes self-regulation. Alternatively, if we already have one foot in the Land of Escapism, we are inclined to pacify our fears by further indulging ourselves—in anything from chocolate to extravagant vacations—this is known as the *anxiety-buffer hypothesis*.[59]

NOTES

57. Exodus 19:12–13.

58. To foster the trait of humility, Ibn Pakudah (*Duties of the Heart*) instructs us to walk the mind slowly and methodically along the full journey of life, from the fertilization of the egg all the way through death and decay. This process is the very essence of perspective.

59. When we face a choice between small rewards and larger but delayed rewards, emotional distress causes us to shift toward the former. See Walter Mischel, Ebbe B. Ebbesen, and Antonette Raskoff Zeiss, "Cognitive and Attentional Mechanisms in Delay of Gratification," *Journal of Personality and Social Psychology* 21 (1972): 204–218.

For this reason, stories on the news relating to disaster and death make viewers respond more positively to advertisements for status products, such as luxury cars and designer clothes.[60]

THE END OF DAYS

The prophet Daniel was told by God that in the end of days, information would be accessed at a dizzying pace: "Daniel, close up the words and seal the book until the time of the end; [when] many will run to and fro, and knowledge will increase."[61]

The end is growing near. Buckminster Fuller's "Knowledge Doubling Curve" shows that up until the 1900s, accumulated knowledge doubled every century. By the end of World War II, it was every 25 years. Estimates today suggest that knowledge doubles every 1 to 1.5 years, and the startling forecast by IBM is that in the next couple of years, it will double every 11 hours.[62] Statistics like these highlight the phenomenon of an information explosion and its consequence—information overload.[63]

The intensity of the times is further magnified by a world that is becoming chaotic and turbulent at a violent speed. This period in history and the coming events are ominously summed up by Rabbi Ezriel Tauber:

> The state of suffering is a necessary condition of the coming Redemption. As the Maharal explains, a seed starts to sprout after rotting and breaking down totally. The "sprouting of the Geulah [Redemption] comes through the total breakdown of the whole world." The Footsteps of the Messiah are not merely indicators; they are necessary conditions. When the frameworks of security, economy, society, and morality fall apart, when all falsehood collapses ... the light of Mashiach begins to sprout.[64]

NOTES

60. See Naomi Mandel and S. J. Heine, "Terror Management and Marketing: He Who Dies with the Most Toys Wins," *Advances in Consumer Research* 26 (1999): 527–532. After the terrorist attacks on September 11, 2001, there was a reported increase in overeating, drinking, and smoking. Equally notable was an increase in time spent with family and friends, as well as religious attendance. See Brooks Barnes and Andrea Petersen, "As Priorities Change, Some Question Why They Eschew the Fat," *Wall Street Journal* October 5, 2001, A1, A4.

61. Daniel 12:4.

62. Buckminster R. Fuller, *Critical Path* (New York: St Martin's Press, 1981), 273.

63. Bernhard Jungwirth and Bertram C. Bruce, "Information Overload: Threat or Opportunity?" *Journal of Adolescent & Adult Literacy* 45, no. 5 (2002).

64. Rabbi Ezriel Tauber, *Thoughts for a Jewish Heart* (New Jersey: Israel Bookshop Publications, 2006), 231.

The veneer of civility and decency has been all but stripped away. Unspeakable atrocities fueled by global unrest and rampant depravity have put humanity into a moral tailspin.

As life becomes increasingly unpredictable and bizarre, a shrinking world compounds the prospect for emotional distress. *Terror management* is no longer confined to our own lives and experiences, but, thanks again to the technological age, our brains are forced to process a confounding degree of calamities and catastrophes—all of which become logged and lodged as a clear and present danger.

For example, in a given year, statisticians put the odds of being struck by lightning at 1,000,000 to 1. In a typical small town of 1,500 people, we can expect that there will be one such occurrence every 600 years—making it largely the stuff of folklore, at any time in human history up until the early eighteenth century. Yet with instant access to the world-at-large—photos, streaming video, live eyewitness accounts—our community now has 7 billion residents, and the likelihood of this occurrence is 7,000 times a day. As we become aware of the myriad mishaps and misfortunes happening all around us, our brains react as if we are experiencing them in real time.

The dry cough that turns out to be lung cancer for 1 in 3.5 million nonsmokers becomes the source of incessant worry because we "know so many people" who had such a diagnosis. We turn away from the statistically improbable in favor of fear, because of all the people "in our lives" whose stomach aches turned out to be a tumor, who were randomly attacked in broad daylight, or who became paralyzed from a mosquito bite. An endless onslaught of unpredictable and unavoidable horrors awaits us at every turn. It should not surprise us that neurotic has become the new normal.

THE EVIDENCE

The consequences speak for themselves. An estimated 67 percent of the population is overweight or obese. The result: cardiovascular disease, cancer, and diabetes account for nearly two of every three deaths in the United States alone.

Sales of antidepressant, antianxiety, and mood-stabilizing drugs are at record levels, and today, one in four Americans suffers from mental illness (and Americans are ten times as likely to suffer from depression today as they were in the 1960s, even accounting for increased awareness and diagnosis).[65]

NOTES

65. A 2011 study by the Centers for Disease Control and Prevention reports that the use of antidepressants has soared 400 percent since 1988. It is the fastest-growing class of prescribed drugs, second only to

The coping mechanism for physical pain has been similarly compromised. In the United States, the number of prescriptions written for major painkillers rose 90 percent between 2003 and 2011.[66] In total, according to the *New England Journal of Medicine*, 116 million Americans suffer with persistent pain—an astounding 1 out of 3 people.[67] Our tolerance for reality—much less pain of any sort—is crippled.

Technology further pulls on the threads of our mental fibers because when we are most vulnerable—in a moment of intense anger or stress—the press of a button or a tap of a finger lowers the drawbridge to our castle of dignity. In years past, we had time to calm ourselves, to regain our senses. Not anymore. In an instant, the enemy—any number of vices—is within our walls, eating away at our self-respect. As we will discuss in the upcoming chapters, the first rule to curb temptation is to keep what is good for us close and simple to obtain and what is counterproductive out of the way and hard to reach. The reverse has become the insisted-on standard.

The world is no longer available to offer a reality check, to set us straight by ridicule or scorn. More and more, our desires are being repackaged as inalienable rights, with society quick to decry anything that impinges on its unchecked freedom.

This crystallizes the ever-critical necessity to know exactly what we are living for. Nothing other than a clearly defined purpose with meaningful growth will insulate us from the quakes of insanity that would otherwise shake our emotional foundation and force us to flee from reality.

Our lives are filled with ever-vivid reminders of the true nature of this world. Snapped into heightened awareness, so much seems irrelevant—at least in the moment. Our soul wants to attach to the one true reality—where we find permanence

cholesterol medications. According to the World Health Organization, mental disorders are the leading cause of disability in the United States and Canada. See *The Global Burden of Disease: 2004 Update*, Table A2: Geneva, Switzerland: WHO, 2008.

66. According to an Associated Press analysis of statistics from the Drug Enforcement Administration. Narcotic analgesics are prescribed for the relief of severe pain and are the third most prescribed class of medication, according to a national audit conducted by IMS Health, a medical data provider.

67. Philip A. Pizzo, M.D., and Noreen M. Clark, Ph.D., "Alleviating Suffering 101—Pain Relief in the United States," *New England Journal of Medicine 2012* 366 (2012): 197–199. Persistent pain is defined as pain that lasts for weeks to years.

and meaning.[68] Yet without a sense of purpose in our lives, we do not have the anchor of *bitachon*, and without this unspoken assurance, we shift to a mentality of "Let us eat and drink; for tomorrow we shall die."[69] The Achilles heel of self-control—the foundational trigger of all susceptibility—lies in how we manage our fears. The antidote to fear is *bitachon*, trust in God.

68. We read Ecclesiastes on Succos to remind us of the finite nature of this world, lest we get caught up in frivolity and unrestrained merriment.

69. Isaiah 22:12.

PART 9

BEYOND ANGER

We can try to eliminate a host of negative *middos* by pulling on their branches—or we can uproot the *yetzer hara* by choking off corrupted desires. Any vestige of desire that lives on germinates into fear. We will discuss how and why this happens, as well as learn tools to inhibit the fear-based mechanism. Should fear not be contained, we must deal with each situation as it arises, and to this end we will explain how to neutralize our anger (the ego's response to fear) followed by strategies to maintain self-control in all areas of our lives.

29 | EXTINGUISHING THE FLAMES

Just as ice, water, and steam are composed of identical molecules, in varying states, desire, fear, and anger are all emotional states that undermine *bitachon* at different points. Fear stimulates our anger, but the birthplace of fear is desire.

Fear exists because of a corresponding desire. We fear death, for instance, only because we desire life, and we desire death only because we fear life. *Terror management*, then, is more accurately defined as desire management. When the ego-based desires cease, there is nothing left to manage. To rid ourselves of fear (and the resultant anger) and achieve absolute *bitachon*, we must free ourselves of these desires.[1] We cannot become angry or disappointed when we desire only to do God's will. Nothing can disturb the peace of mind of a person who has no expectation or sense of entitlement.

A story is told of two wrongly convicted Jewish men sitting in a jail cell. When the time came for the evening prayers, they could not pray because there was odorous waste in their cell—and Torah law forbids praying in proximity to it. Surprisingly, the attitude of the two men was not the same. One of the prisoners remained cheerful, while the other was glum. The unhappy fellow turned to his grinning cellmate and asked, "Why are you so happy? We can't pray as we are supposed to!" His wise friend countered, "The same God that tells me to pray also tells me that I should not pray now. Either way, I am fulfilling His

---

NOTES

1. King Solomon writes, "Desire fulfilled is a tree of life" (Proverbs 13:12); and, "Desire accomplished is sweet to the soul" (ibid., 13:19). He speaks of meaningful desires that are soul-oriented, rather than passing whims and shallow fantasies—which are self-destructive and damaging. "Die before you die" means that a person must kill such desires in order to be free (Rabbeinu Yonah, *Sha'arei Teshuvah* 2:17).

will." His friend smiled wide, and they both began to dance around the cell with great joy.[2]

Sometimes we question why God does not smooth the path of one who is dedicated to doing His will—but we do not always know what His will is. We must accept that irrespective of one's obvious potential and God-given talents and strength, and regardless of one's sincerest effort and intentions, God in His infinite wisdom may decree that such a person suffer an accident, for instance—to be a shining example of *bitachon* and bring His glory into the world through an unbroken spirit that radiates from a broken body. We do not know—and when we presume to know, we set ourselves up for a fall, because the very presumption itself is built on the foundation of arrogance. Then, when our peace of mind is disturbed or our direction thwarted, we cannot help but become frustrated and resentful.

Unshakable tranquility—the seal of *bitachon*—will come when we accept that all of the sacrifices we are prepared to make for God may not be among those that He requires of us most.

IN GOD WE TRUST

When we know a matter to be insignificant, emotional investment is kept to a minimum, but when we become angry, the insignificant too quickly intensifies in importance. What was once—and will soon again be—trivial grows to consume us.

When wisdom reigns, we no longer grapple with concepts of "good and evil." We do not have to force ourselves to remain calm when, for instance, faced with insult, because there is no pain. One does not have to fight against that which he knows to be irrelevant, much less false. Then, regardless of how low our state and how large our ego becomes in the heat of the moment, we will not succumb to anger. What does not exist cannot grow.

All of our ordeals are designed by God to form us into a vessel that holds our humility, and each situation is a test of our *bitachon*.[3] If we fail to rise above our nature, we miss the opportunity to see God—to emulate God—and there will be

---

NOTES

2. Fundamentally, *bitachon* is the acceptance of what is, and the recognition that what happens in our lives comes to us by God, out of His love for us. Until we are able to acknowledge the Source of our plight, our attempt to alleviate it or to move through it is made more difficult.

3. A lack of *bitachon* compounds our troubles. The Rambam explains that if a person thinks that his difficulties are due to happenstance, then God will add to the wrath of that happenstance (*Hilchos Ta'aniyos* 1:3).

little meaning in the battles we have weathered or will endure, because they are all designed with this primary intent.

The Sages say, "There is nothing left for an angry person except his anger."[4] It is not simply that our anger is futile. If we become angry, our struggles are suffered too often in vain. Imagine a person working day and night to save up for a sports car, and then he uses the vehicle for storage. No one could say that he is not getting some use from it, but all would agree that he is foolish, because he does not come close to maximizing his efforts and rewarding himself for his work.

BRINGING FEAR TO LIFE

To become upset is not only an emotional-spiritual failing, but it is also counterproductive because it impairs our ability to optimize the outcome. Trust is not simply accepting the assumed outcome, but it can actually change the outcome. The Chazon Ish explains,

> When a person encounters an event that according to the ways of the world involves a personal danger to him, it is natural to fear the ways of the world … when one exercises self-restraint at such a difficult time and internalizes the truth that this is not a chance misfortune but rather it is all from God … then one has achieved the trait of trust in God…. [H]e who trusts in God will examine his deeds and turn to repentance, prayer, and charity, in order to remove the evil decree from himself.[5]

A lack of trust in God is not only impairing, but it unwittingly helps bring into reality the very thing that we most fear. Worry is a misuse of the imagination, with potentially dire consequences. The eighteenth-century Kabbalist Rabbi David Solomon Eibenschutz writes,

> "What I feared will come upon me" (Job 3:24). Fear is like a magnet that attracts metal. It has the ability to direct the object of a person's fear toward that person. As the *pasuk* says (ibid., 3:25), "[T]hat which I feared has overtaken me." That is the nature of fear: it draws forth the object of our dread and makes it real.[6]

NOTES

4. *Kiddushin* 40b–41a.

5. *Emunah U'Bitachon*, Ch. 2.

6. *Sefer Arvei Nachal, Parashas Vayeitzei.* The power of imagination is discussed further in Chapter 31, "The Mind's Eye."

Thoughts have power. The great mystic and Kabbalist Rabbi Nachman of Breslov said, "If you believe that you can cause ruin, then believe that you can fix." A similar well-known account comes courtesy of Rabbi Menachem Mendel Schneerson, the Lubavitcher Rebbe, who was once asked to pray on behalf of a seriously ill person. He advised, "Think good, and it will be good." The Torah recounts,

> Now it came to pass in those days that Moses grew up and went out to his brothers and looked at their burdens, and he saw an Egyptian man striking a Hebrew man of his brothers. He turned this way and that way, and he saw that there was no man; so he struck the Egyptian and hid him in the sand.
>
> [Moses] went out the second day and behold two Hebrew men were fighting. He said to the wicked one: "Why do you strike your friend?" [The wicked one] replied: "Who appointed you to be a man, an officer, or a judge over us? Will you kill me as you killed the Egyptian?".... Moses became frightened and said, "Indeed, the matter has become known!" Pharaoh heard of this incident, and he sought to slay Moses.[7]

Moses became frightened, and then Pharaoh heard of the incident. Commentators explain that it was the potency of his fear that created the very reality that he wished to avoid.[8] Worry saps us of our strength but, more dangerously, also energizes the negative forces that are only too eager to accommodate our worst fears.[9]

Likewise, the Gemara teaches that dreams follow their interpretation, and that one dream can be interpreted in two completely opposite ways, with the possibility for either way to come true.[10] The *Zohar* notes the response of Joseph's brothers to his dreams: "Said his brothers to him, 'Are you then to be king over us! Are you to rule over us?' At that moment, they themselves gave the dream its definition and destination."[11]

The above scenarios are reminiscent of our discussion on quantum mechanics,

---

NOTES

7. Exodus 2:13–15.

8. Rabbi Menachem M. Schneerson, *Likutei Sichos*, Vol. XXXVI. "Were he to have had complete *bitachon* in God, and not have worried at all about the situation in which he found himself (that "the matter had become known" and would be discovered by Pharaoh), that would have caused the matter to have been forgotten and for him to have realized apparent and manifest good" (ibid.).

9. Among a wide range of benefits, multiple studies show that optimists enjoy an increased life span and better psychological and physical well-being.

10. *Berachos* 55b.

11. *Zohar* 1:183b.

but irrespective of how reality unfolds, fear adversely affects our judgment and performance.[12] The Torah states, "The officers will further address the people before battle and say: 'Whoever is afraid or faint-hearted, let him go and return home, and let him not destroy the resolve of his brothers like his own resolve.'"[13] The Maharal explains that his weakness, which is ostensibly a lack of trust in God, may lead to his death and the deaths of others on the battlefield.

In all areas of life, the bridge between effort and results is not direct. Even in a situation of clear and objective importance, we must not forget that our sole task is to invest the proper effort and to trust that the results come from God.[14] Anything less is laziness. Anything more is a potentially dangerous breach of trust. While we are obliged to maximize our effort to ensure success, we should never feel that we are the maker of our success.

THE ONLY QUESTION

The Talmud explains that Sinai "put an end to the toxicity" that poisoned human consciousness after Adam ate of the Tree of Knowledge.[15] With the giving of the Torah, we had complete and total clarity. No doubt whatsoever existed in our minds, and then doubt (via the *yetzer hara*) crept back in, and clarity was lost.

Doubt occurs when we have an internal conflict, and fear—the opposite of trust and the main weapon of the *yetzer hara*—is what breeds doubt, not the other way around. A person who has complete trust in God has no fear. Only when fear creeps into our mind does energy-sapping doubt assert itself. *Amalek* and *safek* ("doubt") have the same *gematria*.[16] Amalek is the symbol of evil, and his poison is the venom of doubt that he injects into a person's mind and heart.

We must know that at times the path before us seems like a choice between bad and worse, and while there may be no perfect choice, there is always a responsible

NOTES

12. J. M. Burger and R. Arkin, "Prediction, Control, and Learned Helplessness," *Journal of Personality and Social Psychology*, 38 (1980): 482–549.

13. Deuteronomy 20: 1–6.

14. King David asked for a test and failed it (*Sanhedrin* 107a). He had vanquished his evil inclination and his only desire was to be closer to God; but the request itself, although perfectly intentioned, contaminated his relationship with reality: God is the One Who grants success. The test became impossible to pass as soon as it became a request.

15. *Shabbos* 146a.

16. *Mavo Lechochmas Hakabbalah*, Vol. I, 4:4. The Amalekites were the most despised because they embodied the warped dogma of one who fears man but not God. They ambushed the Israelites to gain a tactical advantage over their enemy, without concern that they were going against the will of God.

one. The prerequisite for growth—and the way to purge the ego—is not to blame or to rail against the perceived injustice, but rather to ask ourselves one question: "What does God want of me now?"

Many people have a deep intellectual misconception about this world and our purpose. They fail to understand that by design, the world is inherently flawed and is populated with tests at every turn.[17] "Everything in this world is a test," and the key is not to dwell incessantly on how to emerge from a challenge unscathed or unburdened.[18] Every situation offers the opportunity to become angry and to blame, or to trust in God. It is our only real choice. It is our only real power.

Techniques will help us succeed in our aspirations, but they cannot create awareness. Only the full and urgent recognition of what is at stake will motivate us to pull and cull from every available resource in order to achieve our sole objective: to act responsibly and maintain our calm. When our fear of becoming angry outweighs our nature to become angry, we have achieved mastery over our emotions. Then, when faced with a difficult person or situation, we recognize that it is God's will for us to trust in Him and to take responsible action. Regardless of what else happens, we win. We pass the test.

17. Perhaps it is more fitting to say that the world *appears* flawed. Creation is perfect in its imperfection, or, expressed differently, it is so perfect that it comes with the illusion of imperfection.

18. *Mesillas Yesharim* (*The Path of the Just*), Ch. 1.

A JOURNEY OF A THOUSAND MILES

30

When we become angry—or refuse to let go of our anger—it is because we are, to some degree, fearful.[19] We are fearful because we have lost control over a certain aspect of our life—our circumstances, our image, and so on. The response to fear—the ego's attempt to compensate for this perceived loss of control—is anger. When we feel threatened, we go into defense mode; anger emboldens the ego and peddles the illusion that we are in control. Let us crystallize the sequence of events:

First, there is the **event** or **catalyst** that results in (or reminds us of) an **undesirable** outcome; this produces a **loss of control**, which make us anxious and **fearful**. The lower our self-esteem, in general (the closer to the nerve center of our self-image, in particular), the more fearful we become. As a result of our fear, we become **angry**. This destructive emotion often serves as a mask for other negative emotions, such as jealousy, envy, thirst for honor, and the like. For this reason, the Rambam emphasizes that a person should seek the middle of the road in all of his traits and behaviors, with the exception of anger.[20] He writes,

---

NOTES

19. The National Highway Traffic Safety Administration estimates that one-third of all fatal car crashes could be attributed to road rage (aggressive or violent behavior toward another motorist). Why is road rage more common than supermarket rage? A near-miss between two grocery carts does not provoke the same indignation that surrounds a near-miss on the highway. The reason is that the fear created on the highway is greater, and, as such, the resultant anger is intensified. Also, there is greater anonymity, and the driver does not have to worry about running into the person in the next aisle. The ego is freed of the potential embarrassment over the ensuing outburst.

20. Rambam, *Hilchos De'os* 1:4. The exact wording is intriguing. He advises that one finds the "exact middle path, equidistant to the extremes of each trait." The surface reading suggests a balanced approach, but there is more. The Gemara (*Shabbos* 133b) states, "One should be similar to [God]." But how is walking the middle path emulating God? When a person is equidistant to the extremes of each trait, he is not leaning in one

There are certain character traits that one must distance oneself from to the extreme. In fact, it is forbidden to take [the standard approach of] the "middle path" regarding these character traits.... Anger is an extremely negative character trait, and it is fitting for a person to distance himself from it to the opposite extreme. One should train oneself never to become angry, even regarding things for which anger might be justified.[21]

Among the most important triggers of self-regulation failure are negative emotions, particularly fear (which has been discussed) and its offspring, anger.[22] While all negative emotions betray a lack of *bitachon*, they all feed from the trough of anger. The following excerpt from a landmark research paper summarizes the unsurprising range of self-destructive behaviors that anger spawns.[23]

When people become upset they sometimes act aggressively,[24] spend too much money,[25] engage in risky behavior,[26] comfort with alcohol, drugs or food, and fail to pursue important life goals.[27] Anger is related to relapse for a number of addictive behaviors, such as alcoholism, gambling and drug addiction;[28] and increased eating by chronic dieters[29] and greater smoking intensity by smokers.[30]

NOTES

direction over the other; only then is he able to choose—to exercise his free will. In this way, he is like God.

21. Rambam, loc. cit.

22. G. Alan Marlatt and Judith R. Gordon eds., *Relapse Prevention: Maintenance Strategies in the Treatment of Addictive Behaviors* (New York: Guilford Press, 1985). Rajita Sinha, "Modeling Stress and Drug Craving in the Laboratory: Implications for Addiction Treatment Development," *Addict. Biol.* 14 (2009): 84–98.

23. Todd F. Heatherton and Dylan D. Wagner, *Cognitive Neuroscience of Self-Regulation Failure.*

24. Craig A. Anderson and Brad J. Bushman, "Human Aggression," *Annu. Rev. Psychol.* 53 (2002): 27–51.

25. Sabrina D. Bruyneel, Siegfried Dewitte, Philip Hans Franses, and Marnik G. Dekimpe, "I Felt Low and My Purse Feels Light: Depleting Mood Regulation Attempts Affect Risk Decision Making," *Journal of Behavioral Decision Making* 22, no. 2 (2009): 153–170.

26. Leah H. Somerville, Ph.D., Rebecca M. Jones, and B. J. Casey, Ph.D., "A Time of Change: Behavioral and Neural Correlates of Adolescent Sensitivity to Appetitive and Aversive Environmental Cues," *Brain Cogn.* 72 (2010): 124–133.

27. Viktoriya Magid, et al., "Negative Affect, Stress, and Smoking in College Students: Unique Associations Independent of Alcohol and Marijuana Use," *Addictive Behavior* no. 34 (2009): 973–975.

28. Rajita Sinha, "The Role of Stress on Addiction Relapse," *Current Psychiatry Reports* 9, no. 5 (2007): 388–395. Katie Witkiewitz and Nadia Aracelliz Villarroel, "Dynamic Association between Negative Affect and Alcohol Lapses Following Alcohol" (2009).

29. Todd F. Heatherton, C. Peter Herman, and Janet Polivy, "Effects of Physical Threat and Ego Threat on Eating Behavior," *Journal of Personality and Social Psychology* 60, no. 1 (1991): 138–143. Michael Macht, "How Emotions Affect Eating: A Five-Way Model," *Appetite* 50 (2008): 1–11.

30. Sherry A. McKee, et al., "Stress Decreases the Ability to Resist Smoking and Potentiates Smoking Intensity and Reward," *Journal of Psychopharmacology* (2011) DOI: 10.1177/0269881110376694.

It is significant that anger releases a stress hormone called cortisol. The long-term impact of elevated cortisol levels is detrimental, both physically and mentally.[31] Specifically, cortisol damages cells in the hippocampus and results in impaired learning.[32] In the short-term, cortisol interferes with our ability to think and process information.[33] Herein lies the physiological workings behind the Torah's revelation that when a person is consumed with rage, he cannot think clearly.

Consider the Egyptian response to the Plague of Frogs. According to the *Midrash*, one large frog emerged from the Nile.[34] The Egyptians tried to kill it, but each blow released dozens of tiny frogs. They kept hitting the great frog until Egypt was filled with frogs. The Steipler asks, "Didn't they see that they were only making things worse?" Why did they keep hitting the frog if each blow brought more of what they didn't want? The answer is: they were angry.[35] They were so furious and frustrated that they kept hitting the frog even though they were bringing the Plague upon themselves.[36]

While the Egyptians provide an example of blind anger, those on the highest level must also exercise extreme caution.[37] Even where justified, our Sages state, "The

---

NOTES

31. A great Rabbi was once asked, "How did you achieve longevity?" [He answered,] "I would never get upset in my home" (*Ta'anis* 20b). Indeed, there are hundreds of verifiable studies that link anger to physical illness.

32. "Do not appease your fellow in the time of his anger" (Ethics of the Fathers 4:23). Such a person cannot listen to reason when he is under the grip of his emotions.

33. "Silence is a fence for wisdom" (Ethics of the Fathers 3:13). When we keep from angry words, we hold onto our wisdom.

34. *Tanchumah, Va'eira, Siman* 14, brought by Rashi, Exodus 8:2.

35. Rabbi Yaakov Yisroel Kanievsky, *Birchas Peretz* 25.

36. Jacob did not prophesy during Joseph's absence because prophets lose their prophetic ability in times of anger or mourning.

37. Joshua, Moses' successor and most dedicated student, lost a portion of his knowledge and power of reason when he displayed a slight bit of arrogance: "Rabbi Yehudah said: Just before Moses passed on to *Gan Eden*, he said to Joshua, 'Ask me any questions you have.' Joshua said, 'Did I ever leave you, even for a moment and go elsewhere? Did you not write about me, "The servant Yehoshua Bin Nun never left the Tent"?' Joshua's strength immediately weakened; he forgot 300 laws and 700 questions occurred to him" (*Temura* 14a).

Moses himself forgot laws on the three occasions he showed anger, even though he did so only for the sake of Heaven. In Deuteronomy 31, the soldiers of *Klal Yisrael* returned victorious from their campaign against Midian, and they took captive the very Midianite women who had caused the Jewish people to sin. Moses showed anger and thus forgot the laws of kashering vessels of gentiles. Similarly, in Leviticus 10:17, on the day of the inauguration of the *Mishkan* ("Tabernacle"), Aaron and his two remaining sons intentionally refrained from eating the meat of the sin-offering of the Jewish people. Moses showed anger when he discovered the sin-offering had been burned and not eaten, and thus he forgot the law of *aninus* ("*halachic* guidelines for a mourner before the burial of the deceased"). We find (Deuteronomy 20:10) that Moses showed exasperation when the people clamored for water and thus he hit the rock, instead of speaking to it, as God had commanded Him to do. For this, he was denied entry into the Land of Israel.

Shechinah [Divine Presence] is blocked to those who become angry."[38] Elsewhere in the Talmud, it is written: "Whoever is conceited, if he is a wise Sage, his wisdom will leave him."[39] Loss of wisdom in a state of anger is not a punishment. It is an automatic consequence of an egocentric state.

A LEARNED RESPONSE

In the midst of a taxing circumstance, it can be difficult to present a composed demeanor—let alone to feel calm—but little by little, our capacity to do so develops. By choosing a different response to anger now, we will be able to better control ourselves the next time we feel provoked.[40]

For many years, conventional thinking likened the mind to a steam kettle—where pressure would build until the lid blew off. Psychologists thus encouraged people to release the buildup of pressure by venting their anger. Yet after extensive research on the subject, it turns out that expressing anger is not only unproductive, but destructive. "When people vent their feelings aggressively they often feel worse, pump up their blood pressure, and make themselves even angrier."[41] Multiple experiments confirm that "fits of rage are more likely to intensify anger."[42] This happens because we unconsciously validate our reaction by convincing ourselves that the situation requires our wrath. In turn, our anger flares, and self-justification increases aggression.[43]

On the lighter side, this is evidenced by research showing, for instance, that if we hold a pencil in our mouth—characteristic of a smile—while we're reading something, we're likely to find the material funnier.[44] Our mind seeks to reconcile

---

NOTES

38. *Nedarim* 22b.

39. *Pesachim* 66b.

40. "He who conceals his hatred has lying lips" (Proverbs 10:18). Expressing our displeasure is, at times, required and beneficial to our emotional and physical health. But articulating our feelings is not the same as unleashing a torrent of unrestrained anger. See Chapter 39, "Borders and Boundaries" for the proper approach.

41. Brad J. Bushman, "Does Venting Anger Feed or Extinguish the Flame? Catharsis, Rumination, Distraction, Anger, and Aggressive Responding," *Personality and Social Psychology Bulletin* 28, no. 6 (2001): 724–731. Research quoted by Carol Tavris and Elliot Aronson, *Mistakes Were Made, 26.*

42. Shahbaz Khan Mallick and Boyd R. McCandless, "A Study of Catharsis of Aggression," *Journal of Personality and Social Psychology* 4, no. 6 (1966): 591–596.

43. Physiological confirmation of the sage approach of the Rozdoler Rabbi: "When I feel angry against a person, I delay the expression of my anger. I say to myself: 'What will I lose if I postpone my anger?'"

44. If one were to start moving his hands and legs nervously, dart his eyes, and feverishly move his head, he would become anxious. Anxious people do this because they are nervous, and the mere act of doing so

our behavior with our emotional state and concludes that how we are expressing ourselves must be because of how we feel about the situation (or whatever behavior we are engaged in).[45]

The tenet that our emotional world is molded by our external actions is at the root of Ramchal's observation that "the outward act awakens the internal" and the *Sefer HaChinuch's* statement "Minds are shaped by deeds."[46] He explains: "Know that a man becomes who he is based on his actions. Thoughts of his heart, and his intentions, always follow the lead of his actions, whether for good or evil."[47]

In this respect, the Torah forbids bearing a grudge and taking revenge so that our resulting feelings do not intensify.[48] When we hold on to anger, we suffer, and the more we unleash, the more it consumes us. In the well-known lesson to his son "The Ramban's Letter," we see how the "action to attitude" cascade can flow in a positive direction:

> Get into the habit of always speaking calmly to everyone. This will prevent you from anger, a serious character flaw that causes people to sin.... Once you have distanced yourself from anger, the quality of humility will enter your heart. This radiant quality is the finest of all admirable traits.[49]

NOTES

makes one even more so. Contrast this with breathing deeply, smiling, and moving purposefully. Even if one was in an agitated state to begin with, the action causes him to feel more relaxed, balanced, and in control.

45. Aristotle is quoted as saying, "We acquire virtues by first having put them into action." Today, behavior therapy (also referred to as behavior modification therapy) is built on just such an approach. This type of therapy focuses on changing undesirable behaviors by identifying and substituting them with more positive and healthier types of behavior. Not only is the symptom being treated, but the behavior modification can alter the person's personality from the outside in.

46. *Mesillas Yesharim* (Ch. 8). *Mitzvah* 16. Horeb, *Teshuvah* Ch. 79.

47. *Mitzvah* 16. The previously discussed concept of cognitive dissonance is known to have a strong physiological component. If, in our initial response to a challenging situation, we maintain self-control, we actually become calmer and less troubled. This is precisely why self-control (which leads to trust) is so important; it allows for a person to alter both the short-term and the long-term emotional impact. It is not the circumstance but rather our response to the situation that give rise to the emotions that reinforce our perception.

48. "There are four types of temperaments. One who is quick to become angry and quick to calm down—his gain is outweighed by his loss. One who is slow to become angry and slow to calm down—his loss is outweighed by his gain. One who is slow to become angry and quick to calm down is considered pious. One who is quick to become angry and slow to calm down is called wicked" (Ethics of the Fathers 5:11).

49. *Iggeres HaRamban—The Ramban's Letter.*

MIND YOUR BRAIN

We are born with only two fears: the fear of falling and the fear of a loud startling noise. Every other fear is learned. Our emotional response to any situation can be rerouted—for better or for worse. An apt illustration is found in PTSD ("post-traumatic stress disorder"), a severe anxiety disorder that can develop after a psychological trauma. A person who returns from war, for example, can suffer from PTSD whereby the sound of a helicopter or a slamming door may cause sudden panic—because the brain has literally rewired itself, based on a false conclusion. In such instances, adrenaline hijacks the brain and redirects the perceived threat from the prefrontal cortex ("the thinking brain") to the amygdala ("the fear and anxiety response center"). This fear-based disorder bears a striking similarity to an instinctive angry reaction. Our ego identifies a threat to our emotional selves rather than to our physical selves, and we do not think, we just react.

Recent discoveries in molecular biology provide us with an understanding of the connection between behavior and circuits of the brain. While emotional reactions are created by our mind, they are reinforced in the brain. For instance, if we become upset at someone who is impolite to us, we are likely to react more strongly the next time we are in a similar situation, because the neural connection between rude people and our anger has been strengthened.

Whenever we learn something, millions of brain cells ("neurons") are altered, and new connections are forged in our network of nerve cells. Every neuron adapts to its surrounding (even cells are influenced by their environment)—or more precisely, to the signals it receives from neighboring cells. When two neurons fire repeatedly at the same time, the connection between them is reinforced and strengthened. Hence, the common idiom in biology: "Cells that fire together wire together." In fact, this is true for both emotional and physical responses to stimuli:

Just like muscles, brain circuits grow stronger when you use them—great when you're learning to play the piano, but terrible in the case of a constantly aching joint. Pain pathways are like a trail in the forest; if you have a path that is already worn, it is easier to follow and it becomes strengthened.[50] Through the same neurological process that makes you gradually get better at hitting

50. This sentence is a direct quote (within the article) from Dr. Gavril Pasternak, director of molecular neuropharmacology at Memorial Sloan-Kettering Cancer Center in New York City.

a racquetball or driving a stick shift, your brain "gets better" at perceiving the pain—you become more sensitive and more likely to register a poke or a twinge as painful. Eventually, people with chronic pain disorders such as fibromyalgia (which affects joints and soft tissues) can find even mild sensations agonizing. Imaging studies reveal what's going on: A gentle touch causes brain areas that process pain to react. Similar findings have been reported in people with unexplained chronic lower back pain. It's not a conscious process—it's one way the brain naturally responds to repeated stimulation.[51]

Returning to our immediate discussion, learning a new response—such as remaining calm in the face of insult—establishes neural networks by repeating this specific behavior over and again, which stimulates the associated neurons to grow extensions ("dendrites") to connect with one another.[52]

Constant, repetitive action reconfigures our brain once the neuro-pathways are bombarded for twenty-one consecutive days. These findings hardly represent anything new for *Chazal*, who report that it takes thirty days to change a habit.[53] With sufficient repetition, the new behavior becomes automatic and conceivably, in time, it can become our nature.[54]

The inverse is equally potent. Underused connections gradually deteriorate and eventually fade.[55] Using an electron microscope, we can even see how the inactive connections in the brain simply disappear.[56] A person can thereby unwittingly deplete his capacity to restrain himself, due to willful, continuous, and prolonged outbursts of rage.[57]

NOTES

51. Maiai Szalavitz, "The Pleasant Truths about Pain," *Psychology Today*, September 2005.

52. Dendrites are the branched projections of a neuron where information is delivered to and from the cell. The greater the number of dendrites, the faster and smoother is our capacity to understand related information and to integrate what we learn into our knowledge base. We literally become smarter in this area.

53. *Yerushalmi Ta'anis*, brought in *Tosafos Berachos* 12b.

54. The importance of each and every repetition is not to be understated. "If you repeat a lesson one hundred times you can become a *tzaddik* in this matter. If you repeat it one hundred and one times you can become a servant of God" (*Chagigah* 9b).

55. While the unconscious mind stores every thought, sensation, and experience, the brain is no longer able to readily access those stored memories.

56. Craig H. Bailey and M. Chen, "Morphological Basis for Long-Term Habituation and Sensitization in Aplysia," *Science* 220 (1993): 91–93.

57. When a blind person compensates for his lack of sight by developing his sense of touch (to learn Braille), the borders of the brain realign, expanding areas of the cerebral cortex that are responsible for the index finger. By retraining our mind, we actually alter our brains to enable a more refined nature. See A. Pascual-Leone, and F. Torres, "Plasticity of the Sensorimotor Cortex Representations of the Reading Finger in Braille Readers," *Brain* 116, no. 1 (1993): 39–52.

Anger begets anger, and silence begets calm. King Solomon reveals, "A gentle response turns away anger; a harsh response increases anger."[58] Traditionally interpreted as a reference to the person to whom we are speaking, we may appreciate that the anger he refers to is also our own.

Research shows that even in high-stress situations, it takes no more than ninety seconds for our system to process any anger or fear-based emotion. This means that we can clear out physiological influences and regain our full rational status in the most trying of circumstances. The findings explain:

> Although there are certain limbic system ("emotional") programs that can be triggered automatically, it takes less than 90 seconds for one of these programs to be triggered, surge through our body, and then be completely flushed out of our bloodstream. My anger response, for example, is a programmed response that can be set off automatically. Once triggered, the chemical released by my brain surges through my body and I have a physiological experience. Within 90 seconds from the initial trigger, the chemical component of my anger has completely dissipated from my blood and my automatic response is over. If, however, I remain angry after those 90 seconds have passed, then it is because I have chosen to let that circuit continue to run. Moment by moment, I make the choice to either hook into my neurocircuitry or move back into the present moment, allowing that reaction to melt away as fleeting physiology.[59]

A STEP FURTHER

In order to retrain our brain, we can establish a different meaning to the situation (intellectual or cognitive approach), which then resets the emotional response. The other way is to force ourselves to go beyond the neutrality of a calm demeanor and display the opposite behavior—to literally laugh in the face of fear.

Recall that PTSD can be undone when we reroute the flow of information back through the prefrontal cortex. An incongruous expression or response compels the "thinking brain" to re-engage in order to reconcile the discrepancy between the conflicting emotions; because the "external awakens the internal" our feelings will align with our behavior rather than the other way around.

58. Proverbs 15:1.

59. Jill Bolte Taylor, *My Stroke of Insight: A Brain Scientist's Personal Journey* (New York: Viking, 2008), 146.

The Chazon Ish writes, "The habit of patience is a cure for anger and taking offense; the habit of quickness is the cure for laziness and indifference; the habit of accepting the ridicule of others is the cure for seeking honor."[60] This might be considered radical, but the Rambam, as well, advises that in the short-term a person may need to engage in extreme behavior, for only then will he be able to find an appropriate balance and moderation.[61] He writes,

> A person who, for example, has a bad temper should act as follows: If he is struck or cursed, he should not take it to heart at all. He should continue to act in this manner for a long period of time until his trait of anger is uprooted from his heart. [So too] one who is arrogant should degrade himself greatly. He should sit in the least honorable seat and wear worn-out clothes which shame their wearer. He should do the above and the like until the arrogance is uprooted from him.... So too should a person behave regarding all character traits. If he is on one extreme he should move to the opposite extreme and accustom himself to such behavior for a good while until he may return to the proper middle path.[62]

The Talmud similarly instructs: "If [the animal of] a friend requires unloading, and an enemy's loading, you should first help your enemy—in order to suppress the evil inclination."[63] It is not enough to refrain from hating; we are instructed to engage in acts of kindness to foster warm feelings.

Shakespeare wrote, "Comedy is tragedy plus time." Eventually, we will see the whole picture, and when we smile now, it reminds us to put our trust in God, rather than in ourselves. It is not our emotions that distinguish us from the animal kingdom, but our ability to rise above them. We can choose to respond differently, and each and every time we do—either in actuality or through the soon-to-be-discussed process of visualization—we rewire our physiology to work with us and forever tilt the balance of free will.

NOTES

60. *Emunah U'Bitachon*, Ch. 4.
61. Rambam, *Hilchos De'os* 1:4.
62. Ibid., 2:2.
63. *Bava Metzia* 32b.

CHAPTER THIRTY-ONE

THE
MIND'S
EYE

31

In Judaism, great significance is attached to our self-concept—"How precious is man for he was created in the image of God"—because how we see ourselves dictates our thoughts, attitude, and behavior.[65] For this reason, our Sages warn, "Do not consider yourself wicked in your own eyes."[66] If a person sees himself as bad, then his self-concept automatically confines him to behave in this way and to perpetuate the negative behavior.

Moreover, the Talmud teaches that when one sins and repeats it, thereafter he considers the sin permissible.[67] After we make a poor choice, the dissonance between reality and ego widens—we begin to warp our thinking to accommodate our behavior, which only further torques the ego. From the annals of psychology:

> Self-justification is more powerful and more dangerous than the explicit lie. It allows people to convince themselves that what they did was the best thing they could have done. In fact, come to think of it, it was the right thing... . Self-justification not only minimizes our mistakes and bad decisions; it is also the reason that everyone can see a hypocrite in action except the hypocrite. It allows us to create a distinction between our moral lapses

65. See Genesis 1:26, 27.

66. Ethics of the Fathers 2:13.

67. *Sotah* 22a. Commenting on this Gemara, Rabbi Yisrael Salanter writes that after a third time, the sin becomes more than permissible—in our eyes, it becomes a *mitzvah*.

and someone else's, and to blur the discrepancy between our actions and our moral convictions.[68]

The contour of our self-concept in concert with our belief system is sculpted with each and every action; hence, irrespective of the reward or the consequence, the Sages advise us, "Run to perform [even] a minor *mitzvah* and flee from sin, for one *mitzvah* leads to another *mitzvah*, and one sin leads to another sin."[69]

RESHAPING THE SELF-CONCEPT

Posing as safety inspectors, researchers asked homeowners if they would allow the inspectors to place a large "Drive Carefully" sign in their front yards. Only 17 percent gave permission. Other residents, however, were first approached with a smaller request. They were asked to put up a three-inch "Be a Safe Driver" window sign. Nearly all immediately agreed. When approached a few weeks later, these homeowners were asked to place the gigantic sign on their front lawns. This same group overwhelmingly agreed—76 percent consented—to having the unsightly sign in their front yards.[70]

Simply, those who had agreed to the smaller request had reshaped their self-perception to include the definition that they were serious about road safety. Therefore, agreeing to the larger request signified their ongoing internal commitment to the cause.

A revision in our self-concept does not come only through our actions but via the faculty of imagination. The Hebrew word *hirhur* ("a passing thought") is derived from the word *herayon*, which means "conception." A thought plants the seed, and imagination provides nourishment and helps bring forth its potential.[71] Rabbi Yitzchak Hunter elaborates,

> There is a powerful tool that will help you to cope with even the most difficult situations. Mentally picture yourself coming across difficult life tests and see

NOTES

68. Elliot Aronson, *Mistakes Were Made (but Not by Me): Why We Justify Foolish Beliefs, Bad Decisions, and Hurtful Acts* (Orlando, FL: Harcourt, 2007), 4.

69. Ethics of the Fathers 4:2.

70. Jonathan L. Freedman and Scott C. Fraser, "Compliance without Pressure: The Foot-in-the-Door Technique," *Journal of Personality and Social Psychology* no. 4 (1966): 195–202.

71. "Intellect and senses are generally viewed as being completely different from each other. But there is a point at which they converge in a human being, and this is the imagination" (Rabbi Yitzchak Hutner, *Pachad Yitzchak*, Pesach, *Ma'amar* 70).

yourself coping with them … repeat this over and over again in your mind … see yourself feeling great joy in mastering your impulses.[72]

The power of visualization surfaces in numerous Torah references. For instance, the Shabbos before Tishah B'Av is referred to as *Shabbos Chazon*, "The Shabbos of Vision." We are shown a vision of the Third Temple, so that we may visualize its rebuilding, which will help bring about the Final Redemption. The *mitzvah* of remembering the Exodus from Egypt is also fulfilled by using the power of imagination. "In every generation, each person is obligated to see himself as if he went out of Egypt."[73]

Visualization is amazingly transformative because the subconscious mind cannot distinguish between imagination and an actual happening—therefore, at this level, it is all interpreted as real.[74] In fact, neuroscientists have identified which parts of the brain light up when a person has a genuine experience and found that the same region is activated when the person simply imagines the experience.[75]

Parenthetically, experiments show that visualization can produce changes in the body, as well as in the mind.[76] For instance, the effects of muscle strength are similar whether we are actually doing an exercise or merely visualizing ourselves doing it.[77]

NOTES

72. Rabbi Kalonymus Kalman Shapira, *To Heal the Soul*, Y. Starrett, ed. (New Jersey: Jason Aronson., 1995), 253.

73. *Pesachim* 10:5.

74. As we discussed, anger is a response to fear and shares a strong birthplace with phobias and other anxiety disorders, which emanate from irrational fears. Visualization, then, which is often used to treat phobias, can accelerate changes in our response to both fear and anger-provoking situations.

75. Major James Nesmith, a prisoner of war in Vietnam for seven years, maintained his sanity by playing a game of golf in his head every day. The whole eighteen holes. So real was his visualization that it took just about as long to finish his mental game as does a real game. He imagined the trees and the grass, how the club felt in his hand, and so on. What is most amazing is that when he was released and played his first real game of golf, his score had improved—from the low 90s to the low 70s.

76. Research conducted with athletes, including Olympians and professionals, relates that they can actually feel the muscle twinges associated with their actions as they envision themselves executing a variety of tasks. Terry Orlick and John Partington, *Psyched: Inner Views of Winning* (Canada: Coaching Association of Canada, 1991).

77. Repetitive action patterns also have long-term neural consequences, the effects of which have been observed at the cellular and the systemic level, and which extend to the motor cortex, the muscles that were imagined to be exercised, and even related muscles. Roger M. Enoka, "Neural Adaptations with Chronic Physical Activity," *Journal of Biomechanics* 30, no. 5 (1997): 447–455. An analysis of sixty studies conducted on the power of mental imagery shows that the effect was least significant on strict strength tests, better for motor tasks, and best of all for performance with a cognitive component—for example, to effect a change in one's character.

One such study found that imagined finger exercises increased the subjects' strength by an average of 22 percent; actually doing the same regimen physically that the other test group was doing in their imaginations increased strength by an average of 30 percent.[78]

We need not wait for a challenging situation to occur, only to rely on sheer will to rise above our nature. Imagining ourselves responding in a certain way reshapes our self-concept and produces the same changes in the brain that the actual behavior does.[79]

Mentally rehearsing a patient and calm response, for instance, will help our brain reformat itself and can accelerate our ability to maintain self-control, even under the most daunting of circumstances.[80]

Routinely reflecting on actual or imagined instances also benefits us due to a mental peculiarity called *availability heuristics.* Studies regarding memory and behavior explain that people often base their self-concept on availability, or how easily they can bring information to mind. For instance if we were asked to think of several times where we acted calmly and were able to recall these events with relative ease, then we would see ourselves—at least temporarily—as someone who was in control. However, if we had difficulty recalling times when we were calm our self-concept would conform around our inability to quickly access the memories and we would conclude—at both the conscious and unconscious levels—that we are someone who reacts anxiously or impulsively.

It is for this reason that some people have such a warped perspective of themselves. They have a computer-like memory when it comes to remembering their failures and mistakes in life—so this is how they see themselves—as failures. Even if our accomplishments far outweigh our mistakes, it is what we remember that dictates how we see ourselves.

78. Guang Yue and Kelly J. Cole, "Strength Increases from the Motor Program: Comparison of Training with Maximal Voluntary and Imagined Muscle Contractions," *Journal of Neurophysiology* 67, no. 5 (1992): 1114–1123.

79. The mechanism that drives anger is fear, and the two dominant ego-driven fears are: (a) feeling a loss of control, and (b) feeling disrespected. Therefore, visualizing a calm response—while reminding ourselves of reality: God is One, He is everything, and there is nothing besides Him—is most valuable to one who is working on reducing anger.

80. "Mentally rehearse the situation in advance, visualizing yourself handling it well" (*Reishis Chochmah,* Ch. 5).

IN TIMES OF TEMPTATION

Returning to the principle of *terror management*, we remind ourselves that fear impedes our ability to think. Therefore, a powerful weapon in our willpower arsenal is simply to pause and to calm ourselves. This is effective for two reasons: Physiologically speaking, willpower has a biological basis, and slow, deep breathing activates the prefrontal cortex.[81] When our central nervous system is calm, our thoughts become more rational and clear. Second, if we are contemplating engaging in irresponsible behavior, the act of waiting engages *delay discounting*.[82] The window of temptation can close as quickly as it opens, and holding out—in some cases, for just a few minutes—causes us to view the temptation as a future reward, which weakens the pull of immediate gratification.[83]

In this critical space of time—weighing out "Should I or shouldn't I?"—we should visualize where our choices will take us. The Gemara tells us that a wise person is someone who foresees the outcome.[84] This does not mean he is a *navi* ("prophet"). Rather, it means being able to stop and see beyond the immediate, to look wholeheartedly at the repercussions of one's actions.[85] Accordingly, *Chazal* instruct us to "Evaluate the loss of not fulfilling a commandment against its reward, and the reward of committing a transgression against its loss."[86] Rabbeinu Yonah writes,

> Which is the good way to which a person should cling? ... He looks carefully at everything and sees all the outcomes before they happen. When the thing

---

NOTES

81. Law enforcement and military professionals combat stress with tactical breathing, which helps control the sympathetic nervous system. During a high-stress situation, taking several successive deep breaths (and visualizing a calm, controlled response) have been shown to allow personnel to think more clearly and engage more effectively. Dave Grossman and Loren W. Christensen, *On Combat: The Psychology and Physiology of Deadly Conflict in War and in Peace* (USA: PPCT Research Publications, 2004), 88.

82. "He spoke to Korach and to his entire assembly, saying, 'In the morning God will make known the one who is His own'" (Numbers 16:5). Rashi comments that by telling Korach and his followers that God would respond in the morning, Moses sought to give them time to reconsider their thinking.

83. Physiologically speaking, neuroscientists looked at multiple competing systems within the brain and found that parts of the brain that process emotion were highly activated by the choice of immediate or near-term rewards. In contrast, when participants opted to delay gratification in return for a higher return, lateral areas of the cortex involved in higher cognition and deliberation were more active. See Samuel M. McClure, David I. Laibson, George Lowenstein, and Jonathan D. Cohen, "Separate Neural Systems Value Immediate and Delayed Monetary Rewards," *Science* 306 (2004) (5695): 503–507.

84. *Tamid* 32a.

85. King Solomon states, "Who is a wise person? One who sees what lies ahead" (Ecclesiastes 2:14).

86. Ethics of the Fathers 2:1.

is rewarding in the beginning but leads to a loss in the end, he avoids it. By doing this, he will never sin because he considers the reward of a sin in relation to its loss.[87]

We must seize on this moment, recognize what is at stake, and permit ourselves to feel the unadulterated pain of the wrong choice—as well as the purity and pleasure of choosing responsibly. In other words, we must do more than stop and think—we must feel. Moving beyond rational arguments about long-term costs and benefits, it is essential that we immerse ourselves in the travesty of the trade-off and the actual harm to us and to our loved ones—in this world and in the next—in exchange for satisfying a passing urge.

We need to vividly imagine the painful consequences and become realistic about what our behavior has cost us thus far, and what our lives will look like—in five years, in ten years, or in old age—if we do not change our ways. We should also reflect deeply on how we will feel about ourselves and how differently our lives can be, with a single right choice.

Rabbi Simcha Zissel, known as the Alter of Kelm, was the *Mussar* movement's leading proponent of visualization. He asks, "How did our holy ancestors and all great men throughout the generations attain their high spiritual levels? The unequivocal answer is that they did it by means of their immense power of imagination. When a person's imagination summons up a powerful image of God's promised reward and punishment, it becomes impossible for him to commit a sin."[88]

The psychological research is equally definitive. "What matters, when it comes to self-control, is not so much willpower as vision—the ability to see the future, so that the long-run consequences of our short-run choices are vividly clear. In that sense, our shortcomings in this arena are really failures of imagination."[89] Drenching ourselves with total awareness of the consequences is a powerful remedy to impulsivity.[90] Yet this hinges on our ability to pause—if only for a moment—and in that moment to fully absorb where our choices will lead us. Therefore, the most valuable application of visualization is not simply to uproot individual traits but to acquire the habit of stopping, thinking of, and feeling the consequences of our conduct.

NOTES

87. Rabbeinu Yonah, ad loc.

88. Rabbi Simcha Zissel Ziv, *Chochmah U'Mussar*, Vol. 1, 69.

89. Daniel Akst, *We Have Met the Enemy: Self-Control in an Age of Excess* (New York, Penguin Press, 2011), Introduction.

90. Karen Horney, *Our Inner Conflict* (New York: Norton, 1945), 75–76.

As we are aware, consequences matter to us only if we matter to ourselves. Strategies can help us exercise self-restraint, but the only way to rouse our emotional forces is to remind ourselves that we have a higher, more noble purpose.[91] Reaffirming our core values—knowing what we are living for and who we are (a soul, not a body or an ego)—has been shown to be the strongest factor in replenishing strength of will.[92]

Visualization can be used to help create our future selves and to remind us of the cost should we fail to do so. Frequency and intensity are important. The more often we mentally rehearse and the more emotions we invoke, the more quickly our thoughts become embedded into our subconscious mind. God says, "Let us make man in Our image and in Our likeness."[93] The Ramban notes that the Hebrew word for "Our likeness," *kidmutanu,* finds its root in the word *dimyon,* which means "imagination."[94] The Sages refer to our inner world—the world of our mind—as a miniature world, because through the power of imagination we can become a partner with God in our creation and in all of creation.[95]

91. See Mark Muraven and Elisaveta Slessareva, "Mechanisms of Self-Control Failure: Motivation and Limited Resources," *Personality and Social Psychology Bulletin* 29 (2003): 894.

92. Brandon J. Schmeichel and Kathleen Vohs, "Self-Affirmation and Self-Control: Affirming Core Values Counteracts Ego Depletion," *Journal of Personality and Social Psychology,* 96, no. 4 (2009): 770.

93. Genesis 1:26.

94. The Ramban (ibid.) writes that human beings are defined by the power of broad imagination.

95. See Malbim, Genesis 2:7.

CHAPTER THIRTY-TWO

A
QUIET
SELF

32

Coping with any kind of stress depletes willpower.[96] A cluttered, chaotic mind and a tense nervous system strain our efforts to exercise self-control, regardless of our finest intentions.[97] One effective way to relax the nervous system is through meditation, which, interestingly, has deep roots in mystical Judaism.[98] In fact, meditation is at the heart of Kabbalah's spiritual work, with an estimated one million Jews involved in regular schools of meditation and meditative disciplines during Biblical times.[99]

As we learned, calm and self-control are inextricably linked. While there are a variety of effective stress management strategies for maintaining self-regulation, meditation specifically has been shown to be especially useful, and the benefits can be enjoyed remarkably quickly.[100] Findings show that those who meditated for about thirty minutes a day for eight straight weeks had noticeable increases in gray-matter density in the prefrontal cortex. At the same time, MRI brain scans showed a reduction of gray matter in the amygdala, a region responsible for anxiety and stress.

NOTES

96. Matthew T. Gailliot, et al., "Self-Control Relies on Glucose as a Limited Energy Source: Willpower Is More Than a Metaphor," *Journal of Personality and Social Psychology* 92, no. 2 (2007): 325–336.

97. Notice how high-strung and nervous people carry themselves. Their bodies are often tense and stiff. The central nervous system is made up of our brain and spinal cord, and it is difficult to completely relax the mind unless we relax the spinal cord as well. A stretching routine may be highly beneficial to work out the tensions in the physical body and to begin the process of releasing emotional stresses.

98. Aryeh Kaplan, *Jewish Meditation: A Practical Guide* (New York: Schocken Books, 1985), vii.

99. Jewish Meditation Institute Jerusalem, *Introduction to Jewish Meditation & Neuropsychology: How to Meditate Effectively & Joyfully* (Jerusalem: Jewish Meditation Institute Jerusalem, 2009), 12.

100. Sang Hyuk Lee, "Effectiveness of a Meditation-Based Stress Management Program as an Adjunct to Pharmacotherapy in Patients with Anxiety Disorder," *Journal of Psychosomatic Research* 62, no. 2 (2007): 189.

Among an array of remarkable benefits, research shows that long-term medita-tors possess a more developed capacity to dismiss distractions and to voluntarily control attention.[101] Rabbi Kaplan writes,

> The experienced meditator learns how to think what he wants to think, when he wants to think it. He can always be in control of the situation, resist-ing psychological pressures that work on the subconscious. He is always in control of himself, never doing something that he knows he really does not want to do.[102]

More than 1,000 independent scientific studies conducted at 200 universities and institutions in 27 countries, which have been published in leading scientific journals, attest to the psychological and physiological benefits of meditative practice. Herbert Benson, M.D., a professor of medicine at Harvard Medical School who has authored or coauthored more than 170 papers, reports that frequent meditation "reduces the level of anxiety, worries, and unconstructive thoughts and fears, as well as increasing the individual level of happiness."[103] He adds,

> Meditation induces a host of biochemical and physical changes in the body collectively referred to as the "relaxation response." The relaxation response includes changes in metabolism, heart rate, respiration, blood pressure, and brain chemistry.[104]

Other findings show that meditation promotes overall psychological health, with benefits that include enhanced confidence and greater self-control, em-pathy, and self-actualization, as well as decreased anger in high-intensity situations.[105]

NOTES

101. Julian M. Davidson, "The Physiology of Meditation and Mystical States of Consciousness," *Perspectives Biol. Med.* 19 (1976): 345–379.

102. Kaplan, *Jewish Meditation*, 7.

103. Herbert Benson, *The Relaxation Response* (New York: HarperTorch, 2005), 78–91.

104. Herbert Benson, "The Relaxation Response: Therapeutic Effect," *Science* (1997): 1694–1695. PMID.

105. Stuart Appelle and Lawrence E. Oswald, "Simple Reaction Time as a Function of Alertness and Prior Mental Activity," *Perceptual & Motor Skills* 38 (1974): 1263–1268. Jagdish Dua and Michelle L. Swinden, "Effectiveness of Negative-Thought Reduction, Meditation and Placebo Training Treatment in Reducing Anger," *Scandinavian Journal of Psychology* 33, no. 2 (1992): 135–146.

MODES OF MEDITATION

The purpose of this chapter is not to focus on how to meditate, but to acquaint the reader with the importance of why to meditate. Nonetheless, the following offers an overview of four main types of kosher meditative approaches: mantra, visualization, breathing, and nothingness.

❑ Mantra

Mantra meditation is best-known today because it is one of the simplest and most effective forms. The first reference to its usage dates back to Talmudic times and is found in the primary text of *Merkavah* mysticism called *Heychalos Rabbasai*. It seems that Biblical verses or *Zohar* or Talmud selections were used as mantras in later Kabbalistic schools.[106]

This practice of meditation is based on focusing the mind on one particular thing: a word, a group of words, or a sound. It is inevitable that we are interrupted by thoughts, but instead of our becoming distracted and losing focus, the process requires that we simply acknowledge these thoughts and let them go.

❑ Visualization

Visualization is a crucial discipline in meditation because individuals learn how to control images they see when they close their eyes. This approach begins by a person closing his eyes, taking a relaxing position, and permitting the image—which may also be the object's name—to stabilize in the mind's eye.[107] Kabbalistic texts that deal with meditation speak extensively about visualization.

❑ Breathing

Rabbi Kaplan explains that a primary goal of meditation is to gain control of the subconscious mind, and in doing so, we gain a high degree of self-mastery.[108] This is why, he explains, so many disciplines use breathing exercises as a meditative device. He states, "Breathing usually occurs automatically

106. Aryeh Kaplan, *Jewish Meditation*, 56.
107. Ibid., 77.
108. Ibid., 5.

and is therefore normally under the control of the unconscious mind.... Breathing forms a link between the conscious mind and the unconscious. By learning how to concentrate and control your breath you can go on to learn how to control the unconscious mind."[109] With consistent and focused practice, we will notice our breath slowing down, even as our mind becomes more alert.

❑ Nothingness

Nothingness is an advanced form of meditation that was utilized as an initiator of prophecy and cannot be used by beginners or practiced without guidance.[110] The first stage to visualizing nothingness is to try to envision transparent, pure, empty space that lacks background color. Although this method entails visualizing the transparent empty space, the item imagined is still space and not nothingness.

Subsequent stages remove the empty space from our thoughts until we have nothing but nothingness. Rabbi Kaplan writes, "Of all the images one can visualize, the purest vision is of nothingness.... If one visualizes nothingness and at the same time clears the mind of thought, the mind becomes a total bank. The mind is then at its most sensitive, open to even the most ethereal experiences."[111]

A GREATER GAIN

Whatever method we use, the objective is the same: to calm our active mind while raising our state of consciousness. As a result, our prayers are enriched as well. A famed eleventh-century Jewish philosopher and rabbi explains,

You should know that words uttered with the tongue are like the husk, while meditation on the words is like the kernel. The [recital of the] prayer is like the body, while the meditation is the soul. When one prays with his tongue while his heart is preoccupied with [something else], his prayer is like a body without a soul, or a husk without its kernel.[112]

109. Ibid., 6.
110. Ibid., 83.
111. Ibid., 85.
112. Rabbi Bachya ibn Pakudah, *Duties of the Heart*, 691.

The *Gemara* cites that the pious men of earlier generations (*Chasidim Rishonim*) incorporated meditation into their daily prayers. They would sit still an hour prior to each of the three prayer services, then pray for one hour and afterwards be still again for one more hour.[113] The Rambam explains that this meditative practice helped to "settle their minds and quiet their thoughts."[114]

Not only does meditation reduce stress and enhance our prayers, but it also stems the flood of doubts and fears that seep into our higher instincts. Communication with God is a two-way street, and intuition is blocked to the degree that we are consumed with ourselves. Without static from the ego, we "hear His voice" and are guided more directly and with greater clarity and confidence in the right direction. In *Cheshbon HaNefesh* we read:

> As long as a man's mind is settled, his intellectual spirit quietly stands guard.... At such time man has free choice and control, over his spirit to take the time to focus his thoughts upon exercising his sovereignty.... However, when the mind is agitated, a fearful darkness falls upon him and his counsel and strength are taken from him.[115]

An overall higher stress threshold means that stress-related negative behaviors will be triggered less often. Responsible use of free will leads to *bitachon* and calmness, as has been discussed. Now we see that meditation quiets the mind from the inside out, also bringing us an inner calm. Meditation is the opposite of doing. Synergized opposites—both productive action and being still in the moment—fine-tune each other and bring us to a higher level of inner harmony and a clearer connection to God.[116]

NOTES

113. *Berachos* 32b.

114. *Hilchos Yesodei HaTorah*, 7:4.

115. Rabbi Menachem Mendel Levin, *Cheshbon HaNefesh*, 97.

116. **NOTE:** Because threads of *avodah zarah* can too easily wind their way into various methods of meditation, we cannot overstate the need for extreme caution. A competent *halachic* authority must be sought to ensure that all aspects of one's practice are in accord with Jewish law.

PART 10

THE SCIENCE AND PSYCHOLOGY OF WILLPOWER

Where there is clarity of purpose, there is no inner conflict or struggle. Our focus emerges without ambiguity and anything unrelated to our objective is summarily dismissed. But when doubts creep in or progress is elusive, disruptions and temptations soak up our attention and drown our resolve. In order to refine our character and achieve our objectives, we need to harness willpower—the mental energy that enables us to exert self-control. Infusing Torah wisdom into multidisciplinary research, we will discuss here additional strategies to control competing and fleeting desires and to overcome emotional interference and outside interruptions.

33 | MENTAL RESERVES: BUILDING AND PRESERVING

Discipline is not something we're born with. It is an ability that is cultivated. It takes much more than a passing whim to strengthen and sustain willpower—it requires a conditioned mind.[1]

Like actual muscle, our willpower can be built up through use.[2] In fact, any single act of self-control—in any domain, even unrelated and trivial acts—can strengthen self-discipline in the long-term in other areas, providing a biological basis for "One *mitzvah* leads to another."[3]

NOTES

1. While a meaningful life is a pleasurable life, we should note that exerting self-control itself is highly satisfying. Rabbi Moshe Feinstein writes, "Man's vitality stems from self-control. The righteous are in control of their desires, rather than finding themselves governed by their desires. It is the sweetest of pleasures, the greatest of joys, to rule over one's animal instincts. It means constant happiness, and it restores one's soul" (*Igros* 1–13).

2. The same is true for our spiritual muscle. Who feels better? A person who has spent the entire day lying on the couch eating snacks, or one who has worked toward his life's ambitions? The former is conserving energy, but nonetheless at the end of the day he is tired. The latter expended energy, yet feels invigorated. Energy is always flowing in one of two directions. Using our free will in a purposeful direction actually increases it, while one who seeks to conserve energy by doing nothing becomes depleted of it. After a few days or weeks of conserving our physical energies, we begin to atrophy and waste away—the striking opposite of growth. While we need to rest, perpetual rest in this world is self-destructive. Hence the commandment to take a day of rest begins with the words: "Six days shall you work and do all of your creative acts" (Leviticus 23:3).

3. Ethics of the Fathers 4:2. Engaging in simple, everyday acts of self-control (e.g., avoiding knuckle cracking, eating more slowly) *before* attempting to stop smoking led to increased long-term abstinence rates compared to a control group that did not exercise prior acts of self-control. Once our willpower quotient is increased, it can be redirected to self-regulate other behaviors. See Mark Muraven, "Practicing Self-Control Lowers the Risk of Smoking Lapse," *Psychol. Addict. Behav.* 24 (2010): 446–452. Ethics of the Fathers 4:2.

This finding is observed in the writings of Rabbi Samson Raphael Hirsch, who writes that even if someone has sinned so severely in a certain area that he has lost control of himself within that area, he can eventually regain control by exercising self-restraint in other areas.[4] This maxim was expressively rendered by William Butler Yeats:

> *Every conquering temptation represents a new fund of moral energy.*
> *Every trial endured and weathered in the right spirit makes a soul*
> *nobler and stronger than it was before.*[5]

On a transcendental level, the *Zohar* reveals that whatever actions one performs in the positive realm will draw positive influence, and if one performs negative acts, they draw negative influence. Each side will draw in the person more deeply, encasing him in forces that either contribute to, or inhibit, his welfare.[6] A commentary of the *Zohar* explains:

> When a man increases his drives and lusts, he represses his *neshamah* and the ambition to return to its source also disappears. On the other hand, if the *neshamah* overcomes the body's lusts and a man merits harnessing his will to the Creator's, the power of the *neshamah* grows continuously stronger, while the aspiration to cleave to its source is also strengthened. In Kabbalistic language, we state that if a man merits harnessing his thought, speech, and deeds to serve the Creator, his body becomes a chariot for the Creator, blessed is He.[7]

We cannot presume to comprehend the multilayered reasons for various *mitzvos*, but we can say that many commandments are in fact measures to ensure that man's soul rules over his animal self, which paves the path for ongoing spiritual development.[8] The father of psychoanalysis, Sigmund Freund, understood this correctly, calling Judaism "a religion of instinctual renunciation."[9]

Research shows that our mental muscle — willpower — is similar to its physical

---

NOTES

4. Horeb, *Teshuvah* Ch. 79.

5. Yeats (1865–1939) was a writer, dramatist, and poet. He won the Nobel Prize for Literature in 1923.

6. *Zohar* I:195b.

7. Rabbi Y. Bar Lev, Ph.D., *Introduction to Kabbalah* (*Yedid Nefesh*).

8. See Rabbi Samson Raphael Hirsch (*Commentary* to Leviticus 19:27).

9. The Chazon Ish writes (*Emunah U'Bitachon*, Ch. 2) that the one overriding *middah* ("trait") that a Torah-true Jew must have is self-control.

counterpart in another way: it becomes temporarily fatigued with use. Akin to lifting weights, we are weaker immediately afterward, but we become stronger in the process. The Rambam writes,

> The *nefesh* grows tired and its thoughts become befuddled when it constantly delves into difficult things, much the way the body tires when one does heavy work—unless he rests and relaxes, and allows it to return to equilibrium.[10]

Willpower is depleted by a condition known as *decision fatigue*. Self-control is not an infinite resource but is temporarily spent by each act of restraint.[11] For example, studies found that resisting a persuasive message lowered an individual's ability to exercise self-control right afterward, and this depletion increased vulnerability to persuasion (yet another nail in the coffin of living in a toxic environment).[12] Practically speaking, we can take simple steps that effectively shore up, and strengthen, our willpower reserves.

STEERING CLEAR OF TEMPTATION

Findings show that people who are most successful at exercising self-control set up their lives to minimize temptations throughout the day.[13] By not running down our emotional fuel tank fighting off a barrage of impulses, we are able to conserve willpower and employ it only when necessary. *Cheshbon HaNefesh* expounds:

> As long as the generating source of the desire is somewhat removed, the animal spirit is incapable of violently arousing itself to seek the desire. Consequently, when it is possible to remove oneself from the source of the sensation, the intellectual spirit which can see ahead, can overcome the strongest desires by dealing with them in their first stages. It can surely discard them completely— without exertion—if the animal spirit is still unaware of them. However, the

NOTES

10. Rambam, *Shemoneh Perakim* 5:5.

11. Brandon J. Schmeichel and Kathleen Vohs, "Self-Affirmation and Self-Control: Affirming Core Values Counteracts Ego Depletion," *Journal of Personality and Social Psychology*, 96, no. 4 (2009): 770–782. doi: 10.1037/a0014635.

12. Edward Burkley, "The Role of Self-Control in Resistance to Persuasion," *Personality and Social Psychology Bulletin* 34, no. 3 (2008): 419.

13. Wilhelm Hofmann, Roy F. Baumeister, Georg Förster, and Kathleen D. Vohs, "Everyday Temptations: An Experience Sampling Study of Desire, Conflict, and Self-Control," *Journal of Personality and Social Psychology* (2011).

generating source of the desire frequently presents itself suddenly and in proximity, immediately generating a sensation of desire in all its intensity.[14]

The Gemara directs us to caution a *Nazir* to avoid walking through a vineyard so that he will not be tempted to have wine or grapes.[15] The Ramchal writes that this is a lesson for all people to avoid unnecessary temptation.[16]

We have to appreciate just how easily a person can succumb to a passing impulse, even in matters of life and death. Daniel Akst writes that for years, "England relied on coal gas (which is rich in deadly carbon monoxide) for heating and cooking; by the late 1950s it accounted for nearly half of suicides... . But by the early 1970s, when the changeover to natural gas was virtually complete, the English suicide rate had dropped by nearly a third and has stayed down ever since."[17]

While suicide is not always impulsive, findings like this reinforce the prevailing rule: In all areas of life, we should keep what is good for us close and simple to obtain, and what is counterproductive out of the way and hard to reach. "In matters of self-control we see again and again, speed kills. But a little friction really can save lives."[18]

For whatever trait or behavior we are working on, we want to identify when we are most at risk of going off course. When we know our triggers, we can limit the number of times we arrive at the fork of temptation. Some of these critical junctures—times when we are most vulnerable to falling into familiar patterns—are universal. We have already discussed the two pivotal players: fear and anger. (While these emotions may lie at times outside of our immediate control, it is useful to be intellectually aware that our strength is weakened in these states.) Furthermore, there are also behavior-specific triggers, such as boredom to the dieter or idle chatting to one working on pure speech. A detour to avoid confrontation with temptation may make our route slightly longer, but we will increase our chance of

---

NOTES

14. Rabbi Menachem Mendel Levin, *Cheshbon HaNefesh*, 93.

15. A *Nazir* is one who voluntarily takes a vow (Numbers 6:1–21) to abstain or refrain from a number of things, including eating or drinking any substance that contains any trace of grapes (*Shabbos* 13a).

16. *Mesillas Yesharim* (*The Path of the Just*), Ch. 11.

17. Daniel Akst, *We Have Met the Enemy: Self-Control in an Age of Excess*, 181. Research found that many Englanders did not turn to other methods of suicide because carbon monoxide poisoning required the least amount of courage, minimal preparation, and no pain. See Ronald V. Clarke and Pat Mayhew, "The British Gas Suicide Story and its Implications for Prevention". In Michael Tonry and Norval Morris (eds.), 1988. Crime and Justice: A Review of Research, Vol. 10. Chicago: University of Chicago Press.

18. Ibid., 182. A "crime of opportunity" is a related impulse-based phenomenon whereby a hoodlum commits a crime, without premeditation or preparation, largely because an opportunity happens to present itself.

arriving safely at our destination. The following subchapter elaborates on a parallel theme.

DEFAULT TO VICTORY

The prolific inventor Thomas Edison once said, "Five percent of the people think; ten percent of the people think they think; and the other eighty-five percent would rather die than think." This is not just a clever quip but a piercing insight into our nature. Human beings are cognitive misers—we do not want to think too hard.[19] When faced with an important decision—even when options are limited—the most tempting route is to shut down and not to think. Research found that in one company, just 20 percent of employees had enrolled in a retirement plan after three months of employment. The form was then redesigned to make enrollment the default option, and participation vaulted above 90 percent, all without an ounce of outside pressure.[20]

Lest we think that our brains eschew only complicated financial matters, take the following pairs of countries in the chart below: Denmark and Sweden; the Netherlands and Belgium; Austria and Germany; and France and the UK. They are culturally and religiously fairly similar, yet levels of organ donations are quite different. Germany has an organ consent rate of 12%, while Austria has a rate of 99.98%. In Denmark the consent rate is only 4.25% but nearly 86% in Sweden.

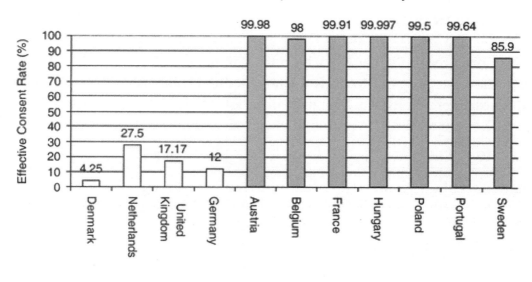

19. The term "cognitive miser" was coined by Susan Fiske and Shelly E. Taylor.
20. Cass R. Sunstein and Richard H. Thaler, *Nudge: Improving Decisions about Health, Wealth, and Happiness* (New Haven, CT: Yale University Press, 2008), 109.

Leading social psychologist Dr. Dan Ariely explains, "The stark difference is due to a small distinction in the design of the form. In countries where the form is set as 'opt-in' (check this box if you want to participate in the organ donation program), people do not check the box, and as a consequence they do not become a part of the program. In countries where the form is set as 'opt-out' (check this box if you don't want to participate in the organ donation program), people also do not check the box and are automatically enrolled in the program. In both cases, large percentages of people simply adopt the default option."[21] He continues,

> You might think that people do this because they don't care. That the decision about donating their organs is so trivial that they can't be bothered to lift up the pencil and check the box. But in fact the opposite is true. This is a hard emotional decision about what will happen to our bodies after we die.... It is because of the difficulty and the emotionality of these decisions that they just don't know what to do so they adopt the default option.[22]

From the standpoint of human nature the less thought and effort the better. Therefore, we should: (a) heed the "out of sight out of mind" policy to reduce unwanted temptation; and (b) structure our routine in a way that minimizes the effort—both mental and physical—that is required to bring us closer to our goal.[23]

THE ENVIRONMENT

The Torah recounts that Korach and 250 members of the tribe of Reuben challenged the leadership of Moses. Korach incited the controversy, but Reuben, as the tribe closest in proximity, was the most vulnerable to his influence. It is for good reason that the Talmud teaches, "Woe unto the wicked, and woe unto his neighbor ..."[24]

NOTES

21. Research cited from Dan Ariely http://danariely.com/2008/05/05/3-main-lessons-of-psychology. Based on a study by Eric J. Johnson and Daniel Goldstein, "Do Defaults Save Lives?" *Science* 302, no. 5649 (2003): 1338–1339.

22. Ibid.

23. Because we have only a limited amount of energy for decision making, a lack of structure forces us to use vital energy in making countless ordinary decisions. See Jim Loehr and Tony Schwartz, *The Power of Full Engagement* (New York: Free Press, 2003). *Halachah*—the laws by which we live—literally means "gait" or "path," guiding us in the proper way to go, encompassing all we do, and in the process, advantageously conserving our mental energy for larger life decisions. Aptly, the Hebrew prayer book is called the *Siddur*, which means "order."

24. *Succah* 56b.

While the influence of environment has been given expansive treatment through-out this book, we cannot underestimate its role in our own behavior—to serve as either inspiration or temptation. A few final studies are worth noting to reinforce how social and environmental factors unconsciously impact on our behavior.

A review of more than three thousand students at the U.S. Air Force Academy found that if half of a recruit's friends became out of shape, he would become three times more likely to fail the final fitness requirements himself. The study concludes with a mind-shaking finale: The most reliable indicator of a cadet's future fitness in the academy is not his entry fitness level—but the fitness of the least-fit cadet in his own unit.[25]

A wide range of attitudes, beliefs, and behaviors are literally contagious. Researchers of the legendary "Framingham Study" found that if a person became obese, his or her friends were 57 percent more likely to become obese.[26] The follow-up paper showed similar effects regarding smoking: A person was 36 percent more likely to pick up the habit if just one close friend started to smoke. Related find-ings found that people are 50 percent more likely to drink heavily if someone they're directly connected to is a heavy drinker. Dr. Nicholas Christakis of Harvard University offered the following analysis:

> We've found that the influence of your friends and people you have connec-tions with can affect your health just as much as your family history or your genetic background.... . With regard to alcohol consumption, your social net-work may have both positive and negative health consequences, depending on the circumstances.[27]

As noted, the environment can also influence us for the better. Christakis and colleagues found that people were 29 percent more likely to completely abstain from alcohol consumption if they were directly connected to at least one person who abstains.

The mentality of those around us seeps into our mindset. If we are serious about our objective, we must consider whether the people we surround ourselves

NOTES

25. Scott E. Carrell, Mark Hoekstra, and James E. West, *Is Poor Fitness Contagious?* National Bureau of Economic Research (2010), NBER Working Paper no. 16518.

26. Christakis and Fowler, "The Spread of Obesity in a Large Social Network Over 32 Years," *New England Journal of Medicine* 2007.

27. Rosenquist, Murabito, Fowler, and Christakis, "The Spread of Alcohol Consumption Behavior in a Large Social Network," *Annals of Internal Medicine* 2010.

with subscribe to the values and ideals that we aspire to, or if we are unwittingly sabotaging our success.[28]

TRIGGERS AND CUES

During Pavlov's famous experiment, he would put food powder into a dog's mouth and, by way of a tube surgically inserted into the dog's mouth, measure the drops of saliva produced as a result. In the course of his work, Pavlov noticed that the dogs began to salivate when he merely walked into the room. This salivation could not be a reflex, because it did not occur the first few times Pavlov walked in; it occurred only when the dog had learned that Pavlov's appearance signaled food. That is, Pavlov's appearance became associated with a future event: food. He called this a *conditioned reflex*.

When we familiarize ourselves with an environment, we create an anchor—we store sensory stimuli or symbols (e.g., sights, sounds, smells) to represent that experience. Subsequent encounters with even one of those sensory symbols actuate our representational systems, and the memories associated with that past experience are triggered. Over time, we begin to respond to familiar stimuli unconsciously. For example, if the traffic light turns red as we're approaching it, we automatically press the brake pedal.

Our Sages speak of the positive applications of anchoring. Regarding the *mitzvah* of *mezuzah*, the *Sefer HaChinuch* writes, "The purpose of this *mitzvah* is to remember God every time one enters or leaves his house."[29] Regarding *tzitzis*, he writes, "The purpose of this *mitzvah* is to constantly remember all of God's *mitzvos*."[30] Indeed, God says, "So that you may remember and perform all My commandments and be holy to your God."[31] While the spiritual depth of these commandments is beyond description, let alone understanding, this surface explanation does offer insight into how these *mitzvos* produce a benefit by providing a visual anchor.

The Gemara teaches that we have different feelings for different places, and, at times, moving to a new location can change our emotional state.[32] Addictive

---

28. An idol-worshipping environment is obviously not conducive toward building a relationship with God. "And God said to Abraham, 'Go for yourself; away from your land, the place of your birth and your father's house'" (Genesis 12:1–8).

29. *Mitzvah* 423.

30. Ibid., 386.

31. Numbers 15:40.

32. *Bava Metzia* 75b.

behavior in particular is highly influenced by environmental stimuli and cues. Analysis shows that abrupt discontinuation of a drug must be combined with a change in one's environment if a successful decrease or elimination of drug addiction is to occur.[33]

Similarly, when we want to break free from self-destructive thoughts or habits (even when they do not rise to the level of an addiction), it is sometimes necessary to remove ourselves from our environment or at least from prompts that keep us locked into negative patterns of behavior.[34] The impact of our physical surroundings—as well as the people in them—on our efforts and objectives cannot be overstressed.

SYNERGISTIC PRIORITIES

The Talmud tells us that every angel can have only one mission.[35] Unlike angels, humans, of course, are meant to take on multiple roles, but there is wisdom in prioritizing our activities.[36] There is a classic demonstration about time management that uses a glass jar, rocks, pebbles, sand, and water to illustrate how to prioritize our day.[37] We first fill a glass jar with large rocks. The jar certainly looks full. Then we add in pebbles that fill in some of the spaces between the rocks. Once again, it seems full. Then we add sand, and as it settles into the crevices, we see that there is still more room.

Finally, as we pour water into the jar, it becomes clear that the jar was able to hold still more. The lesson here is that we should conduct our lives with higher priorities first—the big rocks—and then move on to fill in the space with projects of a lesser priority. We always have room for the little things, but if we began with the smaller items, we could not put in the larger ones without overflowing the glass.

Our energies are too easily frittered away by focusing on trivial matters, and by mistakenly investing great effort in areas that do not produce the most fruitful

---

NOTES

33. See John L. Falk and Chyan E. Lau, "Stimulus Control of Addictive Behavior: Persistence in the Presence and Absence of a Drug," *Pharmacology Biochemistry and Behavior* 50, no. 1 (1995): 71–75.

34. Because these signals are wired directly into the subconscious, it requires great energy to consciously disrupt the current. By short-circuiting these connections, we free ourselves from unwanted urges that seem to appear out of nowhere.

35. *Bava Metzia* 86b.

36. *Chazal* note that one of the seven hallmarks of a wise person is that he does things in order—that is, he answers first questions first (Ethics of the Fathers 5:7).

37. S.R. Covey, *The 7 Habits of Highly Effective People: Restoring the Character Ethic* (New York: Free Press, 2004).

harvest. The Pareto principle, also known as the "80/20 rule," states that for many endeavors, about 80 percent of our results come from 20 percent of our actions—or 80 percent of the effects come from 20 percent of the causes. This means that we need to determine where the return on our efforts is greatest and construct our day accordingly.[38] In doing so, we may just find that some of the "rocks" in our lives should not be in our glass at all.

Success in life requires equal recognition of what needs to be done and what should be left undone. "It's not enough to be busy, so are ants. The question is, 'what are we busy with?' "[39] Having priorities, though, means more than establishing order; it requires objectives that are consistent with our values and in concert with the totality of our lives.[40] Renowned psychiatrist Karen Horney writes,

> We have to make sure our goals are synergistic—living with unresolved conflicts involves primarily a devastating waste of human energies, occasioned not only by conflicts themselves but by all the devious attempts to remove them. When a person is basically divided he can never put his energies wholeheartedly into anything, but wants always to pursue two or more incompatible goals. This means he will either scatter his energies or actively frustrate his efforts... . [N]o matter how potentially gifted he is—[his efforts] will be wasted... . Divided energies also cause him to unconsciously rebel and insist on perfection, forgetfulness, overworking, etc.[41]

When our goals are prioritized and harmonized, and congruent with our values, all aspects of the self are integrated into the larger whole, and our drive is undivided, pure, and potent.

SINGULAR FOCUS

Multitasking is not a skill to be cultivated but a liability to be avoided. Findings show, "People who are regularly bombarded with multiple streams of information do not pay attention, control their memory, or switch from one job to another as well as

---

NOTES

38. The Torah source for this rule is the obligation to always ask ourselves what is the most valuable use of our time now—in other words, what is the most urgent *mitzvah*? And that comes first (*Moed Katan* 9a–b).

39. Henry David Thoreau (July 12, 1817–May 6, 1862) was an American author, poet, and philosopher.

40. See Rabbi Yeruchem Levovitz, *Da'as Torah*, Vol. IV.

41. Horney, *Our Inner Conflicts*, 155.

those who are focused on one task at a time."[42] The researchers expected to find that multitaskers are more productive and successful. "We kept looking for what they're better at, and we didn't find it," said the study's lead author.[43] He explains,

> When they're in situations where there are multiple sources of information coming from the external world or emerging out of memory, they're not able to filter out what's not relevant to their current goal. That failure to filter means they're slowed down by that irrelevant information…. They couldn't help thinking about the task they *weren't* doing. The high multitaskers are always drawing from all the information in front of them. They can't keep things separate in their minds."

The celebration of multitasking encourages a constant need to be busy, consequently the ability to focus on one task, let alone to think without constant interruption and distraction, grows fainter.

In actuality, though, we're not even multitasking. We're abruptly shifting our concentration back and forth with each new interruption. Neurobiologists describe the brain's energy-draining process when it shifts attention between tasks: disengaging, shutting down, rerouting blood flow, assessing the new task—the process repeating itself, constantly forcing the brain to reorient itself each time. This makes us not only weary, but less efficient.[44]

Research concludes, "A person who is interrupted takes 50 percent longer to complete a task. Not only that, he makes up to 50 percent more errors."[45] Findings like these help deepen our appreciation for the Talmudic principle that one who is engaged in a *mitzvah* is exempt from performing other *mitzvos*.[46]

NOTES

42. See Eyal Ophir, Clifford Nass, and Anthony D. Wagner, *Proceedings of the National Academy of Sciences*, August 2009. Stanford Report, August 24, 2009. Quotation and the following passage appear in the Stanford University press release, written by Adam Gorlick.

43. Ibid.

44. Learning Torah requires a clear non-intrusive environment, like that experienced when a north wind blows (*Megillah* 28b). Even the slightest distraction, such as a person's request, detracts from one's learning (*Eruvin* 65a).

45. See John Medina, *Brain Rules: 12 Principles for Surviving and Thriving at Work, Home, and School* (Washington: Pear Press, 2009), 92.

46. *Succah* 25a. "One should be extraordinarily careful not to allow himself to become confused and must condition himself to focus all of his attention on what he is doing at that moment." Rabbi Menachem Mendel Levin, *Cheshbon HaNefesh*, 133.

In the words of the illustrious Winston Churchill, "There is in the act of preparing, the moment you start caring." We again highlight this directive because ultimately only our ability to consider the breadth of consequences that stem from our actions will keep the furnace of determination burning. Still, self-regulation is heavily influenced by a number of factors within our full control, and with some foresight and planning we can take concrete steps to preserve energy and persist more efficiently.

34 | SUCCESS STRATEGIES

A lack of progress is not always due to a lack of will, because a number of hidden forces can influence our success. We will discuss seven additional task-specific factors that can be applied—to varying degrees—to character development, as well as to our long-term objectives.

We should remind ourselves that creation did not happen overnight. In our desire to create ourselves, to be like God, we cannot forget that we are human, after all, and we should not expect to instantly upend our nature or uproot our lives.[47] Let us paint with a broad brush and describe three main categories of personal growth:

Ego-Oriented: Any area that is mostly character-based can be adopted with minimal internal pushback. These are acts that nurture humility over displays of arrogance and anger. The moment the battle is over, and we are victorious, we feel empowered, not drained—and each success builds on the next.[48] Should we fail, the downside is limited. We may be disappointed with ourselves, but it is unlikely that we will completely abandon our pursuit.

This does not mean that we should set ourselves up for failure. Rabbi Yisrael Salanter is quoted as saying: "It is harder to change one bad character trait than it is to learn the entire Talmud." If we want to be successful, we have to be smart. The *mussar* masters repeatedly stressed that our approach should be methodical,

47. As we explained, in some instances a major life or lifestyle change may be necessary in order to break free from the debilitating influences of a destructive environment. Most certainly, these decisions are thought through and not undertaken on a whim.

48. An act of *chesed* that requires effort in the physical world does not fall into this category because it is not entirely character-based.

and we should work on ourselves in only one specific area.[49] Multiple objectives or imbalanced intensity scatter our energies and leave us vulnerable to failure.

Bodily-Based: Although being less lazy or gluttonous would certainly boost our self-esteem, we must proceed with even greater caution than in the above category. A person cannot run a marathon without training. He could try, but he would fail. Worse, it is likely that he would injure himself. *Chazal* explain that trying to change too much too fast can lead to the rebellion of the animal self (*nefesh habaheimis*). In such instances, we may give up altogether and fall deeper into self-destructive behaviors.

Self-Image: The category that needs the most planning and preparation has to do with the mental picture that we hold of ourselves. Recall from Chapter 2 that a person's instinct is to protect the psychological self, in much the same way as we protect our physical selves. As we will go to great lengths to protect our body from harm, we are also alert to threats to change "who we are"—even if these changes are for the better. As a rule, dramatic, wholesale changes in one's lifestyle are therefore ill-advised.[50]

The Sages warn, "A person who attempts to grasp levels of spirituality that are beyond his reach makes himself a target for the forces of *tumah* [impurity]which will make every attempt to push him away from his goal."[51] Regardless of the category, if our efforts to grow generate resentment, anger, or intense frustration, then we must stop and reevaluate. It is our duty to be honest with ourselves so that our expectations do not exceed our limitations.

Of course, it is easy to be misled by our *yetzer hara* into taking on too much or too little. The one thing we cannot obtain on our own is objectivity. Even the wisest of men can benefit from advice from another because the other person's ego is less involved. No matter how a great a person is, it is impossible to escape some bias. This is one reason *Chazal* exhort that one should "acquire for yourself a friend…. Accept a teacher upon yourself."[52]

NOTES

49. See Rabbi Shlomo Wolbe's *Alei Shur*, Vol. II, 191 and 337.

50. Unlike our self-concept, our self-image has to be slowly reshaped. Otherwise, the psyche, not recognizing it as a part of itself, rejects any attitude, value, or belief that it perceives as foreign, similar to a transplanted organ being rejected by the body. Reshaping the self-image is equivalent to an anti-rejection drug, so that our new outlook feels familiar and is slowly integrated into our personality.

51. Rabbi Avraham Danzig, *Nishmas Adam*, Section 145.

52. Ethics of the Fathers 1:16.

SUCCESS STRATEGIES

1. *A Clearly Written Goal*

Formulating a precise definition of what we want to accomplish helps us focus on relevant activities and avoid diversions that distance us from our objectives.[53] In fact, research finds that we are on average ten times more likely to succeed by making a firm resolution to a specific commitment.[54]

We can further increase our success rate by adding one small step: putting pen to paper. [55] The power of a written goal is expressed throughout the *Mussar* tradition. *Cheshbon Hanefesh*, (lit., "an accounting of the soul") offers a precise formula for personal change, based on the principle of having a written statement of what we aspire to, in a particular area of spiritual growth.[56]

"*Shema Yisrael*," our personal mission statement, is traditionally recited three times a day and is the declaration of our belief in One God. Thus, we are commanded to write it, to speak of it, and to place it, so that we can keep ourselves constantly reminded of this one true reality. The first paragraph reads:

> *Hear, O Israel, the Lord is our God,*
> *The Lord is One.*
>
> *(Blessed is the name of His glorious kingdom*
> *Forever and ever.)*
>
> *And you shall love the Lord your God,*
> *With all your heart, with all your soul, and with all your possessions.*
> *And these words which I command you this day shall be upon your heart.*
>
> *And you shall teach them to your children*
> *And speak of them when you sit in your home,*

NOTES

53. God made Abraham's journey to the Land of Israel more difficult by concealing from him the precise location of the Land to which he was to travel: "Go ... to the Land that I shall show you" (Genesis 12:2, Rashi ad loc.). Rashi explains that this was so Abraham could receive greater merit, illustrating that our journey is arguably more trying when we do not have a clear path laid out for us.

54. See J. C. Norcross, M. S. Mrykalo, and M.D. Blagys, "Auld Lang Syne: Success Predictors, Change Processes, and Self-Reported Outcomes of New Year's Resolvers and Nonresolvers," *Journal of Clinical Psychology* 58, no. 4 (2002): 397–405. PubMed PMID: 11920693.

55. We need look no further than the Ten Commandments to see the value in committing to writing the all-encompassing theme. Rashi (Exodus 22:12) explains that all of the 613 Torah commandments are alluded to in the Ten Commandments.

56. Authored by Rabbi Mendel Lefen, an early *Mussar* personality.

CHAPTER THIRTY-FOUR

When you walk on the way,
When you lie down and when you rise up.

And you shall bind them for a sign upon your hand
And they shall be Tefillin between your eyes.
And you shall write them
On the doorposts of your homes
And upon your gates.

2. *Action Steps*

We are taught that "The eyes of a fool are toward the end of the earth."[57] Once a path has been chosen, we want to break down our objectives into a series of specific, clear steps, so we can focus our attention on what needs to be done.[58] In one study, two groups of students were shown the importance of exercise in overcoming coronary heart disease. One group was made to plan exactly where and how to get its physical exercise, while the other group was left to its own devices. The group that made concrete plans succeeded more than 91 percent of the time, compared with a success rate of less than 20 percent for the second group.[59]

Rabbeinu Yonah writes, "From the moment a person awakens in the morning he should examine everything he does. One should divide his daily schedule into manageable segments that are easily monitored."[60] God created the universe with ten statements. He could have done it with one—or with none. Let us emulate God in this way and divide our goals into practical and doable increments to help create our new selves.

3. *Constant Payoff*

The advice of the Sages is, "Celebrate every small victory you have over the *yetzer hara,* and this will lead you to greater victories."[61] Likewise, we are better able to make short-term sacrifices for long-term gains when there is an immediate

---

NOTES

57. Proverbs 17:24.

58. Thomas L. and Paschal Sheeran, "Can Implementation Intentions Help to Overcome Ego-Depletion?" *Journal of Experimental Psychology* 39 (2003): 279–286.

59. S. E. Milne, S. Orbel, and P. Sheeran, "Combining Motivational and Volitional Interventions to Promote Exercise Participation: Protection Motivation Theory and Implementation Intentions," *British Journal of Health Psychology* 7 (2002): 163–184.

60. Rabbeinu Yonah, *Sod HaTeshuvah* (also called *Darkei HaTeshuvah*).

61. *Chovos HaLevavos,* ad loc.

payoff—even when the reward is self-conferred.[62] We should therefore not only divide our goal into specific steps but also incentivize ourselves for reaching each milestone. This gives the *yetzer hara* something to play with, while we focus on the real objective and the real payoff.

Children have a similar mentality. Due to insufficient perspective, both the child and the person caught up in the moment crave what is improper and incompatible with their long-term objectives. Immediate rewards help modify one's behavior, with the ultimate goal of setting into motion a new pattern of behavior. When we are stuck in the "here and now," we must entice ourselves with compensation commensurate with the currency of our mindset.

Even for a highly valued goal, a small short-term reward can drastically increase our motivation. For example, according to a study published in the *Journal of the American Medical Association*, those who have an immediate financial incentive to lose weight are five times more likely to reach their target than are dieters who have no money at stake.[63]

4. *Revisiting Visualization*

Visualization helps us to achieve all types of goals because, as we explained, it can produce actual changes in the brain. For maximum efficacy, the process uses a dual-layered approach. *Outcome simulation* requires us to visualize our objective as if it has already happened, and we use *process simulation* to mentally rehearse the steps and actions needed to reach our objective. Findings show that those who engage in both types of visualization are significantly more likely to start a project on time and complete it on time, and visualization of the action steps, specifically, can cause us to find the task to be less difficult and tedious.[64]

5. *Avoiding Overreaction*

A common pattern of self-regulation failure is having an overreaction to the initial indulgence, which escalates into a full-blown binge and succumbing even more to the unwanted behavior. The resultant overindulgence (or relapse, in the

---

NOTES

62. Yaacov Trope and Ayelet Fishbach, "Counteractive Self-Control in Overcoming Temptation," *Journal of Personality and Social Psychology* 79, no. 4 (2000): 493–506.

63. The incentive does not have to be significant. In this study, 50 percent of those motivated by cash (the total average net incentive earnings was $88.18) attained their 16-pound weight-loss goal, whereas only 10 percent in the control group lost 16 pounds or more. See Kevin G. Volpp, M.D., et al., "Financial Incentive–Based Approaches for Weight Loss," *Journal of the American Medical Association* (2008).

64. Shelley E. Taylor, Lien B. Pham, Inna D. Rivkin, and David A. Armor, "Harnessing the Imagination: Mental Simulation, Self-Regulation, and Coping," *American Psychologist* 53: 429–439.

case of addiction) is not triggered by the first lapse, but by the ensuing feelings of guilt and shame. And the more ensconced we are in these negative feelings, the more likely we are to continue engaging in the behavior. It is the ability to forgive ourselves, not self-flagellation, that increases accountability—which then leads to regaining our self-control and initiating a course correction.[65]

Using an MRI, the neurobiological basis for why self-compassion helps us to self-regulate is explained. When we show warmth and compassion to ourselves, we elicit *neuroaffective* responses similar to those that are stimulated by an encouraging, supportive other.[66] This then helps us feel loved and supported, creating an awareness that we deserve better, and it instills in us the will to invest in our long-term care and benefit.[67]

The previously discussed process of *teshuvah* (to gain forgiveness from God and to forgive ourselves) is instrumental in helping to break the cycle. Rabbeinu Yonah, author of *The Gates of Repentance*, the classic work on *teshuvah*, writes that one should aspire to do *teshuvah* because we are descendants of the Patriarchs and worthy of great spiritual potential.[68] He is describing a path of *teshuvah* based on a positive—rather than a negative—self-image.

6. *Instituting Consequences*

The above-mentioned point notwithstanding, appropriate self-imposed consequences can be an effective tool to regulate one's behavior.[69] There is a copy of the journal of Rabbi Yeruchem Levovitz, in which he committed to fine himself ten *kopecks* (a Russian currency) if he failed to meet his daily goal.[70] The following APA abstract summarizes a range of findings:

> How do anticipated short-term costs affect the likelihood of engaging in an activity that has long-term benefits? Five studies ... manipulated short-term

65. Mark R. Leary, et al., "Self-Compassion and Reactions to Unpleasant Self-Relevant Events: The Implications of Treating Oneself Kindly," *Self-Forgiveness and Accountability* (2007) 92: 887–904.

66. Paul Gilbert, *The Compassionate Mind: A New Approach to the Challenges of Life* (London: Constable Robinson, 2009).

67. Paul Gilbert, et al., "Having a Word with Yourself: Neural Correlates of Self-Criticism and Self-Reassurance," *Neuroimage* 49 (2010): 1849–1856.

68. *Sharei Avodah* 1.

69. Trope and Fishbach, "Counteractive Self-Control in Overcoming Temptation," *Journal of Personality and Social Psychology* 2000 79, no. 4.

70. The *Mashgiach* ("spiritual supervisor of *Yeshivah* students") of Mir in Europe. *Da'as Chochmah U'Mussar*, Vol. I, 9.

costs (e.g., painful medical procedures) and assessed a variety of self-control strategies (e.g., self-imposed penalties for failure to undergo a test). The results show that even moderate short-term costs help people to act according to their long-term interests.[71]

Emotional pain is also an effective consequence and can be used to spur us on to positive behavior. One of countless such stories includes a well-known Torah personality who, determined to stop smoking, hung a note on his office door stating his intention to quit. That way, he would be embarrassed to smoke in front of his students and colleagues.[72]

7. *Monitoring Progress*

Recording and reviewing our behavior has been shown to be effective across a wide swath of areas. For example, one such study found that dieters who kept a food journal lost twice as much weight over a six-month period as those who didn't. Moreover, follow-up studies conclude that they kept it off. The simple act of writing everything down (a) motivates people to consume less, and (b) makes it difficult for them to ignore their slip-ups.[73]

The previously referenced *Cheshbon HaNefesh* was an essential text of the *Mussar* movement. The main theme is that each week, the reader focuses on one of the core thirteen traits and each day records how well he succeeds in expressing or repressing the particular trait.

Keeping a journal or charting progress is a way to move the emphasis from a single incidence of behavior to an overall pattern. It is easier, too, to sustain progress if we see evidence in writing. Memory is far more biased when we feel discouraged, and we have a harder time recalling our successes.[74] Additionally, tracking our progress allows us to adjust our tactics because we can examine what's working and what's not working. While we may be unwavering in our pursuit, we want to be flexible in our approach.

NOTES

71. Trope and Fishbach, "Counteractive Self-Control in Overcoming Temptation," *Journal of Personality and Social Psychology* 2000. Passage edited for brevity and clarity.

72. Referring to Rabbi Meltzen in Siddur *Eishai Yisrael*, page 53 in the 2008 Z. Berman edition.

73. Jack F. Hollis, "Weight Loss during the Intensive Intervention Phase of the Weight-Loss Maintenance Trial," *American Journal of Preventive Medicine* 35, no. 2 (2008): 118–126.

74. Ibid. Rabbi Nosson Tzvi Finkel, better known as the Alter of Slobodka, kept a daily log of his activities (*Tenuas HaMussar*, Vol. III, Ch. 17).

These stated principles for success coalesce around one requirement: we must make a firm commitment and do it with joy. Success requires that for a specified period of time, we do not reconsider the decision in any way.[75] Precious energy trickles out every time we consider, "Should I keep it up or not?" Moreover, a decision made half-heartedly or with a heavy heart is doomed from the start. It is necessary to make our declaration with joy! As we learned, *simchah* charges our commitment with a near limitless fuel supply. When we make a joyous decision that is non-negotiable and not dependent on circumstance and free from any and all conditions, we exercise the muscle of free will in its most powerful form.

NOTES

75. By making a commitment for a fixed period of time, we allow ourselves the option of revisiting our decision after the set time. In this way, we do not have to tackle a lifelong decision, and whatever gains we have made will be viewed appropriately so, as gains, rather than causing us to consider ourselves failures because we did not to succeed in completely eradicating the behavior.

35 | THE FORCE OF HABIT

The Sages say, "Let us seek out our ways and examine them, and we will return to God."[76] All well and good, but we are also reminded that "Bad habits start off like a spider web and end up being like the ropes of a wagon."[77]

The force of habit runs deep through our emotional veins and distinguishes itself from an ordinary behavior, in that it is automatic.[78] As such, in addition to the previously discussed strategies, it requires special attention. We will explore the psychological factors once we discuss two critical biological features.

GLUCOSE EFFECT

Another muscle-like quality of willpower is that it is fueled by glucose.[79] Exercising self-control uses up large quantities of this cognitive resource, and we are most susceptible to temptation when glucose levels are low or not metabolized properly. The following APA abstract summarizes the research:

> The present work suggests that self-control relies on glucose as a limited energy source. Laboratory tests of self-control ... showed that: (a) acts of self-control

---

NOTES

76. Lamentations 3:40.

77. *Succah* 52a.

78. "Intelligence is given; morality is acquired; habit rules" (Rabbi Shlomo ibn Gavirol, *Sefer Tikkun, Middos Hanefesh*). "It's easier to resist at the beginning than at the end" (Leonardo Da Vinci).

79. Matthew T. Gailliot and Roy F. Baumeister, "The Physiology of Willpower: Linking Blood Glucose to Self-Control," *Personality and Social Psychology Review* (2007): 303.

reduced blood glucose levels; (b) low levels of blood glucose after an initial self-control task predicted poor performance on a subsequent self-control task; and (c) initial acts of self-control impaired performance on subsequent self-control tasks, but consuming a glucose drink eliminated these impairments. Self-control requires a certain amount of glucose to operate unimpaired. A single act of self-control causes glucose to drop below optimal levels, thereby impairing subsequent attempts at self-control.[80]

In one of hundreds of such studies, researchers asked volunteers to answer a series of seven questions regarding their preference to receive a small sum of money the next day or a larger sum at a future date. For example, "Would you prefer 120 dollars tomorrow or 450 dollars in 31 days?" They answered these questions after drinking either a regular soda (containing sugar) or a diet soda (containing an artificial sweetener).

The experiment found that the subjects who drank the regular soda prior to answering the questions—and, as such, had higher blood glucose levels—were inclined to choose the wiser option of receiving more money at a later date, while the subjects who drank the diet sodas were more drawn to the immediate, and smaller, sum.[81] The far-reaching implication drawn by the researchers: "Reducing the degree of fluctuation in blood glucose may offer a possible means for the treatment and intervention of some impulsive disorders, anorexia, drug addiction, and gambling addiction."[82]

SLEEP EFFECTS

The temporary effects of sleep deprivation on the prefrontal cortex—the area that regulates impulse control and decision making—are similar to the symptoms of

NOTES

80. Matthew T. Gailliot, et al. "Self-Control Relies on Glucose as a Limited Energy Source: Willpower Is More Than a Metaphor," *Personality and Social Psychology Review* 92, no. 2 (2007): 325–336.

81. Although sugar may give us a short-term willpower lift, it is common sense to eat a nutritious variety of foods that can help decrease the possibility of long-term fluctuation, which leads to mental fatigue. Counterintuitively, glucose levels actually drop when we consume sugars or refined carbohydrates and high-glycemic foods. These foods initially cause a rush of glucose in the bloodstream, but then our body releases insulin, which stores the glucose (leading to weight gain) and causes glucose levels circulating in the body to plunge—commonly referred to as a *sugar crash*.

82. X.T. Wang and Robert D. Dvorak, "Sweet Future: Fluctuating Blood Glucose Levels Affect Future Discounting," *Psychological Science*, published online January 20, 2010. Adapted from the news release by the Association for Psychological Science, 2010.

people who have suffered an actual brain injury. A lack of sleep weakens our ability to think things through. We then too easily default to autopilot and fall into familiar, self-defeating patterns. Research confirms that people who sleep four hours a night (and require at least six hours) are less likely to make responsible choices regarding their health and well-being.[83]

Most adults sleep an average of 6.4 hours or less per night—that's an hour less than a decade ago.[84] According to the National Sleep Foundation, more than 80 percent of Americans do not get enough sleep each night (around 47 million people qualify for the medical label of "sleep deprivation" but do not know it), and almost all experience one or more of the signs and symptoms of sleep deprivation, including irritability, restlessness, lack of focus, anxiety, and depression.

THE BEST DEFENSE

The mind can be compared to a field. A farmer can plant anything he wishes. If the farmer decides to plant corn, then corn will grow. If he chooses to plant wheat, then wheat will grow. However, if the farmer chooses to plant nothing and decides not to tend to his soil—then weeds will grow. So, too, a mind that is not active will be filled with negative thoughts.

It is prudent to be proactive. As the saying goes, the best defense is a good offense. Since the human mind can focus on only one thought at a time, the greatest method to deal with unwelcome thoughts is to fix one's mind on Torah study and to expand one's mind with wisdom.[85] We have Six Constant *mitzvos* that are, in part, designed to keep our minds constantly focused on God and the true nature of this world.[86]

However, when the vise of temptation tightens and our thoughts begin to drift into unsafe waters, we need to actively redirect our attention elsewhere and not allow these feelings to find root.[87] The Torah states, "The tree was good to eat and

NOTES

83. Tony T. Wells and Dean G. Cruess, "Effects of Partial Sleep Deprivation on Food Consumption and Food Choice," *Psychology and Health* 21, no. 1 (2006): 79–86.

84. The Rambam writes that no more than eight hours of sleep are required, unless a person is sick, and studies show that people who sleep between 6.5 hours and 7.5 hours a night live the longest.

85. Rambam, *Hilchos Issurei Biah*, 22:21.

86. The *mitzvos* are: (1) know there is a God; (2) don't believe in any other power; (3) believe in God's Oneness; (4) love God; (5) fear God; and (6) don't be misled by your heart and eyes (*Chayei Adam* 1:5, *Biur Halachah* 1:1).

87. See Rabbi Simcha Zissel Ziv, *Chochmah U'Mussar*, Vol. 2, 224.

desirable to the eyes."[88] The Rambam writes, "As soon as [Adam] began to think about transgressing, he was swayed by his physical desire."[89]

We want to divert our train of thought as quickly as possible, by whatever reasonable means possible. The faster we do this, the greater the odds of success. To cement our strategy, we also need to set up a protocol in advance—a prearranged course of action to follow.[90] This has been shown to be effective even when our willpower reserves are drained, because we do not have to think about what to do.[91] It is also best to follow up our escape plan with an immediate reward (as discussed in the previous chapter) to prevent our thoughts from drifting back.

PATTERNS IN MOTION

Professor Howard Rachlin at Harvard University explains how undoing a habit has less to do with individual acts and more to do with establishing a new pattern of behavior. He uses the example of a smoker who contemplates quitting:

> Suppose you decide to stop smoking for the rest of your life. Then there are only two possibilities. On the one hand, you may keep the resolution and never smoke again. If you do, it hardly matters whether you have one last cigarette tonight; smoking that last cigarette would give you immediate pleasure. After that, if you never smoke again, you will derive all the long-term benefits as well. On the other hand, it is also possible to make the resolution but fail to keep it. If this second possibility comes to pass, if you are simply making one more empty promise to yourself, does it really matter whether you smoke this cigarette tonight? Why suffer the pain of abstinence tonight if tomorrow you are going to smoke anyway? In either case—whether you keep the resolution or not—it makes sense to smoke this cigarette tonight. Secure in your reasoning, you light your cigarette. What is wrong with this argument?
>
> The problem is that the two questions are not independent of each other. A person could begin acting on a resolution tomorrow or today. But while the physical independence of today and tomorrow is real enough, the fact

88. Genesis 3:6.

89. See Rambam, *Guide for the Perplexed*, Ch. 1.

90. Paschal Sheeran and S. Orbell, "Using Implementation Intentions to Increase Attendance for Cervical Cancer Screening," *Health Psychology* 19 (2003): 283–289.

91. Thomas L. Webb and Paschal Sheeran, *Abstract: Can Implementation Intentions Help to Overcome Ego-Depletion?*

remains that actions today affect actions tomorrow. Not smoking tonight makes it easier not to smoke tomorrow, and not smoking tomorrow makes it easier not to smoke the next day, and so on.[92] To smoke the "last" cigarette tonight (or eat one more steak dinner or drink one last scotch and soda) is to fail to perceive the degree to which tonight's act is embedded in a pattern of acts over many nights and days. The decision to stop smoking is in effect a decision to begin a pattern of behavior. The decision to smoke one last time is in effect a decision to maintain a different pattern of behavior—that of smoking. "Shall I begin a new pattern tomorrow or today?" is a psychologically false question. The real issue is whether to begin a new pattern at all or to keep following an already existing one. To smoke the cigarette tonight (or eat the second dessert, or drink the fourth scotch) is to fail to perceive the connection between tonight's act and the pattern of acts over many nights and days—to be "shortsighted" (or "myopic") about both past and future behavior.[93]

The vitalizing force behind both the development and the dissolution of a pattern is momentum. Newton's first law of motion speaks to the tendency of a body in motion to stay in motion, due to the property of inertia. He might as well have added that people in motion tend to stay in motion, and people at rest tend to stay at rest.[94]

We often adopt a "one time won't make a difference" mentality, but when we feel inspired to take a leap—or even a small step—in the right direction, we should move with fervor, swiftly and decisively.[95] This is a principle in Torah known as *zerizus* ("alacrity"). The Ramchal explains that a person's enthusiasm and inspiration to act may not translate into action because of lack of *zerizus*. Rabbi Tzadok

92. He adds here that there is another fault in the logic that views the questions as independent. In twenty-four hours, tomorrow will be today. If it always makes sense to smoke one last time, we will never stop smoking (ibid.).

93. Professor Howard Rachlin, *The Science of Self-Control* (Kindle Location 125). Kindle Edition.

94. The paradox of momentum is that when things go poorly, we want nothing more than to retreat and hide from the world. Yet when things go particularly well, we want to savor the moment, stop, and bask in our success. In both cases, we thwart momentum, our most precious self-generating gift. We build our *succah* right after Yom Kippur—going immediately from one *mitzvah* to the next—rather than taking time off and losing momentum (*Shulchan Aruch, Aruch Chayim* 624:5).

95. "All of your acts should be preceded by deliberation; when you have reached a decision, act without delay" (Rabbi Menachem Mendel Levin, *Cheshbon HaNefesh*). Napoleon is quoted as saying, "Take time to deliberate; but when the time for action arrives, stop thinking and go in."

HaKohen of Lublin writes that in the same way that the Jews left Egypt with haste, so must we act with haste any time we start a new endeavor.[96]

The energy of each window of opportunity in every moment of time carries with it a unique potential. In hesitation, the opportunity itself is lost and the engine of momentum fails to start. To quote the familiar English aphorism, *Strike while the iron is hot*.

THE BLAME GAME

Make no mistake. Just about any habit that goes unexamined is an abandonment of responsibility masquerading as an out-of-control desire. Even addictions do not cast some magical spell over our willpower. Some in academia propose:

> Maybe it would be better to acknowledge ... that a lot of behavior we call addiction is really a love of pleasure that carries the force of habit. We become addicted mostly because of the central issue in all self-control problems, which is the disproportionate value we place on short-term rewards.[97]

While it is ludicrous to suggest that every type of addiction is within the purview of self-control, we must not resign ourselves to automatic victimhood.[98] The dueling theories of addiction are as follows: On one hand, we fault the addicted for having gotten carried away with the behavior in the first place—prompted by curiosity, selfishness, or stupidity—or any combination thereof. On the other hand, considerable research shows that those who have developed a disruptive addiction are the casualty of insurmountable circumstances, perhaps genetic predispositions, which never allowed them a fighting chance.

At what point our free will emerges is a subject of ongoing—philosophical, psychological, and biological—debate, but it remains timelessly indisputable that the beginning of all change comes when we make a conscious decision to accept personal responsibility. In unambiguous terms, this means that we put our ego aside and seek out whatever help we need in order to regain control of our lives.

NOTES

96. *Tzidkas HaTzadik* 1.

97. Daniel Akst, *We Have Met the Enemy: Self-Control in an Age of Excess*, 124.

98. People can be amazingly rational even when it comes to addiction. Research finds that reductions in cigarette consumption occur when a price increase is expected but before the price actually rises. See Gary Becker and Kevin Murphy, "A Theory of Rational Addiction," *Journal of Political Economy* 96, no. 4 (1988): 675–700.

Learned helplessness, a term coined by psychologist Martin Seligman, occurs when a person feels that since he is not in control, he might as well give up. Seligman details how society in general, and the recovery movement in particular, offers up a variety of ready-made explanations for our woes. He writes, "Personal troubles, you're told, do not result, as feared, from your own sloth, insensitivity, selfishness, dishonesty, self-indulgence, stupidity, or lust." Rather, we are taught to believe that the rest of the world is to blame for our failings. In this way, "we have become victims, 'survivors' of abuse, rather than 'failures' and 'losers'." He continues,

> We are now underdogs, trying to fight our way back from misfortune. In our gentle society, everyone roots for the underdog. No one dares speak ill of victims anymore. The usual wages of failure—contempt and pity—are transmuted into support and compassion.... When we fail, we look for consolation, one form of which is to see the setback as something other than failure—to interpret it in a way that does not hurt as much as failure hurts. Being a victim, blaming someone else, or even blaming the system is a powerful and increasingly widespread form of consolation.[99]

The quality of our lives is directly proportional to the amount of responsibility we are willing to accept for what we *can* control. Blame has never moved anyone forward in life—it cannot. Inherent in the assigning of blame is the power to restore what has been lost, taken, or harmed. So goes blame, so goes our power.

King Solomon writes, "A *tzaddik* falls seven times and he gets up [each time]."[100] Note that he does not say that *if* he falls, but that he *does* fall. Failures do not prevent greatness; they are prerequisites to it. Being great is not about falling down but about getting back up.[101] As a prime example, despite Judah's faults and misdeeds, his willingness to admit his sin and recognize its consequences qualified him for kingship. Taking responsibility, not lack of sin, exemplified his true greatness.[102]

NOTES

99. Martin Seligman, *What You Can Change and What You Can't: The Complete Guide to Successful Self-Improvement* (New York: Random House, 2007), 245.

100. Proverbs 24:16.

101. There were four people who never sinned: Benjamin, son of Jacob; Amram, father of Moses; Yishai, father of David; and Kilav, son of David (*Shabbos* 55b). While they are all extraordinary men, they do not quickly come to mind when we speak of the Torah's greatest figures. This is a function of their capacity, which is a reflection of their *neshamos*. Although they maximized their potential and never once fell short, who they could become and the heights they could reach were fixed by their purpose in God's plan.

102. *Tosefta, Berachos* 4:17.

While the spiritual benefits of *teshuvah* have already been discussed, this is the proper place to add that the emotional component is equally compelling. According to research—and common sense—guilt gives rise to self-destructive tendencies; and makes us desire to suffer or to be punished.[103]

A person who holds onto guilt, even though God Himself has given us the means to release it, indeed, to transform it, is not being noble, he is being selfish. He wraps himself in self-pity—the drug that's always within reach and never runs out—to avoid facing himself, his actions, and his life. It is the height of irresponsibility, well beyond whatever action led to his feelings of guilt.

When we find ourselves at the brink of temptation, we need to move quickly to interrupt the pattern, engage in a different pre-planned behavior, and reward ourselves with an instant payoff. Ultimately, accepting full responsibility and capitalizing on even a passing moment of inspiration will help shift momentum and launch a new pattern. Profound change may not happen overnight, but it will happen. To paraphrase Mark Twain: A habit cannot always be tossed out the window; sometimes it must be coaxed down the stairs a step at a time.

NOTES

103. See Gerhart Piers and Milton B. Singer, *Shame and Guilt: A Psychoanalytical and Cultural Study* (New York: Norton, 1971).

PART 11

RELATIONSHIP RESCUE

In the previous chapters, we found techniques to maintain self-control, with a focus on anger management, but when it comes to unleashing our most basic nature, no area in life tries us more than our relationships. Judaism, though, does not embrace the notion of man separating himself from society (with some notable pious exceptions) because a sanitized, frictionless environment offers little opportunity for personal development. Character cannot be cultivated in serenity or solitude. The true measure of one's greatness and growth is found in the domain of relationships.

CHAPTER THIRTY-SIX

THE LADDER
OF
HARMONY

36

The following description is a Kabbalistic representation of Creation and is not to be interpreted literally: In the beginning, the "light" of God—the distinct expression of His Omnipresence and Omnipotence—filled all of existence.[1] A finite world could not exist, because it would be nullified within the Divine light.[2] In simple parlance:

> The essence of the *Ein Sof*'s [Infinite God's], light, as it reveals itself and emerges from its Source, is so superior that no man can grasp such a lofty essence, regardless of his soul's level. This may be compared to a tiny transistor radio connected to a high-voltage electric cable. Of course the appliance will burn out instantly, since it does not possess the capacity to receive such a high voltage.[3]

In order to allow for creation, God "contracted" or "concealed" His light—an act described as *tzimtzum*—thus creating an empty space.[4] This process by which

1. The notion of an all-encompassing infinity is plainly beyond the reach of a finite perspective. Georg Cantor (1845–1918) was a German mathematician and is best known as the architect of set theory—a fundamental theory in mathematics. To give us a taste of his work on absolute infinity, imagine a thin black line stretching to infinity in both directions. How much ink does it take to draw this line? An infinite amount is the answer, of course. Now imagine a thick black line beneath this thin line. How much ink does it take to draw this line? Also an infinite amount, but since it is thicker, does it not require more ink than the thin line? Although he was a genius and well-intentioned, Cantor might have been wise to heed the advice of the Sages, "Do not investigate matters that are beyond you" (*Chagigah* 13a). He died in a mental institution on January 6, 1918.

2. Even a filtered exposure to the light of God, the light of *Ein Sof* ("Infinite"), is not possible: "No one can see Me and live" (Exodus 33:20).

3. *Yedid Nefesh*, Rabbi Y. Bar-Lev, 49.

4. Cf. *Nefesh HaChaim*. Aptly, the word *olam*, "world," comes from the root *helem*, "hidden." Even though

God hides His countenance makes possible the simultaneous existence of two completely incompatible realities: the Infinite and the finite.

He then allowed a *kav* ("single line") of light to penetrate this void, through which flows a Divine energy.[5] Moving in a circular fashion, this ray of Divine light progressively produced a spiritual dimension, which, as we noted, is referred to as the ten *Sefiros*—the ten modes or attributes through which God manifests Himself and interacts with creation.[6]

God created this mechanism as an alternate way for us to experience His Oneness, true unity: we call it harmony.[7] While we cannot fathom the former, we can taste the indescribable pleasure of the latter. Any time we experience pleasure, it is because of harmony—which permits the greatest context for meaning to emerge.

Indeed, many disciplines—from psychology to philosophy to physics—begin with the premise that there is order, a single unified theory; so they seek laws, rules, and theories to explain how disparate pieces fit into a larger, integrated whole.[8] Their soul recognizes the truth—that everything returns to the One.[9] They are seeking God but do not know it.[10]

NOTES

we are speaking figuratively, we must clarify that we are referring to apparent concealment—from our perspective—and not actual concealment.

5. Our understanding of how a finite universe can exist within the Infinite is explained by Rabbi Yitzchak Luria (*Da'as Tevunos* 26, 27, 52).

6. Rabbi Chayyim Vital, *Sefer Eitz Chayyim*. Rabbi Kaplan writes, "It thus forms a bridge between God and creation and acts as a step-down mechanism which prevents creation from being overwhelmed by God's essence while still being infused with it" (*Inner Space*, 8).

7. It may be more accurate to consider the *Sefiros* as an emanation, rather than a creation. *Chazal* explain that before creation, God's indefinable and indescribable name YKVK referred to all ten *Sefiros* as a single unity concealed in *Ein Sof.* "Before they were emanated … the *Sefiros* were one-in-His-essence to such an extent that we may not attribute any [separate] existence to them whatsoever.… Only when it arose in His will to reveal His *Elokut* ('Divinity') in order to bestow His goodness to another via His hidden powers/attributes—did He bring forth non-form into form, and non-existence into existence." Rabbi Moshe Cordovero, *Seder Atzilut.* Quoted by Rabbi Avraham Sutton, *Spiritual Technology* (Hebrew Books, Inc., 2013), 346.

8. On the relevance of delving into non-Torah subjects, the Rambam (*Shemoneh Perakim* 5:4) states that one may do so "as a means to an end"—to bring him closer to his ultimate goal, the recognition of one God. He notes that subjects such as mathematics and engineering can sharpen the mind and "train oneself on the art of theorems, so as to distinguish between valid and invalid proofs. For in fact, that will enable one to comprehend God's essence."

9. The Talmud relates that before we are born, while still in the womb, God sends an angel to teach us all the wisdom for living that we will need to know. Then, just as we enter this world, an angel taps us on the mouth (forming an indentation call the philtrum, which we all have under the nose), and we forget everything the angel taught us. This creates a strong desire to seek out the truth and explains why we are inexplicably drawn to it, and when we come into contact with true wisdom, we don't just see it, we recognize it.

10. This main-text sentence and the unity versus harmony model were framed and formulated by Rabbi Yitzchok Feldheim.

SEPARATE, BUT NOT ALONE

If white light is unity, then the seven colors of the rainbow are harmony. Quantitatively, all of the colors of the spectrum exist inside white light and nothing is missing, yet qualitatively the two are quite different.[11]

White light does not permit individuality. What separates one thing from another is how it differentiates itself. Without some distinction, there would be no separation, much less independence.[12] This would undermine the very purpose of creation, which is to reveal the glory of God—for we cannot reveal what is already in plain sight. To choose to nullify the "I" to reveal the One requires an "I" and a "One."[13]

Harmony is like a puzzle that fits together perfectly, and while each piece interlocks with complete precision into the surrounding pieces, one piece does not melt into the other or lose its shape. The picture is not—can never become—one, even though it is whole and complete.

CLIMBING THE RUNGS

Even within harmony, there is a hierarchy toward a greater representation of unity. We experience harmony in our world in one of three modalities. The lowest level is physical perfection and is expressed through the five senses. The musician brings together notes; the chef, ingredients; the artist, colors—all in a creative process to harmonize separate components into one complete work. Creativity itself is the process by which we fashion a "master piece" (in English, suitably called a *masterpiece*) where everything not only fits together, but where everything works together, to bring forth the potential of each and to produce something else entirely.[14]

NOTES

11. In the ethereal light spectrum, the presence of all color produces white light. When color moves into the physical world, however, it becomes permanently downgraded, such that mixing together a rainbow of paints, for example, produces an earthy brown, representative of physicality.

12. For this reason, the Rabbis tell us that even the angels have bodies, but their souls and bodies are both heavenly. Angels exist only to serve God, but the very fact that they exist means that they feel themselves separate from God. See Rabbi Y. Bar Lev, Ph.D., *Introduction to Kabbalah* (*Yedid Nefesh*), 17 [referencing *Sifre*, beginning of *Parahas Ha'azinu*].

13. The fewer barriers between man and God make a person more Godly (Rambam, *Shemoneh Perakim* 7).

14. Judaism does not suggest, much less encourage, asceticism. In fact, the Talmud says that if a person declines the opportunity to taste a new fruit, he will have to account for that in the World to Come. Physical pleasures are to be fully enjoyed, and this comes through elevating them with a sense of spirituality and enjoying properly and responsibly in the service of God.

Emotional harmony is expressed through love, which is as perfect and absolute as physical beauty, yet it exists on a higher level. For who would not sacrifice something they own for someone they love? And who would risk the well-being of a loved one for an acquisition, no matter how beautiful or perfect?

An even higher level of quasi-unity exists and is found in intellectual harmony (itself in three gradations). At this point, we do what we believe is right, even when it is difficult or unpopular and perhaps even against our own immediate self-interest. It requires discipline and clarity of purpose to forgo creature comforts—much less to risk life and limb—for a higher, meaningful objective. We admire, even revere, the principled person, who is guided by his convictions and not his cravings.

But the truth does not take sides, and "what is right" is inherently tainted by the "I"—our own sense of justice. As such, we cannot say that this, too, is not a competing desire—rather than an act of genuine free will. As we learned, the objective world of "truth and falsehood" supersedes the subjective world of "good and bad" and "right or wrong." The sum of all finite knowledge does not equal truth—qualitatively, truth is something else entirely, because it is beholden not to information, but to reality.

A more refined intellectual harmony is expressed through *emes* ("truth"). The prototype of the *Sefirah* of *Tiferes* ("harmony" or "beauty") is Jacob, who also symbolizes truth.[15] He is referred to as the *whole man* and represents the spiritual beauty that is inherent in unity, in contrast with physical harmony, which is represented by the five senses.[16] In Genesis, Potiphar's wife attempts to seduce Joseph.[17] The Talmud explains that what prevented Joseph from sinning was his being suddenly reminded of his father. The Baal Shem Tov expounds,

> Seeing the physical beauty of Potiphar's wife, Joseph realized her beauty was a reflection of the spiritual beauty of *Tiferes*, the hallmark of his father, Jacob. This awareness immediately cooled his ardor… . He ran away from the physical *Tiferes* of this woman, and rushed out to the higher spiritual *Tiferes*, epitomized by his father, Jacob.[18]

NOTES

15. The Prophets tell us, "Grant truth to Jacob" (Micah 7:20).

16. Genesis 25:27. Ancient Greek society—the antithesis of a Torah mindset—celebrated the physical form as an end unto itself. Absent spiritual substance, the Greeks could not perceive of beauty as anything that extended beyond physicality.

17. Genesis 39:7–9.

18. *Sefer Baal Shem Tov, Vayeishev* 6.

It is feasible that one can make an intellectual error similar to that of Adam HaRishon. We are commanded, then, to both love and fear God, because while love is established by an intellectual bond, fear will keep us from making a decision that may be logically sound, save for the fact that it is not what God wants us to do. Therefore, where a conflict exists between *chochmah* ("wisdom") and fear of God, one should let the latter prevail. Our Sages remind us, "There is no wisdom of Torah without one's intellectual abilities merging with the sense of fear of sin."[19]

King Solomon exhorts, "Trust in God with all your heart and do not rely on your own understanding."[20] The Torah is an instruction book for living. It tells us what is right, even when we cannot begin to grasp the depth of logic behind God's commandments. As we know, Abraham was commanded by God to offer his son as a sacrifice. This command seemingly made no sense. God had promised Abraham that his offspring would multiply like the stars in the sky. Yet Abraham did as God commanded, because he trusted in Him.

One who operates in this sphere abides by *halachah*, even when it conflicts with one's deepest emotions and finite sense of justice. To do the will of God is to live in the world of absolute truth.[21]

THE FINAL LEVEL

The five levels toward unity loosely parallel the five levels of the soul.[22] *Nefesh* is the animating force of the physical body and the five senses; *ruach* is the vitalizing force of emotions; *neshamah* is the vitality of intellect; and *chayah* is the "Divine life force" that channels *chochmah*—an ego-free, unadulterated truth. These four levels are often regarded as extensions of the essence of the soul called *yechidah*, which is also considered a fifth level and is expressed as complete and total unity.

NOTES

19. *Emunah U'Bitachon*, Ch. 1.

20. Proverbs 3:5.

21. Referencing Rashi (Deuteronomy 11:29, regarding idol worship), Rabbi Moshe Feinstein relates that if a person observes all of the *mitzvos* only because his reason tells him that it is worthwhile, his observance is meaningless, because he may at any time change his mind and do something else that appeals to him more. Furthermore, even those *mitzvos* he does observe are not founded in truth, because he does not care if he makes mistakes in his observance, as long as he is not aware of them (*Darash Moshe*, Artscroll, 1994).

22. The five levels of the soul also correspond with Heavenly realms in an ascending chain, referred to as "worlds" or "universes," but more precisely described as planes of consciousness. They are identified as follows, using a loose translation: *Assiyah* ("physicality"), *Yetzirah* ("emotions"), *Beriyah* ("intellect"), *Atzilus*, ("spirit"), and *Adom Kadmon* ("the primordial source").

The Torah is referred to as the Tree of Life because it has many branches, all connecting to one trunk.[23] Ultimately, there is no division; one thing unites everything. Two simultaneous truths can exist, but only one who seeks peace—the final level of harmony—can unite them.

The Talmud states, "The seal of the Holy One Blessed be He is truth;" and "'Peace' is His Name."[24] Peace and truth are not mutually exclusive. Peace is the highest level of truth—to bring unity where there is division.[25] The deeper sources explain that God created the world with the "middle row" of the *Sefiros*. *Gevurah* ("might," represented by Isaac) is on the left side of the *Sefiros*, while *Chesed* ("lovingkindness," represented by Abraham) runs on the right side. *Tiferes* (the middle row, represented by Jacob, as noted above) is the path to peace and to God, because *Tiferes* ascends to the inner dimension of *Keser*.[26]

Almost every major Jewish prayer resonates with a request for peace, illuminating God's love for harmony.[27] Peace wipes away the misperception of multiplicity and reinforces the pervading unity of our reality.[28] For this reason, our Sages proclaim, "All that is written in the Torah was written for the sake of peace."[29]

NOTES

23. See Genesis 2:9.

24. *Shabbos 55a; Shabbos 10b*, based on Judges 6:24.

25. We arrive at this recognition, because Peace is His Name, and as such it is a higher level than truth: His seal. In fact, the Torah allows one to distort the truth for the sake of peace; and it is not only permissible, in some instances it is obligatory (*Yevamos 65b*). We can never, however, cast aside truth in favor of a peace that is inherently false because authentic peace is an extension of truth. See Chapter 39, "Borders and Boundaries" for additional commentary.

26. *Shaarei Tzedek; Likutei Torah, Bamidbar.* Our Sages teach that Jacob was the greatest of all the Patriarchs (*Midrash, Sekhel Tov*).

27. Such prayers include the *Amidah* ("Standing Silent Prayer"); *Kaddish, Birkas HaKohanim* ("Priestly Blessing"); and *Birkas HaMazon* ("Grace after Meals").

28. The Sages write, "Anger, lust, and honor-seeking remove a man from this world" (Ethics of the Fathers 4:28), as do "an evil eye, the evil inclination, and hatred of others" (ibid., 2:16). The shared thread is the illusion of multiplicity and the denial that the Creator is all that exists. They take us out of this world because the true nature of reality does not permit division.

29. *Tanchumah Shoftim* 18.

37 | A WORLD OF CONTRASTS

Before we discuss insights to help foster peace, it is advantageous to heighten our desire to seek peace. This chapter crystallizes the pleasure and latent power that come through bringing together contrasting, opposing energies and depicts the primordial bliss found only in the pursuit of peace.

The Kabbalistic work *Sefer Yetzirah* explains rather cryptically that the *Sefiros* consist of a union of five pairs of opposites, which, the Arizal explains, provides the energy for all of existence: "The nature of *Sefirah* is the synthesis of everything and its opposite. For if they did not possess the power of synthesis, there would be no energy in anything."[30]

Machlokes ("strife" or "conflict") contains great power and causal energy, and, like all forces, it must be directed with proper intentions. The Sages write:

> Any dispute which is for the sake of Heaven will ultimately endure [i.e., will have a constructive outcome], and one which is not for the sake of Heaven will not ultimately endure. What is a dispute for the sake of Heaven? This is a debate between Hillel and Shammai. What is a dispute not for the sake of Heaven? This is the dispute of Korach and his assembly.[31]

Machlokes is the opposing, dividing force that delineates and thus allows uniqueness to emerge.[32] It need not be divisive, and with proper motivation it helps to bring

---

NOTES

30. Kaplan, *Sefer Yetzirah* 1:5, 44. Azriel, "The Explanation of the Ten *Sefiros*." In Dan, *The Early Kabbalah*, 94.

31. Ethics of the Fathers 5:20.

32. It is taught that the letters of the word *machlokes* can be broken down and rearranged to spell *mes chelek*, "death of the parts." The disease of multiplicity contains within it the cure—which is unity.

out the fuller, larger truth—to foster peace, which itself is a means to the greater end: to reveal the Oneness of God, vis-à-vis revelation of our true ego-free selves.

THE MOTIVE

Being right is not a determining factor in whether an argument will endure, only whether our motivation is pure. When we seek to assert ourselves, rather than the truth, our argument is no longer for the sake of heaven but for the sake of ourselves. We observed that as we move away from reality, we move toward suffering; so rather than coming to define the truth, we have cut ourselves off from it. The *Zohar* states,

> Korach followed *machlokes*—but which *machlokes*? Rift. He brought a rift above and below, and he who wished to separate the wholeness of the universe deserves to be estranged from the universe. For this *machlokes* is the fracturing of Peace, of the Whole. He who argues with Peace argues with the Holy Name itself; the name "Peace."[33]

The previously referenced dispute between Hillel and Shammai lasted three years. Then the Talmud clarifies that while both sides are right, "the law is in agreement with *Beis* Hillel." Why does the law follow *Beis* Hillel, if both sides are right? Because their scholars were more accepting and tolerant and would always speak of the opinions of *Beis* Shammai before their own.[34]

It was not the correctness of their thinking but their ego-free conduct in presenting their position that allowed for their truth to emerge as reality. In actuality, *Beis* Shammai's reasoning was often considered to be more sound, but *halachah*, reality itself, bends around the humble of spirit.[35] Peace trumps a finite truth because peace is the Infinite's expression of the one true all-encompassing reality. Let us examine this idea more fully.

POINT, COUNTERPOINT

A person blind from birth has no concept of light or of darkness, but experiencing a momentary flash of light forever changes his lifetime understanding of both

---

33. *Zohar* 111:176a.
34. Cf. *Chagigah*, 22b; see also *Pesachim* 88b and *Gittin* 41b.
35. Ibid.

light and darkness. In order for us to know the full essence of anything, we need to see its contrast, if only for a moment. For this reason, "God has made one thing opposite the other."[36] The *Zohar* states, "If there was no folly there would be no wisdom… . White is known and valued only by contrast to black… . A man does not know what sweet is until he tastes bitter."[37]

For example, through Shabbos—the day of rest—we come to know movement. There is no potentiality on Shabbos: it is complete. Creative acts are prohibited, and anything that highlights our identity or independence is muted. Without Shabbos, we cannot truly comprehend growth—and vice versa—each completes the other. We are thus commanded: "Six days shall work be done, but the seventh day is a Shabbos of rest … you shall do no manner of work."[38]

Shabbos is the ultimate in abandonment of the ego—a taste of the World to Come. We discard any delusions that we are in control of anything, other than our own will. Shabbos, then, was first in thought, because it enables the crown of creation—a human being with potential, to be realized.

Yet opposites do more than define each other; they liberate distinctions that would go otherwise unclaimed, allowing for the sum and substance of each to emerge.[39] Abraham, Isaac, and Jacob all faced tests that went against their most basic nature, and, in doing so, they refined their unique and personifying traits, which helped them realize their potential. The *Zohar* expounds,

> Why is the *Akeidah* presented as a test to Abraham [rather than to Isaac]? Because it was Abraham who needed to be included in *Din* [judgment], Abraham who until that moment had no *Din* at all… . Abraham was not complete until now, when he became invested with the power to exercise *Din*![40]

This is why challenging relationships are at the cornerstone of pivotal events and spiritual awakenings throughout the Biblical narrative. Even Jacob, particularly Jacob—who is the archetype for peace and unity—found conflict and confrontation

---

NOTES

36. Ecclesiastes 7:14.

37. *Zohar*, Leviticus 47b.

38. Leviticus 23:3.

39. Of his two wives, the Torah tells us that Jacob "loved Rachel even more than Leah" (Genesis 29:30) and that "God saw that Leah was hated" (ibid., 29:31). The former statement is not untrue; however, in contrast to Rachel, Jacob's love for Leah leaves us—and, according to some opinions, Leah—with the impression that she was hated, relatively speaking.

40. *Zohar* 1:119 b.

at every turn. A person can master a *middah* only when he endures adversities that involve the opposite of that *middah*.[41] Indeed, a kite flies higher against a strong wind.

Newton's third law explains that if body A exerts a force on body B (an action), then body B exerts an equal and opposing force on body A (a reaction) ($F_a = -F_b$). These two forces have the same oomph but are opposite in direction. A force acting on a body is always the result of its interaction with another body, so forces always come in pairs. In other words, when you push on something, it always pushes back—expressing itself more thoroughly and completely.[42]

It is the height of arrogance to presume that if all of the difficult people in our lives would simply disappear, we would be more productive, happier, and successful. We bemoan these emotional vampires who drain our life blood and exhaust our time, money, and energy. But these custom-made, God-given relationships provide the necessary soil for us to develop our full potential.

TWO SIDES OF THE COIN

Opposites not only refine the essence of each other but, on a deeper level, reveal a higher unity. For example, a parent may rebuke a child for running carelessly into the street only to speak tenderly to him afterward, expressing deep affection. These incongruent behaviors each reveal the same truth: love.

Of course, not all seeming contradictions can be understood from a finite perspective. Kabbalists use the term *achdus hashvaah* to denote that *Ein Sof* is a "unity of opposites," one that reconciles within itself even those aspects of the cosmos that are contradictory to one another.[43] More familiar, but still outside our cognitive bandwidth, are the striking opposites designed to reveal the greater truth: good and evil. The Oneness of God will be revealed, and we will see that evil was merely a tool used to make known that "God is One and His Name is One."[44]

NOTES

41. Rabbi Eliyahu Dessler, *Strive for Truth*, Vol. 5, 54–55.

42. In the human body, negative resistance is used to stretch out a muscle. We push in the opposite direction, while applying external pressure to prevent movement. This increases the range of motion and the the limb is able to extend farther in the desired direction.

43. See Gershom Scholem, *Origins of the Kabbalah*, R. J. Zwi Werblowski, trans. (Princeton, NJ: Princeton University Press, 1987), 312. Cited by Sanford L. Drob, *The Doctrine of Coincidentia Oppositorum in Jewish Mysticism*, 2000).

44. Zachariah 17:9. "That you will know that God is the Supreme Being and there is none besides Him" (Deuteronomy 4:35).

In his work *The Pattern Recognition Theory of Humour,* author Alastair Clarke explains that "humour occurs when the brain recognizes a pattern that surprises it, and that recognition of this sort is rewarded with the experience of the humorous response."[45] Our forefather Isaac, whose name literally means "he will laugh," personifies the attribute of strict justice.[46] Laughter and justice are opposite sides of the same coin, and both depend on our ability to recognize truth.[47]

When we see a paradox from both sides, it produces spontaneous delight. Thus, in order to serve God with *simchah,* we must be let in on the joke—we need to see the full picture.

The definition of *da'as* is "knowledge," but more precisely it is knowledge that is borne out of a connection. As such, Purim is identified as the holiday of *da'as,* because, as Rabbi Wolbe observes, any time there is a connection between opposites there is *simchah.*[48] This is why Purim, despite the looming threat, is also the most festive day on the Jewish calendar.

The same may be said about the fox the Sages saw emerging from the ruins of the Holy of Holies. All of the other Rabbis wept, but Rabbi Akiva laughed. The Rabbis wept because the fox impressed on them the desecration of that holy place. Rabbi Akiva laughed because God had fulfilled His promise: "Foxes shall walk upon [the Holy Mountain]." This is a sure sign that God will also bring about His other promises, to redeem His people and rebuild the Temple.[49] Rabbi Akiva saw both sides of the coin and perceived the pattern.

The Ramchal writes, "Man was created for the sole purpose of rejoicing in God and deriving pleasure from the splendor of His Presence; for this is the true joy and the greatest of pleasure that can be found."[50] The pleasure that he speaks of can be sampled in this world and fully enjoyed in the next world. In light of our immediate discussion, we witness how His Presence brings us pleasure and crystallizes the underlying relationship between the revelation of God's glory and the experience of pleasure.

We explained that a person who is not fully living forces a chasm between the

45. Pyrrhic House, 2008.

46. His birth itself was shocking, for his mother, Sarah, was barren. "Abraham fell on his face and laughed" (*Targum Yerushalmi* 17:7). "This was certainly something to laugh about; it was totally astonishing" (ibid., 17:17, s.v. *Vayitzchak*).

47. "The Holy One laughs ... with His creations, never at them" (*Avodah Zarah* 3b).

48. Rabbi Shlomo Wolbe, *Alei Shur,* Introduction.

49. Cf. *Makkos* 24a.

50. *Mesillas Yesharim,* Ch. 1.

body and the soul. This lack of harmony is felt as depression.[51] Since multiplicity and oneness are incompatible, as we begin to tear down the "I," (through a meaningful soul-directed life) the more of God—reality, unity, the complete picture—we reveal. In the process, the soul and the body move into more perfect harmony, and harmony is the very definition of pleasure.

OURS TO GIVE

Rabbi Aryeh Kaplan writes, "One of the ultimate goals of man is the imitation of God. We do this in every good act, paralleling God's own creation of good. The most direct way that we can do this is in our actions toward others."[52] Let us keep in mind, then, the words of Hillel the Elder when asked to sum up the Torah: "What is hateful to you, do not do to your fellow man. This is the whole law: all the rest is commentary."[53]

The Torah likewise commands, "Love your neighbor as yourself," but we cannot love others if we do not love ourselves, and we cannot make peace with others when we are at war with ourselves.[54] Self-esteem is required for a genuine act of *chesed*. We cannot give of the self, if we have no sense of self. [55]

Only when we are whole can we ascend to the highest rung of harmony, because putting our own ego aside for the sake of peace is an incontestable prerequisite. When we love ourselves, we automatically love and trust (and fear) God. As a result, we embody all of the necessary characteristics to bring peace, such as we do not take things personally; we forgive and apologize with ease; we see others' points of view; we are not prone to anger or offense or inclined to jealousy or envy; we can empathize, see the good in others, and judge favorably; and certainly, we

---

NOTES

51. If the experience of harmony brings pleasure, then disharmony—the antithesis of a synergistic connection—must bring pain. Whether it is a cacophony (a harsh and meaningless mixture of sounds) or a clash of colors, illogical opinions, or outright strife, a lack of harmony is innately unpleasant.

52. Rabbi Aryeh Kaplan, *If You Were God* (New York: NCSY, 1983), 61–62.

53. Shabbos 31a. The Sages ask, "Which is the correct path for man to choose? Whatever is harmonious for the one who does it, and harmonious for mankind" (Ethics of the Fathers 2:1).

54. Leviticus 19:18.

55. *Shalom* is not the absence of difference but the symphony of individual expression. A forced diminution of individuality does not produce peace—it produces problems. We easily acquiesce when we subjugate our true selves, but inevitably resentment builds and relationships suffer. A person can give because he wants to do what is right or because he wants to be liked. These two forms of giving leave opposite emotional imprints. The distinction is intention, and it's the difference between being robbed versus giving a donation. In both cases, money is going from one person's hands to another, but one experience is empowering, while the other is weakening.

do not need to be right. More neatly summarized, being created in the image of God means that our spiritual potential is to reflect the Thirteen Attributes of God's Mercy spoken of in the Torah:[56]

> *Hashem, Hashem,* E-l, Compassionate and Gracious, Slow to Anger, and Abundant in Kindness and Truth; Preserver of Kindness for thousands of generations, Forgiver of Iniquity, Willful Sin, and Error, and Who Cleanses …[57]

In the seminal Kabbalistic work *Tomer Devorah,* Rabbi Cordovero emphasizes that we, too, must follow in God's pathways, and he explores how these very traits should manifest in a person's thoughts and deeds: compassionate, gracious, slow to anger, abundant in love and truth, merciful, and so on.

God Himself tells us that peace is His priority, so much so that the Torah permits the Holy Name of God to be erased in water (in the course of the *sotah* ritual), in order to restore peace to the relationship between husband and wife.[58] He allows His name to be negated to show us our obligation. An obligation that is rooted in creation itself. "Just as God contracts his infinite Presence to make a place in which the finite world can exist, so, too, man contracts his self-centeredness so that Godliness can be revealed."[59]

UNITED WE STAND

God does not leave the key to our success and well-being in the hands of any other person, let alone someone who is sick, selfish, or cruel. We do not need to have a relationship with every unhealthy person in order to remain whole; we need only to make sure that our ego does not keep us from behaving responsibly within these relationships. (In no way does this mean that we become a doormat and welcome every intolerable person into our lives. Ego negation means that we bring our true self out and into our relationships, where our singular allegiance is to the will of God. Whether that takes us deeper into or further away from a

---

NOTES

56. Exodus 34:6–7.

57. The Rambam (*Guide for the Perplexed,* Ch. 53–60) implores one to understand that these attributes should not be taken literally. His concern is that they undermine God's Unity and that describing Him in terms used to describe Man invites comparison to the finite nature of Man.

58. *Chullin* 141a; *Nedarim* 66b. Even a public vow that cannot normally be annulled can be annulled in this case in order to maintain peace between spouses (Rema, *Yoreh De'ah* 228:21).

59. Rabbi Eliyahu Dessler, *Strive for Truth,* Vol. V, 21.

particular relationship is not at issue. Doing what is responsible is.) Should that not be enough to maintain, or to make peace, we may experience sadness over the broken state of the relationship, but we remain whole—emotionally and spiritually intact, undivided by shame or resentment. It is only when we refuse to let go of ego-based emotions that we move to a mode of dependence and to suffering.

After decades of estrangement, Jacob finally made peace with his brother Esau. Afterward, the Torah states, "Jacob arrived whole (*shalem*) to the city of Shechem."[60] The word for "peace," *shalom*, derives from *shalem*, which means "whole" or "complete."[61] Our willingness to do what is legitimately required to foster healthy relationships is ultimately what gives us peace—allows for us to remain whole— *regardless* of the outcome. Moreover, each time we rise above our nature for the sake of peace, we fortify our wholeness; because all acts of giving refresh our emotional reserves and boost our self-esteem.[62]

The Ramchal writes, "The one stone on which the entire building rests is the concept that God wants each person to complete himself."[63] Individually and collectively, the path to holiness is through wholeness. The Infinite is not divisible. Our relationship with ourselves, God, and His world are each a reflection of a whole reality. Fittingly, the Hebrew word for "anything" and "everything" is identical, *kol*. The word for any part of the whole and for the entire thing, which includes all parts, is the same—revealing the interrelationship between the sum and the parts.

We should not see our relationship with God as two halves coming together. Only a complete and independent person can become close with God, Who is whole and not lacking in any way. We then resonate in near-perfect harmony and spiral higher, toward absolute unity.[64] The Ramchal writes that only a union with

---

NOTES

60. Genesis 33:18.

61. The Talmud (Shabbat 33b) explains that Jacob was *"shalem"* because he was "whole in body, whole in money, and whole in his Torah knowledge." Rashi (ibid.) expounds: (1) Jacob was physically healed from his struggle with the *malach*; (2) he was financially sound, despite the expensive gifts he gave to his brother Esau; and (3) he was spiritually intact even though he spent many years in Laban's home.

62. Complete submission to the will of God makes us whole. The *Midrash* (*Bereishis Rabbah* 56:10) states that the original name of the place where the *Akeidah* took place was *Shalem*.

63. *Da'as Tevunos*, Friedlander edition, 14.

64. "According to Kabbalah, there are three entities—each of a Divine source though existing on the physical plane—whose essence is defined by wholeness: 1. the Torah; 2. the Jewish people; and 3. the Land of Israel. If a *Sefer Torah* lacks even part of a letter, the entire Scroll is invalid (Rambam, *Hilchos Tefillin* 1:2); 'If you save one person it is as if you saved the entire world' (*Sanhedrin* 37a). The 600,000 who went out of Egypt embody the totality of all primordial Jewish souls." (Yitzchak Ginsburgh, *Awakening the Spark Within* [Kefar Chabad: Gal Einai Publications, 2001], 57).

God constitutes true perfection and "if he is victorious on all sides, he will be the 'Whole Man,' who will succeed in uniting himself with his Creator…. And if he rules over himself and unites himself with his Creator, and uses the world only to aid him in the service of his Creator, he is uplifted and the world itself is uplifted with him."[65]

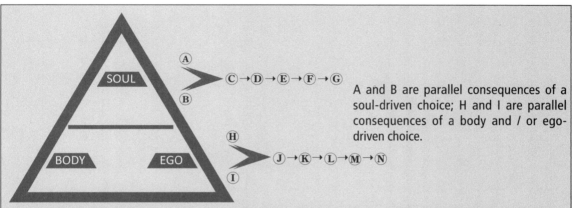

A and B are parallel consequences of a soul-driven choice; H and I are parallel consequences of a body and / or ego-driven choice.

A. Self-esteem increases → ego shrinks → perspective widens → humility stirs → gratitude surges → joy flows
B. More Godlike (reveal God) → closer to God = see God = know God = love/fear God
C. Inner Harmony: connection to true self (soul) = connection to God
D. Increased capacity to love and to be loved
E. Optimum emotional and spiritual health
F. Seek the genuine pleasure found in meaning, growth, and relationships
G. Resonate with Godlike qualities, becoming more whole and moving closer to God

H. Self-esteem decreases → ego expands → perspective narrows → arrogance grows → anger / anxiety / depression follow
I. Less Godlike → further from God = do not see God's hand in our lives = angry with God
J. Inner Friction: disconnected from true self = disconnected from God
K. Decreased capacity to love and to receive love
L. Poor emotional and spiritual health
M. Inability to extract satisfaction from the real world, the ego intensifies and self-destructive behaviors escalate
N. Continue to fracture, becoming more divided and uneven and moving further away from God

The *Zohar* tells us, "The Name of God is Peace, and all is bound together in peace."[66] When we seek peace, we become creators of harmony itself. "With dignity and glory You crowned him, making him just a little less than God."[67] We are now as close to God as humanly possible because we are as whole as possible. The pleasure is an indefinable delicacy to one who has never savored it.[68]

NOTES

65. See *Mesillas Yesharim, The Path of the Just*, Ch. 1.

66. *Zohar*, Leviticus 10b.

67. Psalms 8:6.

68. The blissful experience of this closeness is called *deveikus* and is associated with *neshamah*, the third level of the soul (or, according to other opinions, *chayah*, the fourth level of the soul).

38 | THE SOUND OF SILENCE

We are taught that God created the world through Divine speech, with ten utterances.[69] "By the word of God, the heavens were made; and by the breath of His mouth, all of their host."[70] Man, who is created in God's image, is endowed with a similar ability to create realities. "I put My speech in your mouth ... to plant the heavens and lay the foundations of the earth."[71]

Speech is the conduit between the higher and the lower worlds and the seam between the physical and the spiritual nature of man.[72] Yet the Sages declare, "If a word is worth one coin, silence is worth two."[73] Let us appreciate, then, that the power of speech is eclipsed only by the unmatched power of silence.

The first, sole commandment was for Adam to abstain when God warned him not to eat of the fruit of the *Eitz Hadaas*, the "Tree of Knowledge" of good and evil. Adam was told to "not act." No matter how noble a deed, as long as we are the doer, we soak our actions in a sense of self. Similarly, not speaking—when we are bursting to, but when it is best to remain silent—negates all sense of one's self and brings God into the moment.[74]

NOTES

69. Ethics of the Fathers 5:1.

70. Psalms 33:6.

71. Isaiah 51:16.

72. "The Lord God formed man of dust from the ground, and He breathed into his nostrils the soul of life, and man became a living soul" (Genesis 2:7). The *Targum* (Genesis) explains that what sets man apart from other creations and elevates him above all other life is the power of speech.

73. *Megillah* 18a.

74. Every month resonates with its own spiritual energy and *Nissan*, the Jewish month when *Pesach* occurs, is characterized by kingship. Each year, at this time, the collective ego of the Jewish people is temporarily

Because speech is the spokesman of the ego, we can boast and belittle, with nary an effort—silence offers the greatest leverage to subdue it. Accordingly, the Sages teach that this is our primary purpose. "What is man's task in the world? To make himself as silent as a mute."[75]

Resisting the urge to build up ourselves or to tear down others, has it stated benefits, but there is no better means to imbue ourselves with humility and to eradicate a harsh decree than to remain silent when our ego feels threatened. In the silent prayer *Shemoneh Esrei*, we ask God for this strength: "My God, guard my tongue from evil.... May my soul be silent to those who insult me."

NO EGO = NO INJURY

We are reminded why it is crucial to acknowledge our faults and to do *teshuvah* on our failings. The truth cannot be offended or upended by reality. Images need protection. The truth does not. If we fully accept ourselves there is no need to project an image; we have nothing to protect and nothing to hide from. We become more real, through and through. This creed was lyrically rendered by Shakespeare:

> *This above all: to thine own self be true,*
> *And it must follow, as the night the day,*
> *Thou canst not then be false to any man.*[76]

The eminent psychologist Carl Jung stated that every part of the personality we do not love will become hostile to us.[77] Becoming more courageous is not only a matter of facing our fears. It's a matter of facing ourselves, because it's actually self-discovery that we fear.[78] This is self-evident. We are not easily offended when faced with a truth that we fully acknowledge, nor are we bothered by a blatant,

---

NOTES

deflated, and we have the ability leap beyond our nature—to rule over our base selves—and to bring about powerful, transformative, change. The word *"Pesach"* is in fact a contraction of the words *"peh"* and *"sach"* meaning, "the mouth speaks," which, as the *Sefer Yetzirah* intimates, makes the regulation of speech the gateway to our growth.

75. *Chullin* 89a.

76. *Hamlet*, Act I, Scene iii.

77. The dual themes of acceptance and approval exist in our relationships as well. We often confuse acceptance and approval; if we do not approve of another's actions, we cannot accept him. This erroneous thinking not only negates the concept of unconditional love and results in strained relationships, but also impairs our ability to accept ourselves, faults and all.

78. The Torah commands us to be honest with ourselves, as well as with others. "You shall not lie" (Leviticus 19:11).

bold-faced lie. It is only when presented with a truth that we refuse to accept that we become sensitive or self-conscious.

Total self-acceptance assures that we do not connect the dots from another person's actions to a repressed truth within ourselves. Then, when perceiving an insult, our first thought is one that is perfectly aligned with reality: *thank you, God.*[79]

This is because insult is the gentlest of ways to wash away our sins, the kindest form of suffering. The ego is an illusion, the body is temporary, and our soul is our real self. This shift instantly reframes the offense from painful to joyous. A high level is actually expressed by the person who eagerly awaits insult and embarrassment.[80] Rabbi Avraham Yelin writes,

> A person should tell himself, "I hope I am insulted and [embarrassed] so I can become an object of scorn, and thereby achieve atonement for my sins." Once a person internalizes this outlook, he won't care if he is insulted. Quite the contrary, he will be happy, for it is God's will.[81]

The core of interpersonal success lies in giving honor to others, while the bedrock of personal growth lies in forgoing our own honor and bestowing it on others. Thus, when it comes to our own honor, we are told to run away from it—because those who seek honor will do whatever they can to protect it. The Ramchal states, "Honor is nothing but the vanity of vanities, which causes a man to defy his own mind and that of his Master and to forget his entire duty."[82]

To remain silent, pleasant and benevolent when we want nothing more than to defend our pride not only builds emotional and spiritual immunity, but echoes an attribute of God in the highest sense. In *Tomer Devorah* we read:

> At the very time that a person is sinning against God, God continues to shower him with life and strength. The sinner thus uses that very vitality to insult His Creator. For this reason the ministering angels call God an "insulted monarch." ... Even though God endures such a level of insult, He still does not deprive man of His benevolence.[83]

NOTES

79. Cf. *Tomer Devorah*, Ch. 2.

80. "He who commits a sin and is embarrassed will be forgiven" (*Berachos* 12b). "One who is concerned about becoming embarrassed will not learn" (Ethics of the Fathers 5:23) and cannot grow.

81. Rabbi Avraham Yelin, *Orech Apayim* 3:8.

82. *Mesillas Yesharim, The Path of the Just*, Ch. 16.

83. Rabbi Moshe Cordovero, *Tomer Devorah*, Ch. 1.

Recognizing the value of remaining silent—and, more so, calm—*Chazal* abound with such exhortations: "Everyone who accepts criticism gracefully brings a blessing upon himself; and upon them the blessing of goodness will come"; and "Fortunate is one who remains silent and ignores even many insults. He will be spared a hundred evils."[84]

As noted earlier, the Torah states, "I have put before you life and death ... choose life so that you may live."[85] While silence is the best medicine for our welfare, King Solomon crisply summarizes the awesome power of speech and its restraint.[86] "Life and death are in the power of the tongue."[87] For here is where the free will battle is won or lost, because, as he writes elsewhere, "There is no difference between the righteous and the evil but the mouth's speech alone."[88]

NOTES

84. Proverbs 24:25; *Devarim Rabbah* 1:9; *Sanhedrin* 7a.
85. Deuteronomy 30:19.
86. Ethics of the Fathers 1:17.
87. Proverbs 18:21.
88. *Koheles Rabbah* 9:11.

39 | BORDERS AND BOUNDARIES

The Torah states, "Do not push back your neighbor's boundary."[89] This holds true for emotional boundaries as well. Healthy boundaries are not created to keep people out, but rather to define our space and our sense of personal responsibility.

A poor self-image often translates into porous borders—because if a person does not have a clear definition of himself, he is unable to recognize what is proper between him and another. This may manifest as the chronically needy person, who asks to be rescued from every self-made crisis, or as the controlling, pushy personality who hides his insecurities with arrogance and bravado.

Esau, one of the less-healthy Torah figures, bares his boundary issues. "And he said, 'Travel on and let us go—I will proceed alongside you.'"[90] Jacob declines. Esau becomes insistent: "Let me assign to you some of the people who are with me."[91] When someone refuses to hear the word "No," he is seeking control of the situation or refusing to relinquish control.

THE TRUTH ABOUT PEACE

The Talmud elucidates that one of the reasons Jerusalem was destroyed was due to a lack of sufficient rebuke between people.[92] Indeed, seeking peace does not

NOTES

89. Deuteronomy 19:14.
90. Genesis 33:12.
91. Ibid., 33:25.
92. *Shabbos* 119b.

mean that we let people push past the boundaries of acceptability. At times, the right thing to do is not to remain silent but to exercise our power of speech and to speak up—and stand up—for ourselves and for what is right.

An obligation to the truth at times supersedes a transient peace, and we cannot default to a position of wholesale compliance when *halachah* dictates that our voice be heard—even when it will cause friction.[93] Authentic peace without truth is an oxymoron. It does not exist; and those who would recklessly or sheepishly sacrifice the truth in favor of peace will be bereft of both truth and peace.

Pinchas killed a sinner and was rewarded as a man of peace. "God said to Pinchas: 'I give you My covenant of peace ... a covenant of everlasting priesthood.'"[94] Certainly, homicide and the typical notion of peace are incongruent. Yet on further inspection, we find that Pinchas actually restored peace between Israel and God by putting an end to the Israelites' lascivious behavior. *Shalom*, true peace, is not the absence of strife or conflict but signifies something much more encompassing—perfection and, ultimately, a Divine attribute.

THE APPROACH IS PARAMOUNT

On the Torah passage "Do not hate ... [rather] rebuke your fellow man," the Rambam explains that a victim of wrongdoing should not develop rage and remain silent but rather should confront the person.[95] He explains that such rebuke should not be with the intention of receiving an apology but in order to help someone grow as a person. He also advises us to remain silent if we cannot talk calmly and respectfully or if our words will be unheeded. Furthermore, we must express our feelings with no sense of superiority or vindictiveness.[96] The bottom line: no ego—in our attitude or approach. A prominent *baal mussar* ("master of self-improvement") writes,

> Rebuke someone who has cheated you but do not become angry. After laboring seven years for Rachel's hand in marriage, Jacob was deceived. Most

---

93. In some instances, such as two scholars attempting to clarify *halachah*, the goal is to discover the truth, even if there may be some contention between the parties along the way. But in a great majority of situations, disagreements are simply a matter of opinion and perspective. As such, if we have our priorities straight, the objective is almost always to find a way to get along peaceably.

94. Deuteronomy 25:12.

95. Leviticus 19:17. *Hilchos De'os* 6:6.

96. Ibid., 6:8.

men would have become furious. Jacob, however, did not become angry. He merely admonished Laban and asked him what his motive was.[97]

We should not let our desire to speak our mind derail our ability to successfully plan our approach. Relationship expert Dr. John Mordechai Gottman reports, "96 percent of the time you can predict the outcome of a conversation based on the first three minutes of the fifteen-minute interaction. A harsh startup dooms you to failure. The rule is, 'If it starts negative, it stays negative.'"[98]

King Solomon likewise exhorts, "The words of the wise, when spoken gently, are accepted."[99] When we are not in the right frame of mind or do not have emotional energy to expend, it is prudent to avoid such a potentially confrontational conversation. Just as the Sages put fences around *halachah,* so, too, we should acknowledge our limitations and build practical fences to prevent ourselves from slipping too close to these danger zones.

The wisest of men also writes, "Do not rush to begin a quarrel."[100] If someone continues to overstep boundaries or behave irresponsibly, it is advised to communicate our feelings—but we should let a little time pass first. Time gives us greater clarity because our ego is less engaged, and we are able to view the situation with greater objectivity. This is why we are more likely to become irritated in the heat of an argument. After some time, our anger will generally begin to subside.

Whatever the issue, it is imperative that we convey our motivation. We should let this person know that the reason that we are approaching him at all is because we care about him and our relationship. Only sincere and heartfelt criticism has a chance of being effective. "As water reflects a face back to a face, so one's heart is reflected back to him by another."[101]

Most important, comments of any sort should be offered only when we believe that there is a chance that the person will be receptive to our message.[102] This is particularly true if someone in our life suffers from an emotional illness—diagnosed

---

NOTES

97. Rabbi Yeruchem Levovitz, *Da'as Torah, Limudei Mussrei HaTorah.*

98. Sybil Carrere and John Mordechai Gottman, "Predicting Divorce among Newlyweds from the First Three Minutes of a Marital Conflict Discussion," *Family Process* 38, no. 3 (1999): 293–301.

99. Ecclesiastes 9:17.

100. Proverbs 25:8.

101. Proverbs 27:19. "R. Illa said in the name of R. Elazar the son of R. Shimon, 'Just as there is a *mitzvah* for a person to say words [of reproof] that will be accepted, so too there is a *mitzvah* for a person not to say words [of reproof] that will not be accepted'" (*Yevamos* 65b).

102. *Shulchan Aruch, Orach Chaim* 608:2; *Rema,* ad loc.

or otherwise. The Rambam explains that rather than confront such a person, we can forgive him in our heart and thus use the approach of *middas chassidus* ("pious acts beyond the *halachic* requirements").[103] Let there be no confusion on this point: It is not our responsibility to educate or to cure the person—our emphasis should be on maximizing the relationship. Once we come to terms with his limitations, it will be easier to accept this person for who he is, as he is.

IT ALL COMES DOWN TO THIS

Unpleasant circumstances in general and difficult people in particular, push us toward an irrationally charged response. Choosing to behave properly, irrespective of a negative emotional state, is the epitome of mental health. Even when we feel outrage, the importance of conducting ourselves with a calm demeanor cannot be overstated.[104] Our behavior must not be predicated on anything other than what is right.

God, Who is nonchanging, is independent. If we become angry—or act otherwise irresponsibly—we move to a state of dependency, because someone "causes us" to respond in a way that we do not choose. As we have stressed throughout this work, emulating God is our ultimate aim, and anger specifically undermines this objective, which then destabilizes our emotional, spiritual, and physical health.

Generally, the most responsible—and soul building—course is to remain silent. However, when an objective assessment dictates that we should speak up, both our emotional health and the relationship can be enhanced. Yet without substance and sincerity—much less calm and composure—our words will not prove productive to either the relationship or ourselves.

In the end, should we come to the conclusion that in spite of our best efforts and intentions, the person or the situation is unchanging, we have the ability to simply accept and to trust in God, a task that is made considerably easier when we look beyond the messenger to the meaning of the message.

NOTES

103. *Hilchos De'os* 6:9.

104. When our days are filled with conduct that betrays our trust in God, the ability to put aside our ego for the sake of peace, or even for peace of mind, becomes a formidable task. Recall that the backbone of *bitachon* is responsible action. We remind ourselves that maintaining our calm automatically changes how we feel about the situation because, as we noted, the "external awakens the internal," but fundamentally the act itself reinforces the integrity of our *bitachon*.

40 | GHOSTS
OF
THE PAST

Long after a challenging encounter passes and our feelings subside, we may be covered in a secondary film of emotions—usually anger or guilt. Unquestionably, most of our issues stem from either something someone did to us (producing anger) or from what we did to another (producing guilt—which is anger turned inward). Both burdens contribute to depression and plunk us onto a carousel of self-destructive behaviors. This is especially true when our childhood was less than ideal. For even when we strive in every way—to be good and to do good—we can find a hole in our self-esteem.

FLASHBACK

Our personal sense of right and wrong is not fully developed until our early teens.[105] That is because children do not possess the reasoning faculties to make choices as adults do, and thus they cannot gain positive self-esteem through self-control. Their self-image is bolstered in one way: A child must feel as if he is the path to his parents' happiness and not an obstacle to it. Children, who by nature are egocentric, correlate their self-worth with the way they are treated by others, particularly by their parents. When a parent ignores or begrudgingly endures a child, the child naturally concludes that he is unworthy of parental love or perhaps even love from anyone at all. It is only natural for him to ascribe a failure within himself

---

NOTES

105. The Torah declares a Jewish boy to be of age at thirteen and a Jewish girl at twelve. At this age, a Jewish person becomes accountable for his or her actions and can be punished in *Beis Din* ("Rabbinical court") for his transgressions.

as the reason behind a parent's behavior, and so the child predictably concludes that there is a flaw within himself.

A person who was not raised in a loving home must remind himself that the issue does not lie in him but with his parents. If a mother is full of love, she will be loving to all of her children, even one who is difficult to raise; but if she lacks the ability to adequately love, then even an innocent well-mannered child will be subject to her hostility. The love that parents give children is determined by their own limitations, not those of the children.[106] As adults, we can still find it difficult to appreciate that our self-worth is not contingent on our parents' acceptance of us. We are not less because someone cannot love us.

If we see a person in a wheelchair, we wouldn't get mad at that person because he can't get out and walk. Somebody who is emotionally handicapped is equally challenged. Does it make sense to resent a parent for not being able to give us something that he or she doesn't have? Do we want to hold on to anger because our mother or father was, and still may be, incapable of loving us? People give love; they give respect. If they do not have it, then they cannot give it, regardless of how desperately one desires them to do so.

As adults, when we make the decision to let go of our anger, the breach in our self-esteem is sealed. Once we embrace the above-quoted truism, "We are not less because someone cannot love us," decades of anger and pain begin to melt away.

FORGIVE FOR GOOD

The essence of idolatry is the belief that God is not the only power influencing life. Anger assumes the same belief. "If one breaks dishes in his anger, it is as if he were involved in idol worship."[107] If we do not forgive, then we do not recognize the true Source of the circumstance. The *Sefer HaChinuch* reminds us that a person who causes harm to another is merely an agent carrying out the will of God:

> At the root of the *mitzvah* [lies the purpose] that a person should know and reflect that whatever happens to him, good or bad, is made to happen to him by God, blessed be He. There can be nothing [i.e., no effect] from a human hand,

106. A child's physical or cognitive limitations can increase the parent's love for the child, while emotional issues are more likely to cause anger and estrangement. The reason is that without evidence of an impairment it is easier to assume that the child has control over his behavior and the parent thus has a harder time not taking it personally. Of course, the less self-esteem the parent has the more personal everything becomes.
107. *Shabbos* 105b.

from a man's brother's hand, contrary to the will of God, blessed be He.... . Therefore, if someone inflicts suffering or pain upon him, he should know in his heart that his evil deeds were the cause, and that God, blessed be He, decreed this upon him. Therefore, one should not plan to take revenge from that person, for he is not the [primary] cause of his trouble; it is transgression that is the cause.[108]

God is speaking to us through every person and situation. This is why "One should relate to every person as if he has no *bechirah*, as if he is compelled by his nature, education, habits, and emotional needs."[109] Relationships are a very common area in which people often focus on the messenger, while missing the message. When we fully accept that everyone and everything is ultimately from God for our good, our anger ceases to consume us. Rabbi Avigdor Nebenzhal writes,

> Joseph teaches us a great principle of how we can fulfill the difficult instruction of "Do not bear a grudge" (Leviticus 19:18). We might be able to restrain ourselves from taking revenge, but how is it possible not to even bear a grudge against somebody who does us evil? Yet, if we understand that the person did not do anything, there is no longer room to bear a grudge. "If you would not have sold me to Egypt," Joseph says, "God would have sent somebody else to do it" (see *Ta'anis* 18).[110]

We learned earlier that should we fall below our *madraigah*, experiences are not meted out with precision, in measure for measure. To reconcile these positions, we recall that: (1) we alone are responsible for putting ourselves into the natural world and thus bear shared responsibility, if not full culpability.[111] Note the words of the recently quoted passage: "... he should know in his heart that his evil deeds were the cause ... one should not plan to take revenge ... for [this person is] not the [primary] cause of his trouble; it is our transgression that is the cause"; (2) as we discussed, even when we are used as a *kli*, there is always a

---

NOTES

108. *Sefer HaChinuch* (*Mitzvah* 241, "Do not take revenge").

109. Rabbi Shlomo Wolbe, *Alei Shur*, 1, 156.

110. Rabbi Avigdor Nebenzhal, *Sichos LeSefer Bereishis*, Genesis 50:20, 287–288.

111. "No benefit or damage ever occurs from people without the Creator's permission" (*Orchos Tzaddikim, Shaar HaSimcha*). And Divine permission is granted because of our sins. As the *Zohar* (*Vayeishlach* 179a) states, "If not for the evil inclination, a person would have no enemies in the world."

meaningful message for us, no matter how blunted, and *teshuvah* is the means to reveal the message.[112]

However we view this person—as an agent of God or as a natural world consequence—it behooves us to consider the following: the Talmud teaches us that God relates to us in the way that we relate to others.[113] The *Zohar* explains,

> If one arouses himself spiritually on Earth, Heaven arouses Itself correspondingly above. If a person performs a meritorious act below, he awakens the corresponding force above. If a person does kindness on earth, he evokes kindness toward him from Heaven.... If a person practices mercy, he crowns that day with mercy, which becomes his protector when he is in need [of mercy]."[114]

The Sages ask and answer: "Whose sins does He forgive? The sins of he who overlooks an injustice committed against him."[115] We are further taught: "One who judges others favorably will be judged favorably by God."[116]

The physical and emotional benefits of forgiveness are well-documented. Forgiveness has been shown to be directly correlated to less anxiety, stress, and hostility; as well as fewer symptoms of depression, and lower risk of alcohol and substance abuse.[117] Moreover, forgiveness not only restores positive feelings toward the offender but "may spill over beyond the relationship with the offender, promoting generalized prosocial orientation."[118] In other words, when we forgive someone who has hurt us, all of our relationships seem to benefit. The opposite is also true. Unresolved anger from a soured relationship has been shown to seep into our other relationships.

NOTES

112. These two points notwithstanding, challenges and hardships faced by children—below the age of *bechirah*—are properly attributed to their *tikkun*.

113. *Sotah* 8b, *Shabbos* 151b.

114. *Zohar* on *Emor* 3:92b. The spiritual mechanics are as follows: We recall that an ego-limited mindset is required for empathy; and empathy, naturally, is a requisite for mercy. Therefore, as we divest ourselves of the ego, time and space, as we explained, is suspended and God's mercy, which takes place at the level of *Keser* (which also exists outside of time), is stimulated.

115. *Rosh Hashanah* 17a.

116. *Shabbos* 127b.

117. Everett L. Worthington, et al., "Forgiveness, Health, and Wellbeing: A Review of Evidence for Emotional Versus Decisional Forgiveness, Dispositional Forgiveness, and Reduced Unforgiveness," *Journal of Behavioral Medicine* 30 (2007): 291.

118. K. A. Lawler, J. W. Younger, and R. L. Piferi, et al., "The Unique Effects of Forgiveness on Health: An Exploration of Pathways," *Journal of Behavioral Medicine* (2005).

DISCARDING THE SHELL

Forgiveness does not erase the past, but it does help us let go and ease our lives forward. This is a function of human design, whereby we hold on to painful experiences in order to learn from those experiences and to avoid repeating them. Until we acknowledge them, they remain part of us. Think of those events in our lives that we refuse to release, and contrast them with those we have accepted.

The Rambam writes that there are few transgressions that fall outside the margins of forgiveness: "A person should always forgive others, for worldly matters are only foolish issues ... erase them from your heart."[119] Even in a case of serious and significant wrongdoing, forgiveness does not mean that we deny the hurt; it means that we are not going to allow our anger against this person to harm us anymore. At its core, forgiveness is a choice to give up our role as a victim. That's it.

Forgiving and apologizing both give us a taste of emotional freedom. This is why we typically feel good afterward. We give an apology and we give forgiveness. Only when we are free can we truly give and this single act promotes our independence and builds our emotional immunity.

Before attempting to gain forgiveness for ourselves, we must move forward with the utmost delicacy. If we come into the situation with anything other than complete humility, we will have an uphill battle receiving forgiveness.[120] When Jacob meets up with his brother Esau after having fled for his life more than thirty years earlier, the Torah relates the following conversation:

> But Jacob said, "No, I beg of you! If I have found favor in your eyes, then accept my tribute from me, inasmuch as I have seen your face, which is like seeing the face of a Divine angel, and you were appeased to me."[121]

Humbling ourselves and maintaining the utmost respect help us avoid allowing the other person's ego to become engaged. Approaching the situation with extreme deference, and even reverence, is a requisite for this process.[122] Most definitely, we

---

NOTES

119. *Hilchos De'os* 7:7.

120. "Go humble yourself [before him], and [placate your fellow]" (Proverbs 6:3).

121. Genesis 33:10. According to the *Midrash* (*Bereishis Rabbah* 75:11), God was displeased with Jacob for humbling himself exceedingly before Esau by calling him *adoni* ("my master") a total of eight times.

122. The central themes and wording of this chapter are excerpted from Dovid Lieberman, *Seek Peace and Pursue It* (New York / Jerusalem: Feldheim Publishers, 2010). The full process of how to make peace, as well as other techniques for improving relationships and resolving conflicts, can be found in this book.

do not have to be wrong to apologize. Recall that peace trumps truth, and it is only the ego that insists that our obligation to make peace ceases when we are in the right. This is not so. Rabbeinu Yonah teaches,

> Appease your brothers and friends. Do not go to sleep at night while involved in an argument. Rather, go and appease him even if he is the one who offended you. Do not say, "He is the one who offended me, so let him come and ask forgiveness of me." Rather, overcome your evil inclination and go to him, lest you be considered a haughty person who is an abomination in God's eyes.[123]

If we are meeting with resistance, we should remember that the world is set up as a reflection, direct and pure. We cannot receive if we do not give. If we want to be forgiven, we may be required to forgive others.[124] If we are harboring ill will over what someone has done to us, we cannot be authentic with the person we have injured. For how can we ask for forgiveness from one person, while we are unwilling to give forgiveness to another? If we can resolve any anger we are holding on to—be it toward ourselves or toward another person—we will find a smoother path ahead in resolving the current situation.

Shalom—peace—is the only vehicle through which blessing comes down to earth from Heaven.[125] Intrinsically, whatever brings peace into the world is the purest expression of truth and the highest manifestation of free will. Herein lies the deepest connection between *berachah* and *mazal*. Putting our own ego aside for peace is the essence of *bitachon* and of personal transcendence. Nothing is more difficult, and nothing brings greater reward. A transformed character means a reconfigured *mazal*, a showering of blessings, and pleasure beyond description.

123. *Sefer Hayirah*, Eshkol 1976, 172.
124. "When God favors the ways of a person, even his enemies will make peace with him" (Proverbs 16:7).
125. Rabbi Shimon ben Chalafta said, "The only vessel that God could find to contain the blessings of Israel was *shalom* ("peace"), as it is written: 'God will give strength to His people; God will bless His nation with peace'" (Psalms 29:11) (*Mishneh Uktzin* 3:12).

AFTERWORD

It is impossible to break a four-minute mile. Human beings are not physically capable, experts all agreed. We don't have the endurance, much less the speed. Scientists even conducted studies that proved we could never run that fast—and no one ever did. People ran 4:03, 4:06, 4:04, but no one ever broke a four-minute mile.

But then in 1954 Roger Bannister ran the mile in 3 minutes, 56 seconds—and everything changed. Within months, five other runners accomplished the same feat. The next year, dozens of other men did the same thing, and the following year, hundreds. Today, simply to qualify as a world-class runner, you must break the four-minute mile barrier.

There weren't any startling improvements in running shoes, pavement, or uniforms, and the law of wind resistance wasn't repealed. Yet, a mental barrier was broken down.

In our own lives, we have sold ourselves on a self-sustaining story—"This is who I am, and this is all I can do."

But what if we are wrong?

We are obligated to find out. To ask ourselves, "*Why* have I been telling myself that story?" "*Why*?" We must always ask ourselves, "*Why*?" when we think, "I cannot" or "This is just the way it is."

We may come to realize that we have been following a decades-old script, playing our part to perfection, and we may decide that we have had enough—and that it's time to rewrite our role.

The Torah does not allow a person to count on a miracle, but it does require us to count on ourselves, to believe in our God-given potential, and to know that God believes in us.

Our personal transformation begins the moment we choose to challenge the thoughts that define us and the story that confines us. When we ask ourselves, "Why do I believe this to be true?" then, like our forefather Abraham, our journey to remake ourselves and the world begins.

GLOSSARY

Adam HaRishon—The first man.

avodah—(Lit., work) service of God.

Avraham Avinu—The first Biblical Patriarch, Abraham.

Arizal (1534–1572)—Isaac (ben Solomon) Luria was a transformative figure in Jewish mysticism and Kabbalah.

bechirah—Choice, free will.

beis din—Rabbinical court.

Berachos—(Lit., blessings) Talmudic tractate dealing with blessings.

Binah—(Lit., understanding) one of the ten *Sefiros* (see *Sefirah*).

bitachon—Trust (in God).

Chazal—Acronym for *Chachameinu zichronam livrachah* (Lit., our Sages, may their memory be blessed).

Chovos HaLevavos—A famous ethical work by Rabbi Bachya ibn Pakudah (eleventh century, Spain), presenting the ethical teachings of Judaism.

chesed—Lovingkindness.

Dessler, Rabbi Eliyahu E. (1891–1954)—A leading figure in the *Mussar* movement, who incorporated Kabbalistic and Chassidic disciplines into his approach to *avodas Hashem* ("Divine service"). His essays and letters were published posthumously, under the title *Michtav mei'Eliyahu* ("Strive for Truth").

Da'as—(Lit., knowledge) one of the ten *Sefiros* (see *Sefirah*).

emes—Truth.

emunah—Faith (in God).

Eitz Hadaas—Tree of Knowledge.

Even Shleimah—Compendium of wisdom by the Vilna Gaon (Rabbi Eliyahu Kremer).

Gaavah—Pride.

Gemara—Part of the Talmud consisting primarily of commentary on the *Mishnah*.

Gan Eden—The Garden of Eden.

Geulah—Redemption.

Gevurah—(Lit., might) one of the ten *Sefiros* (see *Sefirah*).

gilgul—Reincarnation.

Hakadosh Baruch Hu—The Holy One, Blessed be He.

Hakhel—Refers to the Biblically mandated practice of assembling all Jewish men, women, and children to hear the reading of the Torah by the king of Israel once every seven years.

halachah—Jewish law.

Hashem—(Lit., the Name) referring to the ineffable name of God.

hashgachah klalis—General providence.

hashgachah pratis—Divine supervision of the individual.

Havdalah—Lit., separation.

Har Sinai—Mount Sinai.

hechsher—Seal that identifies the rabbi or the organization that certified approval of the ingredients used to make the food and the preparation process.

Hod—(Lit., splendor) one of the ten *Sefiros* (see *Sefirah*).

Kabbalah—(Lit., receiving or tradition) the esoteric dimension of the Torah.

Kaddish—Prayer in praise of God recited as part of the daily service and by mourners and those observing *yahrzeit*.

kaparah—Atonement.

kaveid—Liver.

Klal Yisrael—The nation of Israel.

Krias Yam Suf—Splitting of the Red Sea.

Lashon Hakodesh—(Lit., holy tongue) the Hebrew language.

lo lishma—Not for the sake of heaven, for ulterior motives.

madraigah—A person's spiritual level, denoting where a free will choice is within the scope of one's capacity.

Masechta (pl. *Masechtos*)—Volume of the Talmud.

Matan Torah—Giving of the Torah.

Megillas Esther—Book of Esther that contains the Purim narrative.

melech—King.

Mesillas Yesharim—Ethical text composed in 1740 by the influential Rabbi Moshe Chaim Luzzatto.

Michtav Mei'Eliyahu—Rabbi Eliyahu Dessler's classic ethical work.

Middah (pl. *middos*)—Character trait.

Midrash—Early rabbinic compendium of legal or narrative material.

Mishnah—Main source of the Oral Torah, later compiled into six volumes by Rav Yehuda HaNassi.

Mitzvah (pl. *mitzvos*)—Commandment.

mitzvah l'sheim Shamayim—*Mitzvah* for the sake of heaven.

mo'ach—Brain or mind.

navi—Prophet.

nefesh—Soul.

neshamah—Core of the soul.

nisayon—(Lit., a test) a challenge to foster spiritual growth.

Netzach—(Lit., victory) one of the ten *Sefiros* (see *Sefirah*).

Olam Haba—The World to Come.

Olam Hazeh—This world.

Orchos Tzaddikim—*The Ways of the Righteous,* a book on Jewish ethics.

parnasah—Livelihood.

parashah—Torah portion of the week.

Raavad (1120–1198)—Rabbi Abraham ben David was among the first of the early Kabbalists and an eminent commentator on the Talmud and *Mishneh Torah* of the Rambam.

Ralbag (1288–1344)—Levi ben Gershon was a highly regarded philosopher, Talmudist, mathematician, and astronomer.

Ramak (1522–1570)—Moses ben Jacob Cordovero was a renowned thinker and Kabbalist, and author of the Kabbalistic works *Pardes Rimonim* ("Orchard of Pomegranates") and *Tomer Devorah* ("Palm Tree of Deborah").

Rambam (1134–1204)—Rabbi Moshe ben Maimon, also known as Maimonides. He is one of the most well-known Torah authorities of all time. His most famous work is his *Mishnah Torah* ("Review of the Torah"), in which he codified the entire body of Jewish law.

Ramban (1194-1270)—Rabbi Moshe ben Nachman, also known as Nachmanides. He was the foremost halachic authority and Kabbalist of his age.

Ramchal (1707 – 1746)—Rabbi Moshe Chaim Luzzatto was a prominent rabbi, Kabbalist, and philosopher best known for his classic work on piety, *Mesillas Yesharim* ("Path of the Just").

Rashi (1040–1104)—Rabbi Shlomo Yitzhaki is considered the "father" of all commentators; he was a highly esteemed medieval French rabbi and the author of a comprehensive commentary on the Talmud and on the *Tanach*.

rasha—Evil person.

ratzon—Desire, will.

ruach—Spirit.

Ruach HaKodesh—Divine inspiration.

Sanhedrin—In the biblical era, Jewish supreme court.

s'char—Reward.

Sefirah (pl. *Sefiros*)—Channel of Divine energy or life force. It is through the *Sefiros* that God interacts with creation. They may therefore be considered His "attributes."

shailah—Question, especially a question asked regarding a halachic issue.

Sha'ar HaBitachon—"Gate of Trust," a chapter in *Chovos HaLevavos, Duties of the Heart*, by Rabbi Bachya ibn Pakudah.

Shechinah—Divine Presence.

Shemittah—Jewish sabbatical year.

Shemoneh Perakim—The Rambam's introduction to his commentary on Ethics of the Fathers.

shofar—Ram's horn blown on Rosh Hashanah.

Shulchan Aruch—*The Code of Jewish Law*, authored by Rabbi Joseph Karo in the fifteenth century.

Talmud—Largest compilation of Jewish writings of numerous volumes, in which all of Jewish law and thought is represented mainly in dialogue form.

Tanach—Complete Jewish Bible.

teshuvah—Repentance.

Tiferes—(Lit., beauty) one of the ten *Sefiros* (see *Sefirah*).

Tikkun—A fixing or repairing of damage from a previous incarnation.

Tikkun Olam—Restoration of the world.

tochachah—Rebuke.

Tosafos—Critical and explanatory commentaries on the Talmud composed during twelfth to fourteenth centuries.

tzaddik—Righteous person.

tzimtzum—Contraction and "removal" of God's infinite light in order to allow for the creation of independent realities.

tzora'as—Spiritual form of vitiligo.

yahrzeit—Anniversary of someone's death.

Yalkut—Aggadic compilation on the five Books of the Torah.

yetzer hara—Evil inclination.

yetzer tov—Good inclination; moral conscience that reminds a person of God's laws when faced with a choice of how to behave.

yissurim—Suffering.

Yovel—Jubilee year at the end of seven cycles of sabbatical years.

zechus—Spiritual merit.

zerizus—Energetic action; alacrity.

ABOUT
THE
AUTHOR

Dovid Lieberman, Ph.D., is a noted speaker and award-winning author with a renowned insight into the human condition. His ten books, which have been translated into 26 languages and include two *New York Times* bestsellers, have sold more than three million copies worldwide. His works have been featured in dozens of major publications, and he appears as a frequent guest expert on national media outlets.

Blending the wisdom of Torah with the psychological process, Dr. Lieberman's books and lectures are enjoyed by people at all levels and from all backgrounds. His classic *Real Power* and his recent *Seek Peace and Pursue It* (Feldheim Publishers) are available at Jewish bookstores everywhere. He lives with his wife and family in Lakewood, NJ.

Author Contact: DrLieberman@Live.com

Speaking Engagements: ViterPress@Live.com